Houses in the Rain Forest

For Steve Gudeman,
with respect and
gratitude,

Rich Grinker

Houses in the Rain Forest

Ethnicity and Inequality among Farmers and Foragers in Central Africa

Roy Richard Grinker

UNIVERSITY OF CALIFORNIA PRESS
Berkeley • Los Angeles • London

The publisher gratefully acknowledges permission to reprint two essays that appear here in slightly altered form from their original publication; they appeared as "Images of Denigration" in *American Ethnologist* 17:1 (February 1990), and "Houses, Clans, and Cloth" in *Museum Anthropology* 16:3 (October 1993). Both are reproduced by permission of the American Anthropological Association. Not for further reproduction.

University of California Press
Berkeley and Los Angeles, California

University of California Press
London, England

Library of Congress Cataloging-in-Publication Data

Grinker, Roy R. (Roy Richard), 1900-
Houses in the rain forest : ethnicity and inequality among farmers and foragers in Central Africa / Roy Richard Grinker.
p. cm.
Includes bibliographical references (p.) and index.
ISBN 0-520-08357-1 (cloth : alk. paper)
ISBN 0-520-08975-8 (pbk.)
1. Efe (African people)—Hunting. 2. Efe (African people)—Ethnic identity. 3. Hunting and gathering societies—Zaire—Ituri Forest. 4. Lese (African people)—Agriculture. 5. Lese (African people)—Ethnic identity. 6. Agriculture—Social aspects—Zaire—Ituri Forest. 7. Ituri Forest (Zaire)—Ethnic relations. I. Title. II. Title : Houses in the rainforest.
DT650.E34G75 1994
305.8'00967515—dc20 93-36600
CIP

Printed in the United States of America

1 2 3 4 5 6 7 8 9

The paper used in this publication meets the minimum requirements of American National Standard for Information Sciences—Permanence of Paper for Printed Library Materials, ANSI Z39.48-1984 ♾

To
Joyce Y. Chung
and to
Irven DeVore

Contents

Preface

The pair were undoubtedly man and woman. In him was a mimicked dignity, as of Adam; in her the womanliness of a miniature Eve.

Henry Morton Stanley, 1891. In Darkest Africa, *vol. 2:44, on the appearance of an Mbuti [Pygmy] man and his wife*

Although this book is not primarily about foragers, it grew out of my participation in a longitudinal investigation of the Efe (Pygmy) foragers of northeastern Zaire: the Harvard Ituri Project. Since 1980, Irven DeVore has led a series of researchers to explore questions regarding the health, nutrition, demography, child development, and ecology of the Efe, and, to a lesser extent, of the Lese, their farmer neighbors. Despite greater emphasis on the Efe, few of us were able to exclude the Lese from our analyses, for each group is an important constituent of the other, and they are deeply interconnected in every area of social life.

I owe my focus on the Lese not only to the wide-ranging and interdisciplinary research of the Ituri project but to the work of anthropologists who criticize the anthropological fascination with foragers as windows to the Paleolithic, as living fossils, or models of a lost prelapsarian past. R. K. Dentan (1988), C. Schrire (1984), E. Wilmsen (1990), Wilmsen and J. R. Denbow (1990), and H. Vierich (1982) are just a few of those who argue that foragers have a history, that they are intimately involved with farmers and pastoralists, and that the search for a "pure" hunting and gathering society is illusory. As Vierich argues in describing the Basarwa of Botswana, "If the hunting and gathering way of life has survived in the Kalahari it is not because of isolation" (1982:213). The various Pygmy groups, and the San, living in the heart of Africa, where we now locate our human origins, have been seen to exemplify the purest forms of a timeless hunting and gathering way of life shared by the first human beings, and yet we know that they live side by side with nonforager groups. P. M. Gardner (1989) points out that since the beginnings of anthropology as an academic discipline there have been warnings that foragers were neither pristine nor isolated, yet it took years for this fact to be fully appreciated by the field. Even where anthropologists explicitly recognized the complex social and historical contexts in which foragers lived, including relations with farmers, herders, colonial powers, and other political powers, that recognition seldom altered the conventional treatment of foraging societies as closed systems. By 1989, a flurry of articles on the relations between foragers and farmers appeared in most of the major anthropological journals. T. N. Headland and L. Reid (1989) made it clear that foragers and farmers are integrated all over the world; Wilmsen and Denbow (1990) placed forager-farmer interaction in the Kalahari desert of Botswana as far back as A.D. 500, and Robert Bailey and his colleagues (1989) suggested that foragers do not live, and never have lived, independent of farming in tropical rain forest environments. Following recent studies by K. Endicott (1984), and Nurit Bird-David (1988), even the category "forager" has been questioned because its use to designate some societies distorts intracultural variation. For example, some Dorobo foragers of East Africa are also pastoralists, and some Twa foragers from Rwanda and Burundi subsist not by hunting and gathering but by being potters or wandering musicians, among other things (Dentan 1988:279). In short, foragers cannot be considered as social isolates.

Nonetheless, though it has been acknowledged that we must study the farmers with whom the foragers live, the farmers have been more or less neglected. Nearly every ethnographer or explorer to encounter the Lese or the Efe has remarked upon the elaborate relations between the two groups, yet when I began my fieldwork no one had done extensive ethnographic work in the native Lese or Efe language. Jan Vansina points out that, of the one hundred or so scholars working in the central African rain forest between 1875 and 1985, in an area with as many as 450 different ethnic groups, one-third of them worked with the Pygmies:

> There exists an enormous literature indeed about pygmies, and the field certainly suffers from a fatal flaw: it studies only part societies. It studies the hunter-gatherers, but not the farming people with whom they are linked. . . . So, yes, there exists a vast amount of valid information, but it is always incomplete—the farmers are missing—and it is often flawed by strong preconceptions. (1990a:29)

Colin Turnbull recognized this gap, and in the final paragraph of his major publication on the Mbuti Pygmies regretted that no ethnographer had studied the Pygmy-farmer relationship from the point of view of the farmers (1965b:300).

Turnbull's classic works addressed the question of forager-farmer interaction far more completely than any researcher before him (1965a, 1965b, 1968, 1972). He chose to live primarily with the Mbuti, rather than with the Bila farmers, and he presented to his readers the Mbuti perspective on their interactions with the Bila. According to Turnbull, the Mbuti see the farmers and their villages as merely one of several hunting grounds, and they view interaction with the farmers to be a luxury that complements routine exploitation of forest products. Turnbull sees the foragers and the farmers as socially and culturally independent, and he concludes that the ostensible interdigitation of the two groups, as expressed in their cooperative participation in shared rituals, and the political and economic subordination of the Mbuti, is really only playacting by the Mbuti. My study, in contrast, focuses on a group of farmers in the Ituri forest. My view, the opposite of Turnbull's, is that these groups are integral parts of one another—indeed, that they share the same ethnically differentiated social system. My argument is not with Turnbull's choice of the Mbuti perspective—choosing a perspective is a methodological necessity—but with his representation of the Mbuti and Bila as distinct groups whose interactions are meaningful primarily in the service of maximizing the Mbuti's affluence.

This study is not yet another treatise on whether the farmers and foragers "need," "exploit," or "depend on" one another. Arguments about the costs and benefits of their relations, the utilitarianism and practical reason of economic life, are the usual focus in hunter-gatherer studies (Schebesta 1936; Putnam 1948; Turnbull 1961, 1965b; Hart and Hart 1984; Bailey and Peacock 1989). I take issue with the fact that these studies usually stress the terms "forager" and "farmer" as markers of ecological adaptations rather than as markers of ethnicity. Material culture is assumed to be the independent variable in the construction of group boundaries, and the exchange of material goods resulting from subsistence practices is accepted as the dominant discourse of interaction. As a consequence, the ideas and belief systems underlying the interactions between these foragers and farmers, including both the symbolic and social structural aspects of the division of labor between foraging and farming, and the relations of inequality between the two groups, have been largely ignored (Grinker 1990;

Mosko 1987; Ben-Ari 1987). My major concern is with the ways in which the Lese culturally represent their relations with one another and with the Efe; therefore, I shall not deal extensively with the materialist literature on nutrition, optimal foraging, or behavioral ecology.

This book, then, is about the dialectical relations between the Lese farmers and the Efe (Pygmy) foragers as ethnic groups; it is about how the Lese define themselves in terms of the Efe, and how the Lese define the Efe in terms of themselves. It is about how, in the context of intimate interethnic relations, the Lese derive a sense of who they are. My focus is on the ways in which social boundaries are constructed and sustained, and the modes of representation the Lese use to incorporate Lese-Efe cultural differences into everyday discourse and social life. At its most particular, this study argues that the Lese and the Efe must be seen as parts of a larger ethnically differentiated totality. At its most general, this study suggests that ethnicity is tied to inequality and is constituted by the asymmetrical integration of culturally distinct groups. Far from separating groups as distinct entities, ethnicity draws our attention to the *relations* between groups, not to one group in and of itself.

But my theoretical considerations move beyond a recasting of forager-farmer relations to some of the most basic and problematic assumptions in the anthropology of Africa; namely, the separation of domestic and political domains, and an overreliance on lineage theory for the explanation of social relationships. I shall argue that Lese-Efe ethnicity is best understood as a process of social differentiation and integration occurring within the Lese house. The house is characterized by the relations of inequality between its members (spouses, Lese and Efe partners, parents and children), relations that provide the symbolic material for the Lese modeling of society and economy in general. The role of the house in shaping Lese and Efe ethnicity, and therefore constituting large-scale political relationships, thus challenges the conventional structural-functional boundary between domestic and political contexts, between the house and the larger, more inclusive structures of society. Relations between spouses, for instance, are largely constitutive of the relations between the Lese and the Efe. The house, it will be seen, offers a significant advantage over the concepts provided by lineage theory for the comprehension of Lese and Efe ethnicity. While it is clear that clans and lineages are important aspects of Lese and Efe society, these refer to contexts of idealized equality and brotherhood among male agnates. The house, in contrast, is a context of idealized inequality and difference, and so leads us to consider the important role played by gender and ethnicity in the constitution of the society. In paying such close attention to the house, I hope to further discussions of inequality in those societies that might fall easily into the category "egalitarian." I would also argue that the recasting of social organization by a focus on houses could be carried out just as fruitfully with groups that are not associated with hunter-gatherers.

However, studying the relationship between two groups poses difficult methodological problems. I spent my first six months of fieldwork (May–October 1985) living half of the time in a Lese village and half of the time in an Efe camp. This alternation proved unworkable, however, for both groups eventually made it clear that they wanted me to make a choice of allegiance, and I myself realized that dividing my time between residences could negatively affect my relationship with my informants, and that, furthermore, the shifts might make it difficult to explore either group in depth and detail. Turnbull, in fact, describes the same problem in his decision to live primarily with the Mbuti (1965b). I returned to the United States for about six months, during which time I pondered the ethnographic perspective I would take in the future, and constructed a working grammar and dictionary of the Lese language. During the next fourteen months of fieldwork (August 1986–October 1987), I decided therefore to focus my attention on the Lese, and to study the Efe whenever and wherever they became involved in Lese life and thought. If the two groups were indeed completely interlocked, I would eventually come to see the nature of that connection.

Living in a Lese village did not, as I had feared, severely limit my interactions with the Efe. I saw Efe men and women every day and maintained close relationships with Efe informants. But my choice certainly influenced the kind and quality of information I gathered from the Efe and the Lese. Because I lived in a Lese village and spoke the Lese language, Efe informants quite understandably viewed me as a villager, and it seemed to me that they held back some of their more unkind thoughts about the Lese, either out of respect for me, as a "villager," or because they feared I would repeat what they had said. Also, though I eventually spoke the Lese language fluently (a language mutually intelligible with the Efe language), I had a more difficult time understanding Efe speech and sometimes had to resort to Swahili, a language in which most Efe men maintain a degree of fluency. Lese informants, in contrast, seemed to speak to me more frankly about personal and private matters, and to be quite willing to express their feelings about the Efe. For these reasons, this book is more an ethnography of the Lese than it is of the Efe; though it says a great deal about how the Lese manage their relations with the Efe, it does not presume to describe how the Efe manage relations with the Lese, or even, except in certain perhaps superficial ways, how they feel about the Lese.

A work such as this depends not only on day-to-day observation and interviews but also on the compilation and study of maps, censuses, genealogies, collected myths, and oral history. My informants, Lese and Efe, represented nearly every status or social role, including children. The majority of informants' statements and narratives reproduced in the book are my own transcriptions from tape recordings. With the exception of the larger and more extensive demographic data that I collected on the ethnic composition of Lese villages and market sellers, the survey data I present in the text include all Lese adult men and women in my study area, stretching a distance of about three kilometers between two rivers, and including twelve villages. Given the fact that the Lese area is sparsely populated, and villages are frequently situated far from one another, it was impossible for me to carry out more inclusive surveys.

The most frustrating aspect of my research was the absence of either written sources or a collected oral history. Vansina has, in fact, called the equatorial rain forest of central Africa terra incognita for the historian. There are only a few archival sources on the Lese and their history. These include a few documents obtained in Zaire by Robert C. Bailey—four pages of correspondence between colonial administrators of the Kibali-Ituri district, 1920–37; three pages of historical notes on the WaLese-Karo, District du Kibali-Ituri (P.V. No. 222); and a 1947 census conducted by the Belgian administration. The 1920–37 documents mention other reports on the Lese-Dese and Lese-Karo filed between 1911 and 1919, but these and all other documents on the Lese groups and on the Efe were lost or misplaced after independence (1960) and the rebellions that followed. I take heart in the creative and groundbreaking efforts of Vansina (1990a) and hope that anthropologists will eventually come to know more fully this region of the world, not only through ethnography but through its oral history, glottochronology, genetics, and archaeological remains.

Acknowledgments

I am indebted to many people and institutions for assistance at various stages during the research and writing of this study. For generous support of my fieldwork, conducted between May and December 1985 and between July 1986 and October 1987, I am grateful to the Department of Anthropology at Harvard University, the Fulbright-Hays Doctoral Dissertation Fellowship, and Canon, U.S.A. For support provided through the Ituri Project, I am grateful to the National Science Foundation, the Louis Leakey Foundation, the Wenner-Gren Foundation, and the Swan Fund. During fieldwork, I was affiliated with the Institut des Musées Nationaux in Kinshasa, Zaire, under the direction of J. Cornet. I particularly thank Professor Benoit Quersin, who was my liaison. Through the museums, the government of Zaire extended generous permission that made an extended period of fieldwork possible.

My first thanks must go to the people of Malembi who taught me their language and shared their lives with me, and to the other members of the Ituri project. During my periods of study and residence in Zaire, I had the opportunity to work with several researchers: Robert Aunger, John Fisher, Greg Laden, Nadine Peacock, Helen Strickland, and Catherine Sydes, and especially Robert C. Bailey, whose dedication to research was largely responsible for the inception and continuation of the project. I also thank the Centre Médicale Evangélique for taking care of my mail; the Mission Aviation Fellowship for expert mail drops from high altitude and transportation within the forest; the sisters of the Mission Catholique at Nduye and Dr. Joe Lusi of the Centre Médicale

Evangélique for their medical advice; and M. and Mme. Goetz Von Wilde of Isiro for their warmth and hospitality.

In the development of this work, I have profited from the encouragement and suggestions of a number of teachers, colleagues, and friends: Paul Brodwin, Gautam Ghosh, Robert A. LeVine, Sally Falk Moore, and Norbert Peabody. Terry O'Nell provided careful readings and insightful criticisms of nearly every chapter. I also wish to acknowledge the generous and critical comments provided by Stephen Gudeman, Enid Schildkrout, Jan Vansina, and the anonymous reviewers of the manuscript. Thanks also to Nancy DeVore and Meg Lynch for editorial assistance, and to Shirley Taylor and Linda Benefield for invaluable copyediting. Needless to say, I take responsibility for all errors.

Most of all, I thank my wife, Joyce Chung, my late grandfather, Roy R. Grinker, Sr., and my father Roy R. Grinker, Jr.—all psychiatrists, all critical thinkers and readers. Joyce not only read through every word of the manuscript but has consistently offered superb and constructive criticisms. Finally, I extend my deepest gratitude to Irven DeVore, a teacher and friend. In many ways, this book belongs to him. Neither this study, nor perhaps the entire Ituri project, would have been possible without him.

R. R. G.

Note on Language and Orthography

The Lese and the Efe consider themselves to speak mutually intelligible languages: *talu Des-ba* (the language of the Lese) and *talu Efe-ba* (the language of the Efe). Both of these are Sudanic languages. I shall refer to them simply as Lese and Efe. Most Lese and Efe men also speak some KiNgwana, a dialect of Swahili, and Lingala, two of the national languages of Zaire. A few Lese men know basic French. At the villages of Malembi, where this study was conducted, the younger Lese men are able to read and write KiNgwana and Lingala, but to my knowledge, few Lese women, and no Efe men or women, are able to read or write these languages. The Lese do not write their native language.

Except where noted, all transcriptions of narrative or terminology are reproduced here in the Lese language and translated into English. I have represented the sounds of Lese terms phonetically in romanized form but have dispensed with tonal markers and other diacritical notation. As no grammar of the Lese or Efe languages has been completed, I leave the difficult task of constructing a proper orthography and phonology to trained linguists.

I note some special pronunciations of Lese consonants: /b/ and /gb/ are implosive; /v/ is also implosive and lies midway between the English /b/ and /v/; finally, /l/ is a lateral flap similar to the sound of a rolled /r/ or /dl/.

Some Lese vowels are different from the vowels used in English or Swahili. However, all those vowels represented here are nearly identical in sound to the vowels /o/, /i/, /u/, /a/, and /e/, as identified in the International Phonetic Alphabet. Long vowels are indicated by a double vowel, for example, /aa/ or /ee/. When /i/ and /a/ appear as /ia/, the sound produced resembles the English semi-vowel /y/. The distinction between /o/ as in "lost" and "go" is not rendered.

All foreign words are italicized in the first use.

All individuals, clans, and phraties have been given pseudonymns.

CHAPTER I

Introduction

From Tribes to Ethnic Groups

"In the hierarchical scheme a group's acknowledged differentness whereby it is contrasted with other groups becomes the very principle whereby it is integrated into society."

Louis Dumont, Homo Hierachicus

The people who call themselves the Lese have had a turbulent history. At times they have been participants in a world rubber and ivory market, at other times they have been almost totally isolated from trade and markets. They have been integrated into nearby plantation systems, missions, and government; then again they have been completely marginalized from them. In almost every decade in the last century, the Lese have endured crises of the worst sort—forced labor and resettlement, destruction of property, beatings, imprisonment, and hunger. But within the context of flux and turmoil, there has been one striking continuity: their long-standing and complex relations with a group of people who call themselves the Efe, and who are known in Zaire by several names—Les Pygmées, Les Nains, BaMbuti, and Les Premiers Citoyens—and in much of the anthropological literature as the Pygmies.

The long-standing partnerships between Lese and Efe men and their families are for the most part hereditary: a Lese man inherits the son of his father's Efe partner as his own partner. Nearly every Efe man has a partner, and while some Lese men do not have partners, for reasons we shall discover later, all Lese men believe that to be an adult and a "true man," a *muto mani,* one must have an Efe partner. To the partners themselves, these relationships are primarily economic. Ask the members of either group what constitutes the partnerships and they will most likely say that the Lese farmers give cultivated foods and iron to the Efe and that the Efe give meat, honey, and other forest goods to the Lese. The division of labor between farming and foraging, along with the transfer of goods that the Lese and the Efe believe follows from that division, is a central ethnic marker distinguishing the two groups. But the social relations that accompany the giving and receiving of these goods extend far beyond material transactions.

Lese men sometimes marry Efe women, and the children of these marriages are considered by both groups to be members of the Lese group. Efe men, however, cannot marry Lese women nor even engage in sexual intercourse with them. The Efe provide music and dancing at Lese rituals, serve as the chief mourners at Lese funerals, and protect the Lese from witchcraft. Efe children are sometimes raised in Lese villages; Efe women may serve as midwives for Lese women, breast-feed Lese babies, and obtain and administer medicines for afflicted Lese. Efe men and women carry out various household tasks in the Lese villages, such as cutting firewood, collecting water, obtaining house-building materials, and weeding the village plaza. In turn, the Lese represent the Efe in dealings with government officials and at tribunals, and they may pay fines that officials level against their Efe partners or partners' families; in addition, besides being legally responsible for the actions of their Efe partners, Lese men are expected to provide much of their partners' bridewealth payments and to aid in marriage negotiations. Efe men may place one or more of their children in the care of their Lese partner, who will feed the children, teach them Swahili and French, and, as the Efe put it, "cause the children to grow."

Many researchers have treated the Lese and Efe as distinct societies, separable and autonomous. The two groups are indeed physically different; they identify themselves by different names; they speak distinct, though mutually intelligible, languages, and employ different customs and rituals; and they maintain a strict division of labor between farming and foraging. But the intricacy of the relations between them that have developed over time has come to unite them in a system that encompasses both the local terminology and cultural differences.

In some ways, the Lese and the Efe resemble many other integrated societies of foragers and farmers in other parts of the world: the various Phillipine Negrito groups, the Mbuti Pygmies of Zaire, the San of Botswana, and the Hill Pandaram, the Nayaka, and the Paliyans of South India are among the many foraging groups that are socially integrated with their nonforaging neighbors. Few if any foraging societies, as Headland (1987) and Headland and Reid (1989) have recently shown, live independent of farmers, and their integration poses a major ethnographic problem in anthropology. The problem is also a theoretical one, however: that is, though we may now appreciate that foragers and farmers live together—which means that the model of foragers as social isolates should be abandoned—we do not necessarily know how to study their relations. How are these relations to be analyzed and represented? What theoretical and analytical concepts are available? Anthropologists who study foragers and farmers are, for the most part, specialists in forager studies, and although they have a long history of scholarship on the subject of "band level societies," "egalitarianism," and the relevance of foragers to the study of the prehistoric past, they have rarely specifically examined the social relations between culturally different groups, especially relations of inequality.[1] Outside of forager studies, anthropological concepts such as caste, class, and ethnicity have been elaborated for the study of intergroup relations, yet these have not been appropriated for the study of foragers and farmers. Anthropologists interested in forager-farmer relations must turn for guidance to regional specializations such as African or South Asian studies, and to social anthropology in general.

The problem of how to analyze interacting but culturally different groups, though a recent concern in forager studies, is not especially new to sociocultural anthropology. Edmund Leach (1954), Robert Redfield and Milton Singer (1954), McKim Marriot (1955), and Clifford Geertz (1960), among others, lead us to consider cultural differentiation as evidence of social integration. Leach, in his analysis of ethnic and structural relations in Burma, notes that "the mere fact that two groups of people are of different culture does not necessarily imply . . . that they belong to quite different social systems" (1954:17), and he remarks that cultural differences can be expressive of social relations (see Berreman 1975). Geertz adds that social subsystems are "incomplete social systems which are interlocked with one another and depend upon that interlocking for the maintenance of whatever distinctive pattern of organization of their own they may have" (1956:523). In other words, one group is simply not intelligible without the other. These studies, relying on contrasting terms such as *urban* and *folk, gentry* and *peasantry, great* and *little* tradition, differ sharply from the research of hunter-gatherer specialists, whose terms *farmer* and *forager* are meant to define groups according to modes of food production. Redfield and Singer, for example, focus on the interaction between cultural subsys-

1. The major exceptions include Gardner (1972), Lee and Leacock (1982), Schebesta (1936), Schrire (1984), Turnbull (1965b), and Woodburn (1988), all of whom address issues in the study of forager-farmer relations.

tems, whereas forager specialists frame intercultural interactions in terms of subsistence patterns or the exchange of material goods. The former studies emphasize the role that cultural distinctions play as markers of social relations rather than of separateness and autonomy.

This work has three central aims. The first is to show that the Lese and the Efe are more fruitfully analyzed as subgroups of a larger social collectivity (Grinker 1990). Even while the Lese and the Efe describe themselves as two distinct groups, they must be analytically treated as one ethnically differentiated group. In an analytical sense, the Lese and the Efe belong together. The second aim is to locate the social contexts in which interethnic relations are institutionalized and the sources for the symbolic representation of ethnicity. As we shall see, ethnic relations are organized at the level of the house. In addition, the Lese draw on the meanings and metaphors of the house to symbolically represent the Efe, and Lese relations with the Efe, in a variety of realms (e.g., mythology, everyday discourse, and beliefs about the supernatural) that includes their differing subsistence practices but goes far beyond them. The third aim is to explore the ethnic logic of Lese-Efe relations within the house, and the dialectical relation between the relationships the Lese have with one another and the relationships they have with the Efe. How do the values and practices of food distribution between Lese influence those between the Lese and the Efe? How do Lese beliefs about themselves influence their beliefs about the Efe? And how do relationships between Lese at the level of the clan influence Lese-Efe relationships at the level of the house?

ANALYTICAL CONCERNS: COLIN TURNBULL AND FORAGER-FARMER RELATIONS

This is not a comparative study. I do not attempt to place my analysis of the structure of Lese-Efe relations within a comprehensive discussion of the many interethnic or patron-client relations recorded by ethnographers (see Schmidt et al. 1977). While I shall make occasional comments throughout the text about the relevance of a variety of ethnographic observations to my own, such a broad and ambitious comparative project must form the subject of a future work. My immediate concern is to describe the ethnographic context within which the Lese and the Efe relate to one another, and to outline, specifically, the contribution that an ethnic perspective on Lese-Efe relations can make to the study of forager-farmer interactions, a field of research that is in itself wide-ranging and varied. And while I shall discuss how the study of the Lese and the Efe, and their integration in the Lese house, can contribute to analyses of both the structuring of inequality in so-called "egalitarian societies" in Africa and the social organization of the many societies that have been described primarily with a lineage model, my main objective is to provide a detailed account of how ethnicity and inequality are structured in one particular ethnographic setting.

The few works that have appeared on aspects of Pygmy-farmer relations in central Africa have been, for the most part, ecological or biological studies (Hart and Hart 1984; Tanno 1976, 1981; Cavalli-Sforza 1987), brief descriptive works of hunting and farming practices and of general forest history (Schultz n.d.; Waehle 1985), or demographic accounts limited to the composition of settlements and Pygmy-farmer marriage (Ichikawa 1978, 1981; Terashima 1983, 1984, 1985, 1987). To my knowledge, since Turnbull (1965a, 1965b, 1983a), the only original ethnographic study of foragers and farmers of the central African rain forest that has concentrated on ideas, symbols, and culture is that of S. Bahuchet and H. Guillaume (1982) on Aka-Bantu relations in the northwest Congo basin, presented in a short article (1982). These authors argue that the Aka foragers have a long history of interethnic trade that involves an integration of societies going far beyond simple exchanges of material goods to the point where the two groups are integrated into a larger totality and become important components of each other's collective identity. For the farmers the Aka, indeed, represent the "civilizing saviours" who enabled the farmers to become cultural beings (1982:194; see also Bahuchet 1992).

Despite the more recent studies, Colin Turnbull's work on the Mbuti foragers and Bila farmers of the Ituri and Jean Peterson's work on the Agta foragers and Puti farmers of the Phillipines still stand as the two most detailed and thorough accounts of forager-farmer relations. According to Peterson (1978a:335, 1978b:42), she and Turnbull were at that time the only anthropologists to consider these relations as a primary object of study. Turnbull's two major publications, *The Forest People* (1961), a popular account of life with the Mbuti, and *Wayward Servants* (1965b), a more scholarly account of the relations between the Mbuti and Bila, both of which are now standard reading in anthropology classes all over the world, have been the basis of a significant number of studies on economic, political, and gender egalitarianism (Begler 1978; Godelier 1977; Meillassoux 1975; among others). These beautifully written texts continue to attract students of all disciplines to anthropology and to stimulate interest in the lives of central African foragers. Partly because of their romantic appeal, but perhaps more correctly because of their uniqueness, the egalitarianism and social harmony outlined by Turnbull have rarely been questioned by other anthropologists (see, for example, Cashdan 1989: 44–45), and Turnbull's other characterizations of Mbuti beliefs and social organization have seldom been subject to critical examination. As I have said elsewhere in a comment on an article by Nurit Bird-David (1992), in which she applies Turnbull's arguments to a comparative analysis of forager economies, I am skeptical of this uncritical acceptance of Turnbull's writing, valuable though his work is:

> I continue to be struck by the persistence with which anthropologists embrace Turnbull's romantic characterizations of the Mbuti . . . Turnbull's work presents few data to support the ways in which he represents Mbuti life and thought; there are few or no narratives, analyses of mythology, or cultural descriptions based on a knowledge of the native Mbuti language. For example, how do we know that the Mbuti feel "reverence" or "compassion" when they are slaughtering an animal? What are the Mbuti words to describe the "affection" given by the forest? How do we know that the forest is the "vital essence" of people's lives when the central word cited by Turnbull (and Bird-David) in the description of this essence is "*pepo,*" a Swahili word used in northeastern Zaire to mean "wind"? To my knowledge, no subsequent fieldwork among the Mbuti or Efe, including my own, has revealed indigenous conceptions of the forest as a soul or life force. Furthermore, as in this paper, the Mbuti are frequently appropriated as immediate-returners without including in the analysis the Bila farmers with whom they live, and without a knowledge of the cultural constitution of the Mbuti and Bila economy. (Grinker 1992a:39)

Unfortunately, Turnbull provides little evidence that he learned the native Mbuti language and thus elicited the kinds of conceptions of the world that form his representations of the Mbuti and their mothering forest. Turnbull presents *The Forest People* as ethnographic realism, but it is in many ways a thinly veiled attempt to use the *idea* of the "Pygmies" as a way to make universally valid statements about human nature.[2] Turnbull played upon a deep-seated need throughout much of the West to invent a "primitive" and original form of human society (cf. Wilmsen 1990), and toward this goal he draws an idealized picture of the Mbuti living a romantic and harmonious life in the bountiful rain forest of the Congo. The Mbuti he describes in *The Forest People* are

2. Berger (1983:13) makes a similar point about Turnbull's *The Human Cycle* (1983b).

simple and childlike creatures, romping in the forest without the violence and inequality of the unpure West. The implied criticisms of Western civilization (in this and other publications), as compared with that of the Pygmies, are fairly obvious (Turnbull 1983a), and in a later ethnography, in which Turnbull went further to contrast his love of the Pygmies with his hatred of the Ik of Uganda, his bias was duly questioned by the international anthropological community (see, e.g., Barth 1974; McCall 1975).

Wayward Servants may be questioned for more specific reasons, namely, some inconsistencies in Turnbull's argument and generalizations unsupported by his data. Perhaps the most glaring problem, and one that relates particularly to my study of Lese-Efe relationships, is Turnbull's use of the concept of dependence. Turnbull wishes to demonstrate that the Mbuti are separate and independent of the farmers, but, at the same time, he says that the Mbuti are actually dependent upon the farmers for cultivated foods, iron, pottery, and fire, among other things (1965b:34–35). Nonetheless, Turnbull gets around these sticky facts by adopting the Mbuti classification of the world into two spheres, the village and the forest world. In the village, the Mbuti choose to be dependent upon the farmers; in the forest they are totally independent of the farmers. In either realm, they are truly autonomous. Turnbull then asks why the Mbuti choose to be dependent in the village context. There is perhaps no more important question in the study of these foragers and farmers. The answers would no doubt tell us much about the structure and motivation of the complex relations between the foragers and farmers. But he does not delve into the question deeply, for to do so would indeed mean studying their complex integration. The entire book, on the contrary, can be read as a study of their separateness. Turnbull writes:

> Accepting, for the moment, that the Mbuti in their forest world are not in any position of necessary dependence upon the villagers for food or material, or technological skill, and admitting that in the village context they are dependent, the question arises as to why they choose to place themselves in that position of dependence. It is certainly not out of economic necessity. The truth of the matter is simply that the village offers, for a brief while, an agreeable change of pace, an opportunity for a relaxation that is not always possible in the forest, and, one might say, better hunting, on occasion. An Mbuti band or an Mbuti family or an Mbuti individual may descend upon a village either because of sheer whim, or because of laziness if the forest hunting gets too strenuous, or because of dissension, or indeed for almost any reason except necessity. Whatever the reason, and most commonly it at

> least involves an expressed desire for relaxation, and freedom from care, the reason is on the side of the Mbuti, the choice is theirs, and the dependence that follows is as voluntary as it is temporary. (1965b:37)

In other words, the forager-farmer relationship is determined and shaped by whim, fatigue, and the desire for relaxation. Although the farmers are also "dependent" upon the Mbuti, they also engage in these relations out of choice. Turnbull concludes, "The most that one can say about the economic aspect of the relationship is that it appears to be one of mutual convenience" (p. 81). Certainly few scholars would argue with the worthy assertion that dependence is culturally constructed, but whim, fatigue, and convenience are not exactly what anthropologists have in mind when they seek to explain the enduring and well-patterned cultural makeup of a complex social situation.

Having thus established that the Mbuti's ostensible dependence upon the farmers is essentially a kind of play performed by the Mbuti, Turnbull dwells on the theme of the forest as a bountiful, never-changing sanctuary, a place that not only provides everything the Mbuti need or desire but also is a completely good place, unlike the village, which is completely bad. There are several problems with this idealized representation, and I will note just two. First, Turnbull contends that the forest gives everything the Mbuti want or need and is a refuge from the dangers outside the forest, yet he also notes that in history the Mbuti were caught between warring "tribes" and had to attach themselves to particular farmer groups (p. 38). If the forest provides such safe asylum, why did the Mbuti need sanctuary, and why did they involve themselves with warring groups? Turnbull's explanation is simply that the Mbuti had "developed a strong taste for plantation foods" (p. 38). Once again, the relationship is explained in terms of a taste or fancy.

Second, Turnbull's idealized view of the Mbuti leads him to accept the Mbuti attitudes toward the village as a place of supernatural malevolence. Rather than explore the meaning or motivation of such a sharp contrast between the forest and village, Turnbull simply accepts the dichotomy at face value. Although the Mbuti have some magic, they associate witchcraft and sorcery only with the village world; hence, the village is an evil place, where even those Mbuti who do not believe in supernatural powers can be persuaded to believe in them: "When an Mbuti dies in the village there is frequently voiced suspicion that somehow the village is responsible; maybe one of the old curses is at work, perhaps a neglected *kpara* [Bila partner] is employing a sorcerer to seek revenge, or more likely, it is simply the village itself that caused the death" (p.74). The forest, in contrast, is a world of total tranquility and peace. It is mother, father, and God. This is, in fact, the most prominent argument in all of Turnbull's numerous books and articles—that the forest is the positive life force and essence of the Mbuti.

In sum, Turnbull enshrines the opposition between the village and the forest. I should say at the outset that I agree completely with Turnbull that this pervasive and ever-present opposition between the village and the forest is one of the most fundamental components of the culture and society of these foragers and farmers, as well as for the Lese and the Efe (see chapter 3). But there are two ways of looking at this opposition, one adopted by Turnbull, the other which I shall advocate. Turnbull embraces the view that the forest is good and the village is bad, and, taking that as the anthropological model, goes on to accept the forest and the village as totally separate and independent spheres of life about which few further questions need be asked. This acceptance allows him to interpret whatever the Mbuti tell him as simply another detail of that divided social situation. But there is another way to look at the division of the world into the forest and the village. We can see the forest-village dichotomy as an ethnic division in which the Mbuti define themselves in terms of the Bila. In this case, the local model is analyzed as a product of intergroup relations rather than group autonomy. According to the latter model, there is indeed a kind of "dependence" here, although it has little to do with food or metal. To echo Geertz's statement quoted above, these groups depend upon one another for "whatever distinctive pattern of organization of their own they may have." Precisely because these groups "depend" upon one another, I resist Turnbull's reification of the village and the forest, indeed of the foragers and the farmers. The essentialist definition of these domains threatens to prohibit us from seeing them as mutually constitutive.

Peterson (1978a, 1978b) makes ethnicity the central concept in her account of the relations between the Agta foragers and the Puti farmers of the Phillipines. Much like the Mbuti and the Bila, the Agta and the Puti have different agendas. Whereas the Agta strive for an idealized economic egalitarianism among men, the Puti recognize and appreciate inequalities. And like the Mbuti and the Bila, these groups compete with each other for forest and garden resources. The similarities seem to end there, however, as Peterson contends that the Agta and the Puti forge their cultural differences out of an adaptation to the environment; ethnicity, for Peterson, is determined by ecology. But the ecological perspective notwithstanding, she leads us to consider the subject of ethnicity as the result of interaction between the two groups. Peterson argues that the competition between them results in a positive reinforcement of their cultural differences: "This asymmetrical competition in a sense supports positive relations between the two peoples. It helps to maintain distinctions between Agta and Puti that reinforce the potential for cooperation" (1978b:89). Peterson echoes Durkheim's theory of organic solidarity and essentially recapitulates a well-known hypothesis that when ethnic groups compete with one another, they may do so, as M. Gluckman (1958) notes, by emphasizing the dominant cleavage between them, a process that distinguishes the groups further. Distinction is not the same as separation, for ethnic distinction is determined by the relations between these groups. Competition and cooperation, cultural distinction and social integration, work side by side toward the construction of ethnic diversity, including diversity in subsistence strategies. Whether or not we adhere to Peterson's essentially materialist conception of ethnicity, one thing is indisputable: the foragers and farmers have to be considered together.

Peterson's conclusions about ethnic diversity have a bearing on a question repeatedly raised in forager studies: Why have the foragers not become farmers? (e.g., Headland 1988; Schultz n.d.). An equally important question, rarely asked, is why farmers do not more frequently become foragers. Because of their mutual participation in each other's economies, most foragers know how to farm, and most farmers know how to hunt. Why, therefore, do they not engage in these activities? Why is there so little overlap between subsistence practices? The answer seems to lie within the broader cultural context of these societies. Within the total context of the hunter-gatherer group, subsistence itself can signify a cultural identity, especially since that identity opposes others, such as farmers and herders. In other words, *the hunter-gatherer/farmer division is a symbolic representation, an ethnic identity framed in terms of the economy* (Grinker 1992b).

Turnbull introduced the subject of forager-farmer relations to an anthropological audience, and Peterson provided a way to conceive of those relations in anthropological terms. Yet both Turnbull's and Peterson's accounts are ahistorical. Wilmsen (1990) advances us a bit further. His comprehensive account of the San-speaking peoples of Botswana focuses on inequality and ethnicity among foragers and their neighbors in historical context. He views the various San-speaking peoples as ethnic groups whose identities and political and economic positions are the result of a long history of interaction between the San and others in the Kalahari. San ethnicity is thus determined not by their isolation but by their participation in a complex political economy. What we see today as forager groups in the Kalahari are not remnants of prehistory but rather the products of a complicated past in which these foragers were geographically and economically marginalized from the centers of power.[3] Dentan (1988: 281) furthers Wilmsen's line of argument in a more comparative context by suggesting that the egalitarianism and peacefulness so often observed among foragers may actually be a creative adaptation to defeat by dominant and oppressive forces, followed by withdrawal into geographically or socially isolated areas.

I am in sympathy with both Peterson and Wilmsen in their attempt to explore the integration of foragers and their neighbors in terms of ethnicity. Peterson's book on Agta-Puti relations deserves recognition because it is one of the earlier accounts of ethnicity in a nonurban context (cf. Barth 1969), and, to my knowledge, one of the first accounts of ethnicity in a foraging society. Ethnicity has been viewed in much of the world, especially in Africa, as a correlate of urban and economic growth. Rural areas were assumed to be somehow immune from the social perils of ethnicity because they were less subject to historical change (Vail 1988). Although Peterson's work remains ahistorical, she takes pains to point out that ethnic ideologies develop in places that conventional theories would not predict. The value of Wilmsen's study is that it gives not only ethnicity but a *history* of ethnicity to a foraging group that has been treated as ahistorical and primordial.

One of the most salient benefits of an ethnic focus is that it draws our attention away from conventional and static notions of group membership, such as the tribe and corporation, and toward analyses of group identity as dynamic and as the product of intercultural relations. Studies of ethnicity thus involve, to some degree, a rejection of the conventional models of group solidarity and continuity. The most popular of these, the descent models, including the model of "tribe," have been shown time and time again to limit our range of observation and understanding (Barnes 1971), to neglect relations between people of different cultures, and to be a product of the specifically Western oppositions (such as state and stateless societies, clan system and territorial system,

3. Wilmsen's notion of history should not be accepted uncritically, however. As I have noted elsewhere (Grinker 1992a:162–163), Wilmsen tends to see most historical change as produced by exogenous forces, and thus his view threatens to rob the San of an endogenously produced history (see also Solway and Lee 1990).

matrilineage and patrilineage) to which we often hold stubbornly. Anthropologists have been particularly susceptible to the notion that descent organizes behavior—as if there might be a perfect fit between an ideology and actual group composition (S. F. Moore 1978). There is already a vast and critical literature on the theoretical and methodological problems of "tribe" and "tribalism" (see, e.g., Gulliver 1971; Helm 1968; Fried 1968; Southall 1970; Kopytoff 1987; Ekeh 1990), and the replacement of these terms with "ethnic group" and "ethnicity."[4] Adam Kuper points out that descent models rarely reflect folk models, the ways that people actually conceive of their own societies, and furthermore, that "there do not appear to be any societies in which vital political or economic activities are organized by a repetitive series of descent groups" (1982:92). Vansina (1980) suggests that the concept of the lineage should be dropped from the vocabulary of historians of Africa. Even Evans-Pritchard, one of the creators of the descent model, could not reconcile his own model based on the lineage and the clan with his analysis of Nuer political organization. He wrote: "What exactly is meant by lineage and clan? One thing is fairly certain, namely, that the Nuer do not think in group abstractions called clans. In fact, as far as I am aware, he has no word meaning clan and you cannot ask a man an equivalent of 'What is your clan' " (1933, part 1:28). Moreover, when he did discover a word that corresponded to lineage, it was translated as *thok mac,* the hearth, or *thok dwiel,* the entrance to the hut, neither of which have to do primarily with lineages or corporate groups, both of which have to do with the house. However, I would not go so far as Vansina or Kuper in rejecting descent groups or lineages. My data show that descent is an important aspect of Lese social life, but that it is merely one part of a complex social organization constituted by many elements, one of the most important of which, I believe, is ethnicity.

A given social organization, when represented in terms of descent, might well be seen to reproduce itself within distinct and culturally homogenous "tribes," and to be easily mapped on genealogies or kinship charts according to biological relationships. To represent the same society in ethnic terms is to see both reproduction and transformation within diverse and ever-changing social totalities. Moreover, whereas a focus on descent can potentially mask the integration of individuals and

4. For review and critical commentary on theories of ethnicty, see Cohen 1978; Thompson 1989; Tonkin, McDonald, and Chapman 1989; and Williams 1989. See also Bentley's bibliographic guide, *Ethnicity and Nationality* (1981).

groups who do not participate together in descent groups (such as the Lese and the Efe), and who may not speak the same language, follow the same customs, or live in the same territory, a focus on ethnicity emphasizes the relationships between cultures as constituting variables in social organization. Lese descent groups (clans and lineages) are concerned with only one kind of social organization—an idealized egalitarian political organization of Lese agnates—whereas Lese houses are concerned with organizing inequality between men and women and between Lese and Efe.

TOWARD THE HOUSE

In the chapters that follow, I shall explore the ethnic processes of Lese and Efe society. By ethnic process, I mean the ways in which these groups define themselves in opposition to each other. But this study goes beyond a simple description of the cultural features that comprise ethnic stereotypes. I want to discern how and why some features are more salient than others and to analyze the relationship between ethnicity and the integration of the Lese and the Efe in both symbol and practice. I shall thus be more concerned with analyzing culture as a conceptual scheme, as culture is constituted by models and metaphors. While I do not diminish the importance of extended case analyses and event histories and descriptions, I must admit that I pay more attention to the cultural structure and logic underlying Lese-Efe ethnic relations than to analyzing those relations as they unfold in practice. I give special importance to the idioms employed by the Lese in their symbolic constructions of society, idioms expressed in myth, narrative, and everyday speech.

I view ethnicity to be a historically constituted process in which the Lese and the Efe integrate themselves into a set of relations of inequality. Though we know very little about the relations between the Lese and the Efe in the distant past, the recent history of political and economic marginalization has, in Malembi, the site of this study,[5] contributed not only to the intimacy and the cohesion of the partnerships but also to Lese conceptions of those partnerships as isolated and primordial. As we shall see, though the Lese have been subject to successive waves of Arab, colonial, and national oppression, many Lese men and

5. "Malembi" is not an official designation of a village or group of villages. I use the name to refer to the villages in which I worked, scattered along the Malembi River.

women imagine that they have created their own isolation, and that they live in a peaceful society that is independent of outside forces and constituted entirely by Lese and Efe. As one Lese woman explained the infrequency with which the Lese interact with ethnic groups other than the Efe, "That is the way we are. We want to be alone. Every house to itself." The intimacy and nonviolence of Lese-Efe relations, based in large part upon their solidary juxtaposition to turbulent exogenous forces, stands in contrast to the many violent ethnic cleavages throughout the world, including, for example, South Africa (Vail 1988) and Sri Lanka (Kapferer 1988, Tambiah 1986). And elsewhere in Africa, C. Newbury's recent study of the Hutu and the Tutsi of Rwanda (1988), argues that historical changes in Rwandan politics over the past one hundred years have created greater ethnic solidarities and violent conflict. At the book's close, I will comment on the relative absence of violence between the Lese and the Efe.

However, my approach differs in at least one important respect from that of some anthropologists who have studied ethnicity (John L. Comaroff 1987, Vail 1988, Wilmsen 1990). Whereas many anthropologists take great pains to explore the actual historical circumstances surrounding the emergence of ethnic sentiments, I am concerned more with cultural representations than with ethnogenesis. Indeed, the bulk of this book is devoted not to a historical analysis of the genesis of ethnic identity but to a detailed ethnographic analysis of Lese-Efe social integration during the years 1985–87. The ethnography entails an analysis of how the historical circumstances of economic and political marginalization have resonated with cultural patterns of isolation—for example, the isolation of clans, houses, and gardens from one another—but I am less concerned with locating the motivations and genesis of Lese and Efe ethnic differentiation than I am with analyzing its composition and representations. These two areas of inquiry—historical genesis and cultural constitution—are, like process and structure, no doubt inextricably linked, but within the scope of this study, and within the scope of the data available to me, I place somewhat greater emphasis on my own observations, on the way the Lese group constructed and sustained cultural distinctions and social boundaries during the mid 1980s. Where and how can we locate ethnicity and the social processes that constitute it? How is identity culturally represented? And how are these representations made available to the anthropologist? Because I believe that ethnicity involves the asymmetrical incorporation of groups into a common social organization, I am especially concerned with uncovering and analyzing Lese discourses about inequality. What are the images of domination, and the discourse about status through which relations of inequality between the Lese and the Efe are constituted? And how is the cultural discourse on inequality enacted in social practice?

In large part, the answers to my questions about the Lese-Efe relationship lie in a careful examination of the countless symbolic meanings that together constitute ethnic identity and the nature of interethnic interaction. This is a project that will, ideally, link up the historicity of ethnicity with its "primordial" constitution. Descent, I shall argue, is not of major importance to our understanding of Lese and Efe ethnicity, because Lese-Efe relations are neither conceived nor constructed at the level of the descent group, in this case, the clan. The Lese reckon descent patrilineally and organize their villages as clans. Within villages, the members believe they are genealogically related, though they cannot always discern the precise relationships and usually do not recognize a single apical ancestor. Furthermore, all clan members are ideally equal in status, with no household producing more goods than any other. The primary social function of clans is to unite and mobilize Lese men for war and marriage alliances and thus to mute inequality and social difference in the service of social solidarity. If the clan is the cultural model for equality, where, then, can we locate the model for inequality? Where can we find the images and forms of male-female and Lese-Efe relations? How are these relations culturally patterned?

These questions have been informed, to a considerable degree, by the house models Jan Vansina and Curtis Keim have proposed for the societies of the central African rain forest (Vansina 1982, 1990a, 1990b; Schildkrout and Keim 1990). Vansina's model rejects lineage and kinship as the central or only forms of political organization and argues strongly that the southern central Sudanic and Proto-Mamvu societies of past centuries, which included the Lese, maintained house-centered political traditions. More specifically, he describes the incorporation of slaves, clients, and other kinds of house members who are not necessarily lineage members. In other words, ethnic relationships might be found in the house rather than in the lineage. The house made possible two ideologies of social organization: an egalitarian ideology that reflected the ideals of the lineage (Schildkrout and Keim 1990:89) and a hierarchical ideology that reflected the ideals of the individual. The house was thus flexible enough to simultaneously permit a "coherent internal organization" as well as hierarchical relations between its members (Vansina 1982:175). My use of the house differs from Vansina's in some very important ways (see chapter 4); nonetheless, his model provides a basic theoretical foundation on which I have constructed this ethnography.

I shall argue that relations between the Lese and the Efe, as well as other relations of inequality, are organized at the level of the house. For the Lese and the Efe, the Lese house is where nearly all production, consumption, and distribution of foods take place. Indeed, the house is the physical locus of economic interaction between the Lese and the Efe, and therefore also the locus of social differentiation and potential inequalities. Lese houses are not coresidential units. They ideally contain a man, his wife or wives, their children, and an Efe partner who does not live in the house. Because the partnership, and therefore house membership, is defined through individual Lese and Efe men, the children of Efe partners are not considered members of the house. Houses are therefore not defined by coresidence or lineage so much as by membership, with membership founded upon the integration of Lese men, their wives and children, and Efe partners into common participation in the production and distribution of cultivated foods. As the center of relations of inequality—between men and women, children and adults, Lese and Efe—the house is symbolically significant in the Lese construction of identity and social boundaries. The house is built upon several interlocking metaphors, the most primary of which are "the house is a body," and "the Efe are female." The relations between men and women are, in fact, modeled upon the actual structure of the house (in which sticks support mud as men support women), and Lese-Efe relations are, in turn, modeled upon gender relations (in which the Efe, as a group, are feminized). Thus, the symbolic material out of which the Lese construct their ethnic and economic relations with the Efe has its origin in that which is closest to every Lese individual: the home and hearth, and the primary relationships contained there.

The house, then, is not only a component of larger sets of social relations but a model that has to do with the conceptual organization of ethnic and gender relations, as well as the organization of social practices. It is a source of core symbols but also an arena for interactions structured by them. Although the core metaphors of differentiation are manifold, they all revolve around the house. The house provides for the Lese and the Efe the metaphors that inform ethnic differentiation, and that come to be experienced as primordial, everlasting, and axiomatic. This does not mean that houses and descent groups are not linked, or that one refers solely to domestic relations and the other to political relations; it means merely that they are *coexisting models:* one for inequality, one for egalitarianism. The social organization is perhaps too complicated to be subsumed under one model, and so different aspects of the social totality are modeled by different idioms.

The important role of the house in Lese and Efe society leads us to rethink the Fortesian jural model. One of the legacies of structural functional anthropology is that anthropologists were pulled toward the study of politics in the "politico-jural" domain as distinct from politics in the domestic domain, usually the household (Fortes 1945, 1949). Public and private domains were analytically separated from one another and seldom linked (Yanagisako 1979, H. Moore 1988). What happened at the level of the household, for instance, could be accounted for by kinship relations, but what happened at the level of the clan could be accounted for by clan, descent, or corporate relations. As Evans-Pritchard suggested, "the relations between the sexes and between children and adults belong rather to an account of *domestic relations* than to a study of political institutions" (1940:178). Relations of inequality at the level of the household, including male-female relations, were not salient features of corporate groups, and so were relegated to the domestic domain. Even the numerous studies that focus specifically on households and their economic functions in sub-Saharan Africa (see Guyer 1981) tend to treat the household as a discrete entity "opposed to wider, exogenous, economic processes" (Heald 1991:131). This distinction between the household/domestic and the corporate/political domains does not hold for the Lese and the Efe. We shall see that Lese houses are concerned not only with reproduction and child rearing but also with determining the structures and meanings of economic and political relationships, including the curious and often misunderstood ethnic relations between the foragers and farmers.

CHAPTER II

The History and Isolation of the Lese

"That is the way we Lese are. We want to be alone. Every house to itself."

A Lese woman commenting on the infrequency of Lese interactions with the neighboring Budu farmers

Discoveries are inseparable from the roads we take to find them. Traveling south from the town of Isiro, across the forest-savanna border, through seemingly endless stretches of green, and into the heart of the Ituri rain forest, one is aware of the dilapidated north-south road as an encumbrance—a barrier to overcome, rather than an integral part of the local human landscape. Many Zairians who live with the road do not think of it as their own; it belongs to the tourists, missionaries, expatriate traders, and scientists, for whom, as some Zairians say, it was originally intended. The foreigners are the ones who have always depended upon it for commerce and mobility. For me, the road was a lifeline that linked me to what I perceived to be "the outside world," and I endowed the road with enormous personal meaning and significance. I tended, therefore, to unwittingly think of the road not only as the route of foreigners, but also as the anthropologists' footing, as an extension of myself. It was many months before I began to conceive of the road as an important element in the everyday lives of the people of Malembi.

The road alongside which the Lese of Malembi currently live is for them a symbol both of isolation and of contact; it constitutes both the limits and the possibilities of isolation. To some extent, Lese and Efe interaction with neighboring societies, and with urban or plantation systems, has been extensive or slight depending upon the condition of the road. In the 1930s, before the road was built, the Lese lived in interaction with a number of different groups, such as the Budu and the

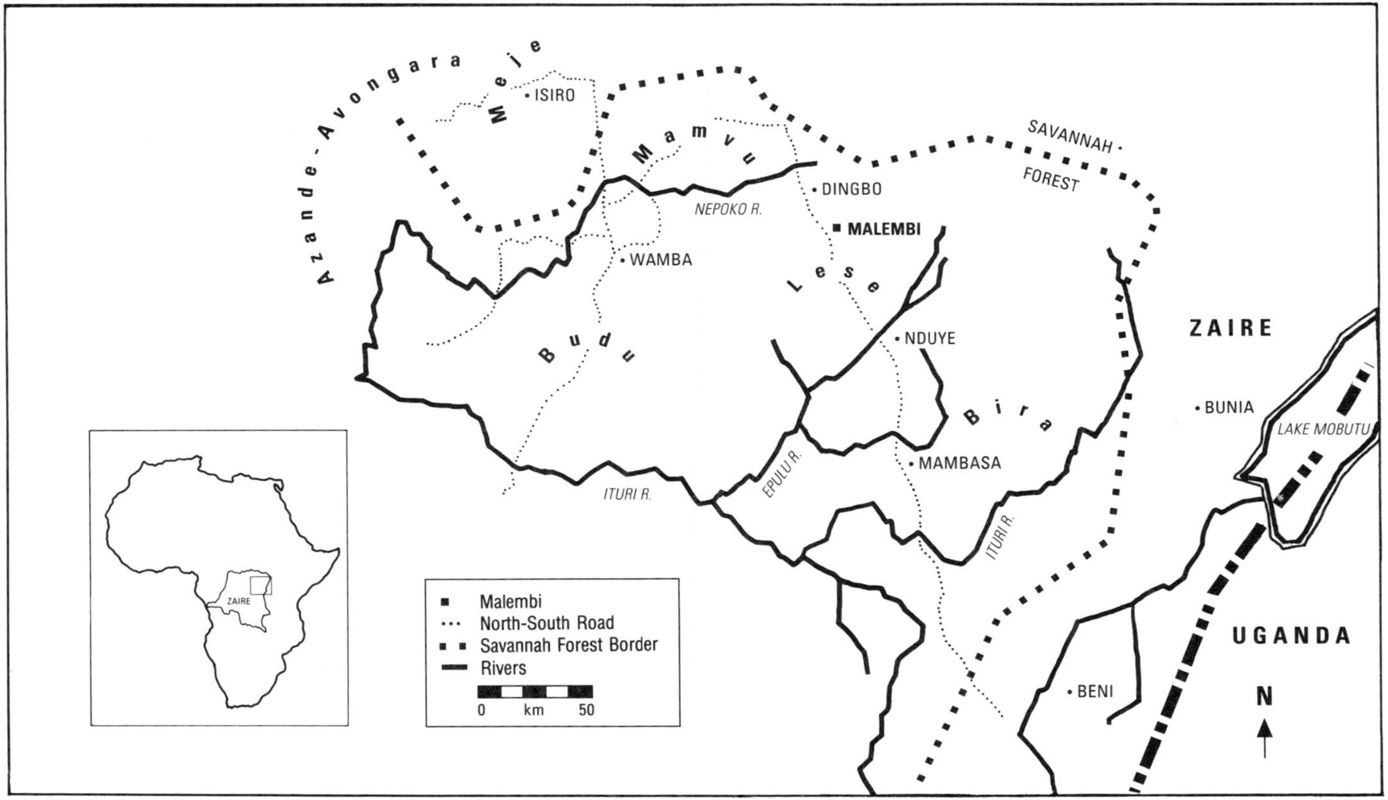
Azande-Avongara
Meje
ISIRO
Mamvu
NEPOKO R.
DINGBO
MALEMBI
WAMBA
SAVANNAH
FOREST
Lese
Budu
NDUYE
Bira
MAMBASA
EPULU R.
ITURI R.
ITURI R.
ZAIRE
BUNIA
LAKE MOBUTU
UGANDA
BENI
N
ZAIRE
Malembi
North-South Road
Savannah Forest Border
Rivers
0 km 50

Mamvu, but interaction must have been infrequent. Even within Lese areas, villages were situated as far as fifteen kilometers apart. During the 1940s, the Belgian administration displaced the Lese from their deep forest villages, resettled them close to where they intended to build the north-south road, and eventually forced them to construct it. By the 1950s, when Belgian colonialism reached its zenith, the north-south road was as wide as twelve meters. Trucks passed daily, going back and forth from Isiro and Mungbere to Mambasa, Epulu, and Kisangani. In those days, the trip from Isiro to Mambasa took less than five hours; from Isiro to Kisangani took just over a day.

By 1987, the road had so deteriorated that the trip to Mambasa took two days, and the trip to Kisangani sometimes took five to ten, depending on the weather and road conditions. All along the route, there are now bridges in ruin, deep holes, and trenches; long stretches are so overgrown that they are hardly passable. There are visible signs of atrophy also in the gutted buildings of the Belgian administration that now house Zairian government offices, in the disused rail lines, telephone and electrical poles, and remnants of the once lush plantations and gardens of the former European owners. At one time, Belgian and Greek entrepreneurs maintained plantations within a short walk from Malembi, and near the gardens of the Lese one sometimes finds old pipes and cement culverts blanketed in foliage.

During the rainy season, in October and November, the road is so muddy that only small motorcycles can get through. Occasionally, perhaps once or twice a month, a vehicle driven by a Catholic missionary comes along. Because of the humidity (even in the dry season at the beginning of the year) and the dense overhead curtains of plant life the road is seldom really dry. Villagers wage a constant battle to cut back the vegetation from their own paths, villages, and gardens, and the police and military continually press the villagers to clear narrow stretches of road, and to widen its borders in the hope that Land-Rovers, if there were any, could pass.

The road in a sense symbolizes what anthropologists have been gradually learning as we begin to explore historical transformations and reproductions, and place the study of social organization, kinship, or the economy, among other things, within a wider historical context. This change is a response not simply to synchronic studies but also to the old notion that communities can be studied in isolation from larger domains, such as the region, the nation, or even the international community. Epistemological changes in anthropology involve reconceptualizing the boundaries of what we assumed to be "closed societies," to one extent or another removed from the larger spheres of capitalism, polities, and the world system. Situating our fieldwork within historical context represents a central paradox in the practice of anthropology; the problem, as Sally Falk Moore phrased it, is that anthropology is practiced not in the world but in the local community, yet the local community exists within the world (personal communication).

If we overemphasize the importance of exogenous forces, we run the risk of viewing the communities we study as encompassed and determined by them, and of perpetuating the analytic dichotomy between the closed and open society, the traditional and the historical, the primitive and the modern (Lévi-Strauss 1976, Comaroff 1984). The north-south road of Malembi was, indeed, built by the Belgians. In the course of the road building, not only were many Lese forced to work on the road but others were made to relocate and work on plantations, missions, and in urban centers that were previously far out of their domain. But the Lese and the Efe also "constructed" the road both literally and figuratively. Many Lese, my informants tell me, welcomed the changes. Some Lese were happy to move to the roadside and engage in plantation and missionary work. Many Lese also enjoyed selling their crops for cash and receiving medical care from the missionaries. In past years, however, many Lese have sought to destroy the road and to insulate themselves from outsiders, primarily for the purposes of achieving safety and autonomy. Instead of trying to maintain the road, they have worked to help its deterioration as a way of reducing their contacts with European and neighboring groups—not only government administrators and Greek traders but also the Ngwana, Budu, Bila, and Mamvu, among others, all of whom are called *ude,* meaning stranger and enemy. More recently they have attempted to minimize the effects of Zairian state and regional domestic policies (especially those concerned with the value of the Zaire currency) on their local economy by participating less in local markets and wage labor. The Lese and the Efe with whom I lived from 1985 to 1987 try to interact almost exclusively with one another. More and more, owing both to their wishes for isolation and to the condition of the road (for which they are in part responsible), they are physically isolated from the missionary, urban, and agricultural systems with which they were so well acquainted before independence.

Lese men and women of all ages are ambivalent about such isolation. The villages, they say with sadness, are today much smaller than in former years. This is due largely to a high mortality rate, and lower fertility (Ellison et al. 1986) resulting primarily from venereal disease. It is hard to determine just how prevalent sexually transmitted diseases are in the area, but gonorrhea and syphilis appear to be common among both the Lese and the Efe. In addition, AIDS, though most prevalent in the urban areas of Zaire, may soon reach the rural areas in which the Lese live. The poor condition of the road means that the Lese have less access than they would like to missionary hospitals and clinics. They also have less access to cloth and Western goods such as shoes and radios. Outside traders rarely enter the area to buy coffee or peanuts from the Lese, and since the Lese themselves show little desire to repair the road, and the Zaire government has neither the money nor the inclination to help the Ituri region, the present isolation will no doubt continue.

But isolation has its rewards in security and sanctuary. The lives of the new generation of Zairian Lese have been filled with anxiety and fear about the role of the state in their everyday lives. The Lese cite frequent imprisonment, poverty resulting from exploitation by government authorities, and the high inflation of the Zairian economy as examples of the dangers of the integration of their lives with what they call the "outside" world. The inside world of the Lese and the Efe is something to be protected and maintained, even if the insulation of that world has its costs. I cannot stress enough the importance and saliency of isolation that I found to be the case for the Lese during my fieldwork, the frequency with which the people of Malembi spoke to me about being alone (*ite*), different (*muamua*), and socially fragmented (*ikau*). Isolation is not something of which only I am conscious, as I pursue an analysis of a social situation; this is how the Lese represented themselves to me.

The Lese of Malembi are isolated in two ways—isolated as a group, as a result of their conscious struggle for greater security and autonomy in the context of a history of oppression and peripheralization, and isolated from one another in smaller social units such as the house and the village, as a result of cultural dispositions. The deterioration of the road, the consequent loss of access to markets, and peripheralization from the centers of Zairian politics and economy forced the Lese into a larger geographical and social isolation, but cultural preference determined the internal social isolation. The tendency toward isolation in social and economic organization (a subject that forms the basis of chapters 4 and 5) cannot be underestimated. Not only the structure and layout of Lese villages but also the beliefs in various forms of witchcraft and local prejudices against the sharing or trading of cultivated foods among themselves reinforce the larger isolation in a way quite different from the process of marginalization and peripheralization in the political economy. However, many Lese, I believe, rationalize their peripheral status in terms of the wishes for the isolation of other more local social domains; that is, although many Lese do not want to be isolated, especially from markets and medical centers, they may say that they do. One young Lese woman, commenting on the infrequency of her contacts with the Budu, a neighboring Bantu-speaking group, said, "That is the way we Lese are. We want to be alone. Every house to itself." She quite clearly confounds two different kinds of isolation—isolation in the larger political and economic context, and in the context of everyday village life—and thus draws a connection between the isolation of the Lese from other ethnic groups, and the isolation of houses from one another. She said, quoting a Lese proverb: "Pigs know each other by their noses," meaning that one should know only those with whom one is living intimately, or, more literally, those to whom one is close enough to smell.

Isolation, then, is one of the constituents of Lese identity. The Lese are, of course, not as isolated as they make themselves out to be, nor does everyone always and unequivocally hold a particular preference for contact or isolation. As we shall see, the Lese have a long history of forced labor, rubber cultivation, and relocation. More recently, and to this day, the Lese sell some cash crops to outsiders and sometimes work as wage laborers at plantations so that they can buy Western goods. Many Lese have also enjoyed occasional friendships with missionaries and the various scientists, including anthropologists, who have lived in the area over the years. Moreover, they continue to be subject to harassment by state officials. Yet the Lese of Malembi insist that they are isolated. Such is the ambivalence that characterizes the Lese within their historical predicament and allows the young woman cited above to overlook the distinction between these two parallel processes of isolation, one imposed from outside, the other imposed from within. Marginalization has become so confounded with smaller-scale social isolation—in the idea of isolation as a general tendency—that it is an integral part of many Lese men and women's self-image.

The concern with what I have referred to as "isolation" is crucial to my representation of the Lese in this study. Recall that one of the central aims of this book is to discover just how the Lese of Malembi derive a

A Lese village with scattered coffee plants and a recently slashed and burned garden. *Photograph by R. R. Grinker.*

sense of who they are, and where they find the cultural material to construct group boundaries and identities. Isolation has become an ethnic criterion, a way that the Lese envisage themselves in relation to their history and to the other ethnic groups with whom they have had contact.

THE LESE "CHIEFDOMS"

More by name than by actual political organization, the farmers living at Malembi today are, officially, members of a "chiefdom." They call themselves the Lese-Dese and make up one of five Lese chiefdoms in northeastern Zaire, the others being the Lese-Karo, living from Nzaro to Mambasa, the Lese-Abfunkotu, living from Komanda to Mount Hoyo, the Lese-Otsodo, living from Watsa to Djungu, and the Lese-Mvuba, living in the vicinity of Beni, near the Ugandan border. H. Van Geluwe (1957) treats all the Lese as if they were one unified group, and the Mvuba as if they were another. G. Schweinfurth (1874), one of the first explorers to encounter the Lese, recognizes an additional group called the Lese-Obi, and P. Schebesta (1952) lumps the Mvuba, Lese, and Mamvu together as the Bvuba-Balese-Mamvu based on their linguistic similarity. To my knowledge, however, those people who call themselves Lese-Obi identify themselves as a subgroup of the Lese-Abfunkotu. The Lese-Otsodo also present some confusion, since many Otsodo identify themselves as Lese-Mangutu. The Mamvu, today considered by Zairians to be a non-Lese group, live north of Malembi and Dingbo. The Lese-Dese, with whom we are concerned here, is the smallest of all the groups. They live in the *Collectivité Lese-Dese,* a Zairian administrative unit that includes approximately twenty-three hundred farmers, about nineteen hundred of whom are Lese-Dese, about four hundred of whom are Mamvu, Lese-Karo, or Azande, and about a thousand Efe who live close to the Lese-Dese villages.

Following Geluwe (1957), A. Merriam (1959) considers the "Mamvu-Lese" as a "culture cluster" either within itself or as a subcluster of the Mangbetu-Azande cluster (based primarily on similarities in material culture). Although the customs and the language of the Mamvu are considerably different from those of the Lese-Dese and the Lese-Karo, their proximity has resulted in extensive intermarriage with the Lese, as well as the mutual exchange of language and ideas. Vansina (1990a), using A. Vorbichler's figure of a 93 percent correspondence between the Mamvu and Lese-Abfunkotu languages (Vorbichler 1971), suggests that the split between the Mamvu and the Lese groups occurred as recently as A.D. 1720. He points out that in the first centuries A.D., several diverse groups of farmers and herders made their way into the rain forest from nearly every direction (Vansina 1990a:169). However, historians and linguists who have looked into the question of dating the arrival of the Lese distinguish the Lese from the early wave of immigrants. The immigrants included speakers of three main language families: Bantu, central Sudanic, and Ubangian; the Lese most likely derive from, or were associated with, the Sudanic speakers.

I refer to the Sudanic Lese language as "Lese," and the language as spoken by the Efe, "Efe." I have purposely dropped the prefix "Ki-," used by many scholars (e.g., Schebesta 1933; Turnbull 1965b; Bailey 1985) to refer to the languages of northeastern Zaire because "Ki-" is a prefix for Bantu rather than Sudanic languages and should therefore not appear with "Lese" or "Efe." [1]

According to the historian and administrator M. Baltus (1949), the various Lese groups before colonization classified themselves into four

1. Readers interested in the morphology of Lese and related languages can refer to Harries 1956 and Vorbichler 1971.

divisions: the Lese-Karo, the Maro, the Masa, and the Lese-Dese. Baltus believed that, as early as the seventeenth century, the Lese were situated north of their present location, in the Uele and Bomokande River area, and that, in the nineteenth century, as a result of Zande and Mangbetu expansion, they were pushed further south. Whether or not the Lese were actually affected by Zande and Mangbetu invasions, we do know that the Lese were living with the Efe, and living within or near the Ituri rain forest, at that time (Keim 1979). The Lese themselves say that they come from a large mountain called Menda, from which all the "black people" of Africa originated. After arguments over sharing fruit, each group went its own way, the Budu traveling to Wamba, and the Mamvu and the various Lese groups traveling southeast toward the Nepoko River.

We do not know where Mount Menda is located; we cannot even be sure that such a mountain exists outside of legend. Most Lese I interviewed, however, are confident that their ancestors emigrated from the north, and Mount Menda may therefore be a metaphoric representation of north. Paul Joset (1949), another historian and administrator, thought the Lese could have traveled south to the Ituri from the Uele/Bomokande region, or, just as possibly, could have come from the Ruwenzori mountain area far to the east and gradually moved west across the Semliki River, from what is now western Uganda.

There is some support for this latter theory. For one thing, the Lese-Mvuba (they appear as "Mbuba" or "Bambuba" in Joset 1949) live today not far from the Semliki, the town of Beni (close to the Uganda-Zaire border), and Lake Mobutu (formerly Lake Edward, on the Uganda-Zaire border) and form part of a larger ethnic group called the Amba. Also, some elderly Lese-Dese informants told me that despite the many people who believe Mount Menda is in the north, it is actually located in the savanna to the southeast of the Ituri forest. Furthermore, Baltus (1949) says that his Lese-Mvuba informants talked of migrating from a great lake (there are no great lakes in the Uele region), following the Mamvu and Lese-Dese across the savanna. There is also support for the Lese legend of migration from a mountain in the fact that, whereas there are few mountains in the Uele or Ituri regions, the area around the Semliki is quite mountainous. In addition, the Lese-Dese language contains words for birds and mammals that live only outside the rain forest, such as hippopotami and lions, large populations of which live in the valley of the Semliki River. Joset writes:

> The Bambuba [Mvuba] are blood brothers of the Walese, and of the Mamvu. They seem to have been the rear-guard of the migration; the

> Mamvu, followed by the Walese, preceded them. . . . According to the commissioner of the Absil district, the Bambuba came from Kitara, in Uganda, by way of Mukeve, to the north of Ruwenzori. In the course of their migrations, they settled in MUHULUNI [sic; Uganda], near the border, then settled in the Abwanza region (currently inhabited by the Watalinga). Under the pressure of the Watalinga, who also came from the east, the Bambuba crossed the Semliki River and settled on its banks.
>
> Sharing the same ethnic and racial characteristics, the Mamvu-Walese-Bambuba also share the same linguistic characteristics. (1949:5, my translation)

The linguistic evidence may be quite unreliable, of course. If the Lese came from the north and traveled through the forest south to the Semliki, and then moved back into the forest, they could have been familiar with mammals in a transitory way. Many Lese groups who live near the forest-savanna ecotone have had contact with a variety of savanna populations, so that words of savanna origin were introduced into the vocabulary at various points in history. Joset, on the other hand, says that the various Lese groups, "the warriors of the forest," as he calls them, did not like the savanna and searched for forest land. He says that the Lese, after living for some time at the edge of a series of mountains, were afflicted with severe hunger. They dispersed and looked for hospitable territory.

> The Walese left Mount Ami, stopped for a short time at Mount Sawa, and settled on Mount Mulabu, in the middle of the forest. They planted bananas there, proof of a prolonged stay.
>
> Several years later there was a great famine that dispersed the Walese. Each family split off from the group, going its separate way, seeking hospitable soil; this would be the last stage of their migration. (Joset 1949:5, my translation)

THE FIRST CITIZENS

Geluwe (1957), a Belgian museum worker who had never been to Africa, but nonetheless assembled reports of explorers, missionaries, and Belgian territorial administrators into a volume on the Lese and Mamvu peoples, agrees with Joset that the Lese came to the forest and discovered the Pygmies, whom she refers to as the ancient inhabitants of the Ituri forest. The Pygmies are, in fact, officially designated in Zaire as "Premier Citoyens" (first citizens), a title that, in addition to lumping these culturally different groups under a single category, accords them the privilege of not paying taxes. Both Joset and Geluwe state with confidence that the Lese represent the first non-Pygmy arrival to the forest.

There is, of course, little evidence to indicate how long the various Pygmy groups have lived in the Ituri, and Vorbichler's dates, based on linguistic evidence, are far from conclusive. If, as some recent ecological data suggest, no hunter-gatherer group has ever lived in a rain forest environment independent of agriculture (Headland and Reid 1989; Bailey et al. 1989; Bailey and Peacock 1989), it may well be that the Pygmies entered the Ituri at the same time or later than farming communities, and the Lese-Efe relationship may therefore be of very recent origin.

The history of the relation between the various Pygmy groups is as unclear as the history of the relation between the Lese and the Efe. The short-statured hunter-gatherers who live with the Lese and the Mamvu in the northern Ituri forest call themselves the Efe. They distinguish themselves from three other named Pygmy groups in Zaire: the Mbuti, who live to the south of the Efe and who are associated with the Bantu-speaking agriculturalist Bila; the Sua, who live on the western border of the Ituri and are associated with the Budu, and the Aka, who live in the northwest with the Mangbetu. The members of each of these Pygmy groups generally associate with one, but sometimes more than one, group of farmers and speak a language that is mutually intelligible to the farmers. Thus, the Mbuti, who associate with the Bila, speak a language similar to KiBila, and the Efe speak a language similar to Lese. When Mbuti and Efe meet, they communicate in Swahili or Lingala.

Despite the differences in language, Schebesta sought linguistic evidence to explore earlier relationships among these disparate Pygmy populations. He intended to show, first, that there were similarities in structure between the language of the Sua and the language of the Efe, and, second, that the Sua and Efe similarly altered the languages as spoken by the farmers. For example, although the Sua and Efe languages are radically different, they both drop the sound */k/* in favor of a gutteral sound; */aka/* as spoken by the farmers thus becomes */a'a/* in Sua or Efe, and */mpaka/* becomes */mpa'a/*. If Sua and Efe could be shown to be similar to one another, and yet distinct from the languages of their village counterparts, this might point to an earlier unity, linguistic or otherwise, between Pygmy groups. Turnbull furthered this line of investigation by stating that an Mbuti from any part of the Ituri can *recognize,* though not *comprehend,* any other Pygmy language. However, there are too few data to support generalizations about prior unity, and the hypotheses are fueled less by scholarly investigation than by the assumption that foragers and farmers entered the forest independently, and that all Pygmies were at one time a single, undifferentiated cultural group.

Finally, the study of the history of the relations between the Lese and the Efe, as we shall see, is in somewhat of a muddle. Recognizing the importance of the relationship between the two groups, however, can lead to several interesting lines of research, including glottochronology (Vansina 1990a) and studies of the historical changes in Lese-Efe relations. One might well question whether the Lese sought relations with the Efe because of the demands foreigners placed upon the Lese to supply forest goods. There is strong evidence to suggest that some patron-client relations in Africa have their origin in imperial or colonial history (Turton 1986). D. Turton, for example, argues that the link between the Mursi pastoralists and Kwegu hunters and cultivators of Ethiopia was forged in recent imperial history primarily to enable the Mursi to exploit the Kwegu for ivory. As well shall see in a moment, both Arabs and Belgians demanded ivory and rubber, and the Lese were able to provide their quotas only with the help of the Efe. Establishing a point of origin for such complex relations is an endless and perhaps fruitless task. Neither this chapter nor this book attempts to answer such questions. However, future investigations must take into account the historicity of ethnicity. It is unlikely that the Lese and the Efe of today resemble those of yesterday.

PRECOLONIAL HISTORY

In any case, Baltus states that by the nineteenth century the Lese bordered the left bank of the Nepoko River, and its southern tributaries, the Uala, Afande, Mambo, and Ngaue rivers. A group of people known as the Masa followed the Lese south, settled east of the Lese-Dese on the Kero River, and would much later be incorporated into the new Lese-Dese chiefdom. The Lese-Karo, and the Maro, occupied the left bank of the upper Bomokande, as well as parts of the Nepoko, Nduye, Epulu, and Ituri rivers. Another group, the Lese-Abfunkotu, who now live southeast of Mambasa, followed the Ituri River and established themselves on what is today the Beni road. For reasons unknown to Baltus or Joset, the Lese subsequently migrated south and west from the Nepoko toward the confluence of the Biasa and Nduye rivers. The Andisopi and Andipaki phratries, which today occupy Malembi, the site of this study, occupied the Afande and Mambo rivers. According to Baltus, Tshaminionge, a man whom the Belgians appointed chief of the Lese-Karo, believed that the Karo were for a time under the authority of the Mangbetu people, who today live far north of both the Lese-Karo and the Lese-Dese. The Mangbetu demanded that the Karo give them ivory and women as tributes, and later demanded rubber for trade with the Belgians and the Arabisés.

The Arabisés, a people of Arab-coastal Swahili origin who were first contacted by Europeans at the Congo River as early as 1870, were actively involved in slave and ivory trading, and their dominion extended throughout the eastern Congo, from Stanleyville (Kisangani) to Lake Albert (Lake Mobutu), and Lake Edward (Lake Idi Amin Dada). Sir Henry Morton Stanley encountered them on his expeditions and helped to establish an Arabisé settlement on the banks of the Ituri River at MaWambi. According to Baltus's informants, the Arabisés kidnapped young boys and girls from various groups for slavery, and mutilated or executed many adults. Joset notes:

> Until the arrival of the Europeans, independently of their numerous internal ways, the Walese had to deal with large fights, first against the Bahema, then against the Arabisés . . .
>
> Five or six years later [after a Hema invasion], came bands of Arabs, slave traders, under the authority of three chiefs . . . It was the first time the Walese came in contact with firearms. The Arabisés resumed, in a bloodier fashion, the massacres that Kabarega [of the BaHema] had carried out. The old men we interviewed—who were between six and ten years of age at the time of these events—asserted that the Arabs killed more than half of the male population and carried off children, livestock, ivory, and young women. (1949:7, my translation)

By the turn of the century, many Arabisés were settled at Wamba, within a day's walk of most of the Lese-Dese villages. Other Arabisés were settled at Andudu (36 km. north of Malembi), Nduye (70 km. south of Malembi), and Mambasa (120 km. south of Malembi). The arrival and penetration of the Belgians brought an end to the Arabisé violence and slave trading, but they continued other forms of trading for many decades. They were the first to engage the Lese in rubber and ivory production, and their presence can still be recognized in the names of the Lese-Dese, among whom names of Arabic origin such as Abdala and Salumu have been passed down over the generations, and in the presence of a Swahili dialect, KiNgwana, that is today the *lingua franca* of eastern Zaire.

RED RUBBER

King Leopold's dynamite-carrying agent Henry Morton Stanley—and later, the whole colonial regime—was popularly known in the Belgian Congo as the "Bula Matari" (literally, "rock crusher"). The Belgians ruled the Congo ruthlessly and comprehensively, penetrating into Congolese societies to dominate, govern, and recruit labor from its members. Leopold II of Belgium began his large-scale exploitation soon after being given the Congo Free State as his personal property at the Berlin conference of 1885. Within five years, the Congo Free State claimed to own all natural products of the Congolese forests (Jewsiewicki 1983), and it had seized all land not "directly occupied" by the Africans. With virtually no financial assistance from his homeland, Leopold would have to seek revenues from even the most secluded of forest populations. Local farmers like the Lese, Bila, Budu, and Mamvu would eventually form the basis of the Belgian colonial economy (Jewsiewicki 1983; Young 1983; Young and Turner 1985).

At first, Leopold II was able to provide funding for colonial rule by exploiting ivory and wild rubber. Western demand for ivory had been high for a long time, and after the development of the pneumatic tire in England in the 1890s, the demand for rubber hosing and tubing spurred rubber production in the Congo. Between 1894 and 1905, the price of rubber doubled (Harms 1975). But there were several problems with rubber production, not the least being a shortage of trees. B. Jewsiewicki cites a 1908 report that shows only six rubber trees on average in one acre of Congo forest, each tree yielding only half a kilogram of rubber. At this rate, the rubber supply was nearly exhausted within a decade after production began. Production was further hampered by wasteful methods. Instead of extracting the sap carefully with small incisions, collectors cut and mutilated the trees, making them worthless for future use. By 1910, the Belgians had run out of rubber in Equateur Province, and the supply was waning in the Ituri. The flood of Southeast Asian rubber three years later was a further depressant. The serious human cost of rubber production also began to emerge, and it helped critics of the Belgian regime, especially the English, to influence Europeans of many nations to halt investments and seek goods elsewhere (see Morel 1906). Jewsiewicki sums up:

> During the Leopoldian era in Zaire history, only 10 percent of income came directly from the Crown domains, the profit from which was mostly used to finance the activities of the Crown of Belgium. Rubber and ivory, which had

> contributed 60 percent of the total value of exports in 1890, were responsible for 95 percent of the total in 1900. Rubber accounted for 84 percent of this figure, but in the long run the system destroyed itself by destroying its own resources of men and rubber trees. (1983:99).

All Congolese were taxed, but since money was forbidden in the Leopoldian Congo, they were "allowed" to pay their taxes with labor for the state or for concessionary companies. In some parts of the Congo, local inhabitants were therefore obligated to give rubber to Leopold's concessionary companies, as a labor tax, also called "taxes in kind" (Louis 1966:274), or the *impot de cueillette*. The formal quota was four kilos of dry rubber (equivalent to eight kilos of wet rubber) every two weeks for each male inhabitant. In actual practice, the Belgians extracted everything they could, and the requirement of a specific quantity of rubber was primarily a way to make the exploitation look ordered and temperate (Jan Vansina, personal communication). Those who did not meet that burden were subject to beatings, and the Arabisés apparently tried to get rubber in any way they could, including violent acts. Congolese sentries guarded the posts, and they were flogged and sometimes executed or mutilated if the villagers under their supervision did not meet the quota. While there is no accurate estimate on the number of Congolese men, women, and children executed, tortured, or mutilated between 1885 and 1906 (some estimates are as high as one million), the number must have been in the thousands.

Although historians have not documented actual methods of violence committed against inhabitants of the Ituri during the rubber collecting period, some missionary reports, and reports from intermediaries responsible for forcing the local populations to produce ivory, rubber, and other goods for the state, suggest that amputated hands were circulated as a currency to make up for shortfalls (Forbath 1977). The Congo Reform Movement in Britain, fueled by outrage at the fact that an individual could control and own such a large amount of land and people, accepted these reports of violence as accurate. For the purposes of his propaganda, E. D. Morel, the leader of the movement, called Leopold's reign the era of "red rubber," rubber stained with blood of innocent thousands. Even if the stories about amputated hands are inaccurate, the reality is that a large percentage of Congolese died as the result of violence and disease.

Oral history suggests that soon after contact with the Europeans, the great-grandparents and grandparents of the Lese of Malembi collected rubber, though whether or not this was a legal obligation is not clear.

Certainly, however, for the Lese as for all Congolese, the dwindling supply of rubber forced men to travel farther and farther from their villages, beyond the boundaries of their clans and phratries. Out of their own territories, various groups often fought violently with one another for rights to the little rubber that remained. In a letter dated June 15, 1915, D. de D. Siffer, a Belgian official, described to the district commissioner in Irumu the local inhabitants' difficulties in procuring rubber. Siffer's letter suggests strongly that the Lese inhabitants of the Nepoko region were under legal obligation to produce rubber; the obligation was, indeed, a general policy in the Belgian Congo; however, I know of no written documents stating explicitly that the Lese were forced to collect rubber. From his post among the Lese-Dese, Siffer (District du Kibali-Ituri Correspondence, 1920–37, Zone de Mambasa archives) writes of the rubber collecting activities of the "people of Nepoko," presumably the Mamvu:

> Their [the WaLese's] forest is just about the last resource of the people of Nepoko. Seeking to take care of their taxes by the harvest and sale of rubber, the people of Nepoko show up in [our] area after walking for five to seven days, already poorly received because they come to exhaust the forests that the Walese would prefer to keep for themselves. They are starving and want to eat; they steal from the plantations, and the Walese have a great sense of property. Quarrels follow, arrows are shot, and there are wounded at every battle. The Walese is constantly vigilant. (my translation)

Siffer goes on to point out that in addition to the human casualties, many houses were burned and destroyed.

My Lese informants were clear in their association of the rubber collection era with a time of feuds that made travel beyond one's boundaries all the more perilous. The period seems to be a significant reference point for the Lese. Three elderly informants (two men and one woman) whom I questioned about the past, though not specifically about rubber, brought up rubber collection as one of the most important events in Lese history. I quote:

> 1. We were feuding, and the Europeans came and said "stop that." "Go and get rubber for us." They sold the rubber we gave to the BaNgwana [part-Arab descendants] grandfathers. Rubber, rubber, rubber. It went to the *ude* [Belgians]. The others called themselves Marabo (Arabisé), and their skin was red. My father called them KodoKokbo because it [KodoKokbo] is a long snake that is red, and the Marabo carried long sticks, and beat us with them. We had to give rubber, and they paid us with cups and beads, and bracelets.

> 2. Our great-grandfathers lived at the time of rubber. They would go out for two days, but stay only two days because they were afraid of being lost or killed. They did get lost, and when Ude-ni, my ancestor, looked for his father, and when he passed the Andisamba Efe, they shot him with an arrow, and killed him.
>
> 3. We were at war with the Maru [phratry]. Azima's father showed my father to a place where there was some rubber left. Our children followed, and went to the river to dig for crabs. Aumbu of the Maru heard the children EdiEdi and Aboreke. He knew they were the voices of children, and killed them. And so there the Maru killed us.

When these and other Lese informants discussed the period of rubber collection from the perspective of their relations with the Efe, they often remembered the period fondly, as a time when the Lese and the Efe shared their lives and food much more fully than they do today. For example, the Efe and the Lese cooperated in rubber collecting. The Efe, in fact, produced large amounts of rubber, and rubber acquisition thus became an essential part of their relationship with the Lese.[2] The Efe accompanied the Lese as guards on most of the Lese rubber-collecting expeditions and guided the Lese on lesser-known forest paths. One Lese man reported: "We lived always with our Efe. Every man cut rubber with his Efe. Every man stopped and stood with his Efe before the *ude* [European] to sell rubber. Everything. We did everything with the Efe." The Efe not only helped the Lese collect rubber, but in later years would protect the Lese from hunger seasons and the violence of Zairian national political strife.

Rubber was such an important item for the colonial administration that rubber markets were placed on the axis of the north-south trail that later became the road through the Lese residences; markets were also established at Nduye, and later at Biasa (only 40 km south of Malembi) and Paoni. Although the Congo rubber market essentially came to a halt after 1910, the Lese occasionally cut and sold some rubber on a voluntary basis until the 1930s. An elderly Lese man said, "Later the Dese stopped selling [rubber] at Nduye, but we sold at the Andikara clan [Biasa]. From there they started to build roads, and we sold rubber at Uetakukbo [Paoni]. They stopped getting rubber when Alambi became chief of the Lese-Dese [in1936]."

2. In sharp contrast to the Lese situation, the Aka Pygmies of present-day Central African Republic did not engage in rubber collection, though why this was the case is not clear, especially since the Aka were the principal producers of ivory, another good demanded by Europeans (Bahuchet and Guillaume 1982:200).

ASPECTS OF THE BELGIAN COLONIAL ECONOMY

Belgium responded to the financial crisis and to increasing criticism in Europe over the brutality of Leopold's regime by assuming control over the Congo Free State in 1908. Soon after annexation, Belgium replaced the brutal station agents and sentries with Belgian civil servants. Congolese soldiers were organized into gendarmeries, and the floggings, executions, and amputations were for the most part halted. Most of the forced labor ceased, as did the imposition of rubber and ivory quotas, and Leopold's monopoly on commerce was open to any and all investors. The Belgian administration focused its attention on two areas: mining and agriculture. By the 1920s, it was exploiting tin, gold, copper, and iron in the Congo for extensive profit, primarily in Katanga district. The new administration did not interfere with the mining concessions created by Leopold, but rather expanded them with a railway concession, and new mines were developed in previously unexploited areas of the colony—gold mines in the east and northeast, near Wamba, Watsa, and Mambasa, where the Budu and the Lese-Otsodo formed the bulk of the labor pool, and manganese mines in the south, partly as a response to the demands of American steelworks. By the 1920s, many of these towns had undergone extensive construction and landscaping. Schebesta noted that by 1933 Wamba was an administrative headquarters, had many factories and plantations, and had "broad streets lined with Coco-nut palms on either side" (1933).

From oral history, my best estimate is that the mines were within a three-day walk of the Lese-Dese villages, far enough away to allow them to escape direct incorporation into the mining industry. Mining development depended on the recruitment of huge labor pools from the hinterland of the colony, but recruitment was purposely carried out locally, within the vicinity of the mines, so as not to mix workers from different "disease zones" (Vellut 1983), and thereby, it was hoped, prevent the spread of disease; mortality rates were already a significant problem at the mines. The Belgian recruiters profited from indigenous food scarcity because hungry farmers sought to work on the mines in exchange for payment in cultivated food and dried, salted fish. Locusts and other natural catastrophes had always forced people to shift residences, and during these times of crisis many Congolese migrated to the mines, where food was more plentiful. The Lese-Dese, though no better off than most in their food supply, lived too far from the mines to get attention from the labor recruiters, and I heard no accounts of any Lese-Dese going into the mining area for any reason.

Indirectly, however, the Lese and other more remote communities were caught up in the mining industry because the mine workers' food came from the agricultural sector, and because agriculture itself suffered from losses of labor as farmers flocked to the mines. When the wild rubber market finally collapsed, the colony needed a profitable and exportable surplus to increase revenues, as well as a surplus of food above the level of rural subsistence systems so that they could feed the miners. By World War I, the colony decreed that each villager had to devote at least 60 days to growing crops decided upon by the administration, and that failure to do so would result in fines, beatings, and imprisonment. Large plantations were established near Wamba to produce food for the miners, but these did not produce enough food for export. Until World War II, the only profitable export crop coming out of the plantations was palm oil, much of which came from palm fruits gathered by local hunters and farmers like the Lese (Young and Turner 1985).

European farmers in the Congo produced little food on their own and were nominally successful in coffee production only; Jewsiewicki (1983) notes that "the production of [other] foodstuffs thus remained in African hands, and its regional commercialization remained within the framework of a free market." European capital was channeled into the processing of cotton and palm oil, rather than into primary production. Recognizing this situation, many in the colonial administration aimed to increase indigenous production, to capitalize on what had already been established. In an attempt to form an agricultural policy, the administration founded INEAC *(Institut National pour l'Etude Agronomique au Congo Belge)*. The goal, never realized, was to have the Congolese develop cash crops such as cotton, palm oil, coffee, and rice, in cooperative *paysannat* (peasantry) collectives, and in that way stimulate an active market economy. The cooperatives succeeded in many instances, but the money was rarely returned to the farmers (Vansina, personal communication). Europeans did not support and encourage, or did not comprehend the logic of, indigenous Congolese agricultural practices (largely, subsistence-level shifting systems). The colonial administration considered these practices to be a hindrance to modernization (Wilkie 1987).

Along with agricultural development came the development of a commercial infrastructure that included, by the time of independence in 1960, some ten thousand miles of navigable waterways, three thousand miles of rail, and eighty-five thousand miles of roads (Wilkie 1987). Infrastructural expansion affected even the most peripheral of Congolese, the Lese and the Efe. In 1941, when the Belgians decided to begin road construction, the Lese-Dese, and specifically the Andisopi and Andipaki phratries, were living near the Afande and Mambo rivers, a short distance from Wamba. The Belgian administration began recruiting Lese labor and forced the members of these phratries out of their villages and into Malembi, a new area east of Wamba where the Belgians intended to encourage Europeans to establish plantations, missionaries to build churches, and the Lese to build bridges and roads. The Belgians brought Lese men thirty to sixty kilometers from their villages to construct a north-south road through the Ituri forest, and, in 1943, forced entire Lese families to resettle at the roadside. The following statement by one of my informants gives us a sense of the authoritative and officious manner in which the Lese were relocated: "The strangers sat atop Malembi. They dug all the way from Mambasa to Mungbere. Five, ten, five, ten. Go there, come here. To the place of the Masa. Someone?! Present! Someone?! Present! Someone!? Present! They measured gardens for us, told us where to plant. Someone?! Present!" The Lese who eventually occupied Malembi were told to plant cotton, palm oil trees, rice, and coffee, and to abandon their practice of shifting residences every two or three years. Residences became much more permanent, with residence shifts of less than one kilometer's distance occurring about every seven years. Few of the Lese or other Congolese produced much coffee or cotton, in part as a resistance to the colonial administration. Some reports state that groups such as the Lese would plant crops following the orders they had been given but then never harvest them because they had not been told explicitly to do so (Jewsiewicki 1983).

ADMINISTRATIVE INNOVATION AND THE ORIGINS OF THE LESE CHIEFDOMS

Early in its rule, the Belgian colonial administration set out to enforce the cultivation of crops by means of the authority of *officiers de police judiciare* and also of a newly developed local administration consisting of African chiefs who were selected as the administrative chiefs of their various ethnic groups. In 1910, the Belgian administration introduced the first organized administration of territories in the Congo as a whole (Jan Vansina, personal communication). This was a decree that would in time become a reality on the ground. The administration would choose one locally respected man from each ethnic group, give him a medallion, and name him chief of a "tribe" (*tribu*). We do not know the process by which these chiefs were chosen, but we do know that they were recognized locally as men with large families, villages, and gardens. Each tribe constituted a chiefdom (*chefferie*), even though many of these groups, such as the Lese, had never recognized a central authority within their indigenous political systems. The chief was to be the "customary head" of a "tribe." In the event that a particular society did not have such authority figures as an indigenous institution, the Belgians nonetheless asked local inhabitants to suggest a candidate. If they did not suggest one, one was chosen by the district commissioner. The position of chief was to be, ideally, that of a "former ruler who has been placed in tutelage" (I.D. 1213, *Manual of the Belgian Congo*, n.d.). Moreover, each village had to nominate someone for the position of a *notable*, or *capita* (headman). Capitas were to be heads of villages, men responsible for reporting to census takers the numbers of residents at villages, and for ensuring that these residents produced their quotas of cultivated foods.

The organization of the Lese into chiefdoms is curious because it occurred at a time when chiefdoms were being abolished by the thousands. R. F. Betts (in Boahen 1985) notes of the European colonization of Africa:

> With the establishment of European administration, chiefs were manipulated as if they were administrative personnel who might be reposited or removed to satisfy colonial needs. Chieftaincies were abolished where considered superfluous and created where considered colonially useful. Perhaps the most striking example of this process occurred in the Belgian Congo (now Zaire) where, after 1918, the number of chefferies (kingdoms or states) was reduced from 6,095 in 1917 to 1,212 in 1938. (p. 147)

In addition, the Belgians were attempting to adopt the Lugardian model of indirect rule, which would recognize "native authorities" and limit the imposition of external or foreign structures of authority. In order to settle disputes and to tax, however, modifications in political institutions were necessary, and for the Lese this involved the invention of the chiefdom. The Lese were more than likely consolidated because they had no indigenous political organization beyond alliances of a small number of clans and had no leadership that could serve the Belgians as liaison for the Lese. The Belgian administrators had considerable difficulty in establishing organized contact and communication with the

Lese—so much, indeed, that it took fourteen years for them to carry out the 1910 decree among the Lese-Dese (Irumu District Correspondence, Zone de Mambasa Archives). Finally, on April 1, 1924, after what must have been a long series of attempts to consolidate the Lese into a chiefdom, their first chief, Mbula (Andimau clan), was "appointed" (Baltus 1949). At the same time, the Lese-Karo received their first chief, Tshaminionge, and the phratries were required to nominate notables to represent the villages in front of the chief. An informant said: "Before, everyone was the chief of his house, and we did not know the ways of the chief. They all got their medallions at *Tutu-ke* [today named Andudu]. Every tribe [*tribu*] was asked 'who do you want to be your chief?' and then 'who do you want to be your *notables?*' The first person to state an opinion became a *notable.*"

How these groups were organized into different chiefdoms, or whether the name "Lese-Dese" was an indigenous term to describe political units, is not known, but my informants suggest that the word "Lese" is of recent origin. They use the words "Lese," "Dese" or "Karo," to describe members of the Lese-Dese and Lese-Karo chiefdoms, and older people describe all Lese-Dese as "Andali," which is the current name of a large phratry, that is, a collection of clans tied together through intermarriage. The Andali phratry may have consisted of over two hundred pople at the time they were incorporated into the Lese chiefdom. According to Joset (1949:5), the term *Andioli,* meaning "the descendants of Oli," was used by the Lese-Obi to refer to all the Lese. Lese-Dese elders I interviewed assert that all Lese-Dese are Andali, and that the term means "the people [or descendants] of Ali."

One informant's rendition of the process by which the Belgians distinguished between the Lese-Dese and Lese-Karo suggests that linguistic boundaries were a significant factor for the Belgians in their construction of chiefdoms.

> The Belgians said the Dese and the Karo should be one people. The Commandant called, "Tshaminionge!" "Present!" "Mbula!" "Present!" The Belgian said, "Who are you?" Mbula said, "I am Andali." Tshaminionge said, "I am Karo." The European asked Tshaminionge, "What do you call a bird?" He said "osa." Then he asked Mbula, "What do you call a bird?" He said "keli." Then they were given their medallions, but they were separated.

Whether Mbula and Tshaminionge used the terms "Andali" and "Karo" to refer to phratries, descent groups, or ethnic groups is not clear, but it is likely that the chiefs were identifying themselves by phratry, since that was the most inclusive level of social segmentation for which there was a word in the Lese language. Each phratry maintained a distinct way of speaking and gesturing, and still, today, the members of one phratry can be identified by their accents, tonality, and vocabulary.

The whole notion of a chiefdom as a politically, linguistically, and ethnically homogenous unit was generated by the colonial administration in its efforts to tighten its control and administration of the Ituri forest peoples. Much of the solidarity that Lese-Dese today experience in opposition to other Lese groups, such as the Lese-Karo or Lese-Mvuba, is no doubt a consequence of the Belgian administration's unification of various Lese phratries into their own form of political and administrative structure. Like colonists elsewhere, the Belgians attempted to fix and classify responses to their questions within their own categories regardless of whether or not those categories reflected indigenous social groups (Cohn 1987:206; Anderson 1991[1983]:168).

Censuses, too, may have played a significant role in fixing ethnic identity, even clan identity. According to my informants, Belgian administrators counted adult men of different clans, excluding the Efe. The vast literature on European images of the Pygmies, written mainly by explorers and missionaries, reveals that the Efe were not seen as potential workers, and, according to my Efe and Lese informants, were further dehumanized as "baboons" and "monkeys." The census takers would thus ask not only how many men were living at a particular clan's village but how many men were members of that clan, even if they were living or working elsewhere. Clan identity, indeed chiefdom identity, can be manipulated, yet the census takers demanded that people maintain (and perhaps, in some cases, invent) one specific set of identities. Censuses can often result in the invention and reification of social categories. In my own efforts to look at fertility and clan death, I replicated a 1947 census of Lese villages, and thus used the identical categories employed by the census takers. I may therefore play a part in producing identities and contributing to the ongoing legitimacy of the ethnic group, phratry, and clan as distinct categories. One can only wonder whether the Belgian denigration of the Efe as animal-like influenced the Lese's view of the Efe.

Oral history and interviews with elders do indicate that the Lese had little difficulty accepting a new identity as members of a chiefdom. Although the chiefdom introduced into Lese society a new category of social groupings more inclusive than the clan or phratry, the chiefdom was a buffer between the village and the state, represented at first by the colonial administration, and later by Zairian police and other state officials. Thus, the government-imposed Lese officials came to be legitimated by the local populations not because they were respected as effective adjudicators or political representatives, but because they could protect the people from the government (see also Turnbull 1983a:59). Since state officials sometimes defer to the chiefs in the adjudication of criminal offenses or concerning fines imposed by the state, the people quite naturally appreciate that it is in their best interests to cultivate amiable relations with the chiefs.

Under the Belgian administration, a chief's duties were, not unlike his duties today, to collect taxes, mobilize labor for portage and road construction, and enforce the cultivation requirements. The colonial administration of the Congo was "organized into a microadministrative grid extending into the farthest village" (Young and Turner 1985), with the intention of controlling the resources of even the most isolated villages. It appointed local chiefs, *chefs de localité,* who would be in charge of a few hundred people at the most, and would report to the central chief. The Belgian administration appointed officials at the most *local* levels of the Congo. To my knowledge, only the Pygmy groups of the Belgian Congo, seminomadic and therefore elusive, uncountable, and considered by many Congolese and Belgians to be subhuman, were never organized into a chiefdom. My Lese and Efe informants report to me that officials during the colonial regime imagined the Efe to be violent and rarely ordered them to collect rubber, to become farmers, or to work on the road. Belgian censuses bear out the colonial view of the Efe; the official Belgian censuses I have seen seldom mention the Efe, and never count or include them as an available work force.

About seven pages of correspondence between territorial administrators and the commissioner of the Irumu district survived independence and the rebellions that followed. These letters attest to the fact that the Belgians had great difficulty dominating and governing the Lese, the Efe, and also the Mamvu, who sometimes lived within one or two days' walk of the Lese.[3] A 1912 correspondence stated, "Except for among the . . . [*sic*] and the Walese and the Mamvu, the political situation had been 'good'." (Irumu, 17 Mars 1912, Benaets to the District Commissioner, my translation. Zone de Mambasa Archives). The same official stated that he had abandoned the Lese until he could gather more mili-

3. Documents obtained by Robert C. Bailey in 1980.

tary support from Wamba in order to "subdue" the population. Several months later, in 1912, he reported that he was not hopeful about the possibility of dominating the Lese, and he remarked that the Lese had more interest in maintaining relations with the "Marabo"—the Lese word for the Arabisés—than they did in establishing new relations with the Belgians.

My informants contend that the Lese were more fearful of the Belgians than of any other group, that the Lese were frightened by the Belgians' "hideous" white appearance and their overt displays of force. Some Lese believed the Belgians to be the *tore,* or evil spirits, some of whom are said to have white faces. Many believed them to be cannibals. Why else, my informants asked me, would they kill so many people whom they did not know? The Lese tell numerous stories of Belgian cannibalism, and the chief of the Lese-Dese even pointed out to me two abandoned buildings in which the Belgians were alleged to have processed Congolese bodies for food. Some anthropologists working in the Ituri have had to differentiate themselves from the Belgians to avoid accusations of cannibalism.

The administrator wrote:

> The situation is always bad, police operations have produced no results; I will soon be prepared to send an officer to Wamba, and a military operation will be led against the Walese.
>
> . . . This region needs to be worked directly by European traders; they are the only ones who will create needs among the natives. But the Walese are still savages. They have hardly had any dealings with us; the go-betweens, rather unwilling, have always been the Arabisés from the Mavambi-Irumu route. (my translation)

We do not know how the region was eventually conquered, but Adjt. Sup. Benaets wrote on June 22, 1913, that sous-lieutenant Rultberg controlled the region, that the area was "calme," and that the inhabitants would no longer run away from colonial officials. There were likely several military sweeps in the region, stimulated in part by the difficulties of controlling the movements of local inhabitants, and in part by the fact that much of the Ituri was controlled by Arab descendants. In 1914, the *Congo Oriental Compagnie* (C.O.C.) was able to found a trading house near the Biasa River, an area that, according to a territorial administrator's report in 1939, was by 1924 the boundary between the chiefdoms of the Karo and the Dese. (Although most of the Lese were living far to the west of Biasa, the administrator's report suggests that many Lese-Dese were already living near Biasa, and therefore near the site of the yet-to-be-built north-south road, and near what is today Malembi). According to an administrator, a Lieutenant Scharff, the Arabisé chiefs helped the Belgians forge more peaceful and cooperative relationships with the Lese at Biasa. In a letter dated August 5, 1914, M. Siffer wrote to Scharff and the Irumu District Commissioner that although not perfect, the situation with the Lese was improving: "La situation chez les Mamvu est très satisfaisante . . . chez les Walese, cela va moins bien" (the situation among the Mamvu is quite satisfactory . . . among the Walese things are going less well). But despite resistance, Siffer said, the Lese were "subdued" and received "whites" with hospitality.

The administrator also notes that the Lese were involved in several wars and feuds among themselves. Oral history I collected in 1987 indicates that several Lese groups suffered food shortages around the turn of the century, and, presumably with the help of their Efe, attacked groups with larger and more productive gardens. Explorer's accounts seem to bear this out: for example, a detailed illustration in Major Gaetano Casati's *Ten Years in Equatoria* (1891) depicts Pygmy women stealing corn from the garden of a Lese group under attack by their husbands. According to M. Siffer's official report, the "dwarfs" (Efe) were constantly attacking the Lese's neighbors, the Mamvu, in order to steal their cultivated foods. He lamented that any extra foods were either given to, or stolen by, the Efe, rather than traded at the C.O.C. post. In May of 1916, the same official wrote that the Belgians would never be the "masters of these forests" until they conquered the Efe, whom he called "Mambuti." He stressed that the individual Lese was "occupied" with his Efe trading partners "de tout son pouvoir" (in every capacity). The Lese, he noted, fed the Pygmies because they served as warriors for the villages of their Lese partners and guarded their Lese partners' houses, villages, and gardens from outside attack. The official concluded, "tous les méfaits qui secommettent [*sic*] sont commis par les Mambuti" (all wrongdoing is committed by the Mambuti).

During the years 1914–20, few reports were made. Joset, however, collected some oral history from the Lese-Obi (who live to the south of the Lese-Dese) around 1916. He stated (1949) that, for the Lese, the age of rubber collecting was one of prosperity, and that during World War I, a number of Lese-Obi served near Kisangani as porters carrying ammunition. Although the Lese-Dese had little contact with the Lese-Obi, they had a good deal of contact with territorial administrators from Irumu. It is likely that some Lese-Dese men were also involved in the ivory trade and helped to transport military goods. It seems that, by 1920, the Belgians had left the Lese-Dese alone, for a 1922 report from the territorial administrator at Andudu states that no Belgian government official had visited them in two years. After 1922 the yearly reports contain usually less than four sentences of general information, with phrases such as "situation bonne," or "situation excellente." Reports filed up to 1937 continued to state that relations between the Belgians and the Lese and Efe ran hot and cold, and that the Lese generally did not obey the laws of the colonial regime. In late 1926, the territorial administrator at Irumu noted that he was having considerable difficulty recruiting Lese-Dese and Lese-Karo men for service in the "F.P." (*Force Publique,* a Belgian-organized army made up of Congolese) or for work with *l'Offitra,* a rail/transport company with offices at Kinshasa and Matadi.

Between 1924 and 1935 there is little mention in official reports of Chief Mbula of the Lese-Dese. Most Belgian reports during this decade focus on Tshaminionge, the chief of the Lese-Karo. Tshaminionge seldom resisted colonial orders and is praised as "paternal," "accredité," and "le plus coutumier des chefs coutumiers" for his efforts to force the Lese-Karo to begin preliminary construction work on the north-south road. This is supported by Schebesta, who writes in 1933 that "Chamunonge [Tshaminionge] is a protege of the Colonial authorities, who have conferred on him numerous honours and tokens of their favour" (1933:225). There is no mention in the brief colonial reports I have seen of the murder of Chief Mbula of the Lese-Dese in 1927, and there is only one mention of his successor, Djumbu, whose name suddenly appears in the records in 1931. Even Schebesta, who stayed with Mbula for two days, wrote little about him, and stated only that "Mbula was valueless from the point of view of my research work, as no pigmies [*sic*] lived anywhere nearby" (1933:225). Mbula was, for obvious reasons, regarded by the Belgians as an ineffective chief. Official correspondence describes him as lazy and uninterested in traveling to the various Lese villages to collect head taxes, and the government in fact considered finding a new man to replace him. But in October 1927, near the Mobilinga River, the Belgian problem with Mbula was resolved when Mbula was killed by one of his own policemen. The story told by my informants is that Mbula got into an argument with the policeman, Batuko—a Lese-Dese man of the Andipaki phratry—either about the way in which Batuko had allegedly mistreated an elderly Lese man named Akilau, whom he had tied up and beaten on charges of disrespect, or, as others say, because Mbula had seduced Batuko's wife, and Batuko had discovered them in flagrante delicto. Schebesta amplifies the story: "Mbula was shot dead some years ago by one of his policemen, whose wife he had seduced. The chief's family group speedily avenged his death. Two women inveigled the assassin into their toils, bound him, and beat him to death with cudgels" (1933:225). Baltus's version is that Batuko tried to escape to Andipaki but was caught and murdered by Lese-Dese civilians (Baltus 1949). One man told me:

> They said, "if we go to the Europeans, they will leave this murderer, so we will kill him." They cut off his nose with a machete. Achakbati of Andipaki sent a letter to the district commissioner at Irumu. Who will be the new chief? Djumbu, Mbula's brother. He slept with the medallion [remained chief for] only a few years. The Europeans took it from him because he was a bad chief, and he tortured people. There was a lot of mud on this chief [he was dishonest and cruel]. They asked who will be chief? And they came with Arambi [of the Andape phratry], who received the medallion [in 1936].

Mbula's brother, Djumbu, succeeded him, but he was ousted by the Belgian administrators within one or two years in favor of a new leader, the chief Arambi. Reports in 1932 and 1933 state that a military excursion had been carried out by the Belgian administration in order to halt "illegal practices." Djumbu, Mbula's fellow clansman and successor, appears to have been involved with large-scale cultivation of marijuana (an illegal activity), which, according to the official reports, he exported from the chiefdom. Due in large part to the impact of the Depression, there were at about this time several shifts in the focus of administrative personnel throughout the colony, away from the local administration of localities and toward large-scale infrastructural work on bridges and roads. One of the consequences of this was that many of the Belgian territorial personnel left the Lese-Dese area in 1932 (Hackars, report to Stanleyville, District du Kibali-Ituri, Historical Papers). In 1933, some correspondence took place between the administrative headquarters at Ituri and Stanleyville. The correspondence followed official reports that a military exercise of 1932, and exploratory reconnaissance with the Dese in the same year, revealed a situation that was less than satisfactory to the administration, which then had to decide whether or not it should unite the Dese and the Karo under one *secteur* or *cheferrie*. Unfortunately, the correspondence says nothing about why the Lese situation was so unsatisfactory, nor what specific actions Belgian military took against them.

The choice of Arambi as the new chief of the Lese-Dese came only after a long and difficult decision in which KopaKopa, of the Andipaki phratry (now located at Malembi), opposed him (Baltus 1949). The administration described Arambi in a 1936 report:

> The forest population of the Dese, who already give rise to fewer concerns than three or four years ago, will reach a level of political and economic evolution equal to that of their neighbors, if one can maintain in Mambasa the long-term presence of a good agent, endowed with as much tact as energy. Arambi, the chief candidate of the Dese, the only one to have garnered nearly all the votes of the Dese *Notables,* is a very calm fellow, very understated, more of a peacemaker and conciliator than one to organize new initiatives. Given the current conditions among the Dese, he is the best man politically. (P.V. 246, my translation)

Within a year, the Karo and Dese were, in fact, united, not under one chiefdomship but into a single administrative unit called the *Frontière de Karo-Dese.* This is the last official report of the colonial administration available to me: "Arambi was sworn in on March 31, 1937. The Karo-Dese border was drawn and recognized by decisions 245 of March 10, 1937, and 246 of March 9, 1937, by the Commissioner of the Kibali-Ituri district; relating respectively to the Karo and the Dese" District du Kibali-Ituri Historical Papers. (P.V. 246, my translation).[4] Arambi served for seven years until his death in 1943. Nekubai of the Andipai clan was named to be the new chief, and his new headquarters of the chiefdom was established at Ngbongupanda, approximately eighteen kilometers to the south of Malembi.

RELOCATION AND REORGANIZATION

During the early 1940s, the Lese who now occupy Malembi were expelled from their villages and forced to relocate around the proposed site of the north-south road; elders were excluded from resettlement, but since few of them wanted to stay alone in their villages, nearly all of them moved with their families. Although the Lese were told that they would have only a short period of obligatory labor, only later did they learn that the residence shift was to be permanent. The area the Belgians assigned to the Lese was one that had formerly been inhabited by the Masa phratry of the Lese-Karo and their associated Efe families, and though the Masa were not at that time occupying the sites that

4. I wish to thank Scott Carpenter for assisting in the accurate translation of documents written in French.

became Lese-Dese villages, they nonetheless believed that the land remained theirs, especially the old abandoned gardens, which could be slashed and burned again and still produced small quantities of yams and tubers. Over the next few years, there were some bitter quarrels between the Lese-Dese and the Masa over access to the palm oil trees that grew near the Masa gardens. One particularly serious quarrel occurred between the Masa and the Andingire and Andingbana clans of the Lese-Dese Andisopi phratry:

> The Europeans named Iapu to be *capita* of Andingire clan, and they gave him the area from Ngodingodi to Abdala's stream Anderu at Andingbana village. Koboni of the Andibuku clan received the area from the marsh to the Malembi River. Everything was Masa. Andingbana had no place. The Belgians tried to give Abasondo hill to Andingbana, but they did not want to go there. Iapu said they could remain next to Andingire, and gave them their current village. But we fought a lot over palm oil, and Andingbana and the Masa do not like each other. We had to give the Masa gifts of elephant, and other things.

Within a decade, the Lese-Dese and the Efe held firm control over their new land and trees. The Masa slowly moved north, began to intermarry with the Lese-Dese, and within a short time had shifted their chiefdom identity away from the Karo to the Dese, probably encouraged by the administration, which sought to keep the peace and simplify ethnic boundaries: if the Masa lived within the chiefdom of the Lese-Dese, they could not be designated as Lese-Karo. The Masa today refer to themselves as the Masa phratry of the Lese-Dese, but they remember that they were at one time Lese-Karo. Similarly, the Belgians relocated the Maru phratry of the Lese-Dese within the territory of the Lese-Karo chiefdom, and today the Maru claim to be Lese-Karo.

On the whole, despite the trouble with the Masa, the Lese-Dese were able to take up their new residences in some peace. Within the general area designated for the new Lese-Dese residences, most of the clans were able to choose their immediate neighbors, and could even reestablish the same kinds of spatial relations between clans and phratries that they had had before in what the Lese today refer to as their *sapu,* or ancestral villages. The main problem for the Lese was the smaller size of the new area. Before relocation, Lese villages were highly independent and for the most part self-sufficient social units, situated as far as fifteen kilometers from one another. This distance made it possible to group phratries well apart. Not all villages were exactly alike, but villages of the same phratry were closer together than villages or clans that belonged to a different phratry. Lese elders remember the days before relocation as filled with feud and violence between villages and between phratries. They say that they sent Efe to other villages as spies to collect information on the availability of food and meat, and the numbers of women and children who lived there. If there was a great deal of food in another village, they might raid it; if there was an inequity in the number of women and children, they might capture or kill them to bring their levels into parity.

After relocation, although the Lese of Malembi were able to reestablish prior sequences of clans and phratries, it was not possible for them to locate their villages at great distance from one another. Instead of the widely spaced villages they had been accustomed to, now nearly twenty clans were resettled on the roadside within an administrative unit only twenty-seven kilometers long, so that few villages were more than two kilometers from another. This closer proximity of villages and settlement on a major road meant increased contact with non-Lese, and new competition for land and resources. Moreover, although these Lese had some choice in the matter of locating their villages, they were told by the Belgians, and then later by the state of Zaire, that they could shift their village sites only every seven years, instead of the customary two or three years. In addition, they were ordered to locate their villages at the roadside. From the point of view of the Lese, settlement at the roadside diminished the size of the forest because the area available for settlement and for clearing was limited by the close proximity of their neighbors.

Another major problem with relocation was the difficulty of maintaining the close Lese-Efe relations. Every Lese village maintained relations with Efe, and most of the Efe groups that were associated with the Lese villages were prepared to move along with their Lese to the roadside so that they could continue the relationships. This was by their own choice, not by any order of the Belgian administration. But many Efe clans did not move right away. Some remained with the few older Lese who did not resettle, others moved closer to Wamba to establish relations with the Budu farmers they had come to know through their Lese partners. Most of the latter never reestablished exchange relations with their Lese partners; some have changed their clan names, assumed specifically Budu names, and learned to speak the Budu language fluently. Efe informants describe relocation as an abrupt shift in their trading relations, a time of turmoil and uncertainty. Whether an Efe camp moved to the roadside or to Wamba, moving meant learning about new stretches of forest and adapting to the demands of new historical conditions. To this day, many of the Efe and the Lese continue to return annually to their former area (sapu), sometimes for visits of one to three months.

DEVELOPMENT IN THE BELGIAN CONGO DURING THE 1950S

Soon after World War II, the Belgians faced increasing criticism abroad and within the Congo over continued colonization. The Congo Reform Movement in England had long exerted pressure on the Belgian government to instigate reforms and to uphold the 1885 Berlin Conference's commitment to "free trade and welfare of the indigenous population" (Louis 1966; Morel 1906), and in response to this and other pressures, the Belgian administration had tried to expand education in the Congo in order to develop an African elite, possibly as a preparation for decolonization. By 1958, a state-run dispensary had been set up at Ngbongupanda (the administrative headquarters of the chiefdom of the Lese-Dese), and trained work elephants and machines had been sent to the Ituri to widen the north-south road to twelve meters and to build long drainage ditches.

Previously, it was the missionaries who had assumed responsibility for most social amenities. Christian missions had been in the Congo since 1890; most of these were Catholic, both Belgian and French, although after 1900 they also included such groups as the Baptist Missionary Society, the Swedish Mission, American Presbyterians, French and Belgian Catholics and, in the northeast, the Catholic Premonstrants. From the start, these missions played the role of a civil government in remote areas the colonial regime had found difficult to penetrate (Slade 1959). By the time of independence, there were eight thousand white missionaries living in Zaire (six thousand of them Catholic), on 966 mission stations (Young and Turner 1985). Many missions began as homes for freed slaves, and as schools, hospitals, plantations, markets, and courts. By 1905, two Premonstratensian missions at Ibembo and Amadi housed a total of sixteen hundred "abandoned children" (Slade 1959). (It is not known how these children were abandoned; their parents may have been executed, and some may have been unwanted children: girls, twins, or products of illegitimate marriages.) Membership in these *chrétientes* was dependent upon literacy and conversion, as well as the formation of permanent homes and gardens. The missions taught specific trades and recruited Europeans to organize departments of industrial training.

Although the goals and aspirations of the missionaries and the colonial administrators differed, many similarities have been noted between them. For example, few authors question that the missionaries were often quite as harsh as the administrators in their treatment of the Congolese. R. M. Slade (1959) cites reports from the early 1900s that document Congolese being denied free movement in and out of Catholic mission property. They were sometimes chained and beaten with a *chicotte* (a whip made of animal hide with thongs twisted and dried on its end). Mary Douglas, in *The Lele of the Kasai,* comparing the Congolese missions with the colonial administration, says, "They were as one. . . . The administration ensured security of life and property, transport, and communications. Without it neither commerce nor missionary development would have been possible. The commercial interest subsidized the missions, who trained their staff in schools and gave extensive medical services. The state supported the missionaries in the course of their normal enforcement of the laws of the colony, some of which were framed in response to missionary demands" (1963:259).

But by the 1950s, the Belgians had turned things around, as Young and Turner (1985) explain:

> Clinics, hospitals, and rural dispensaries pushed from the major centers out into the remote hinterland. Whereas it could be said in 1920 that "African medical service did not exist," by the late 1950's the Belgians could justifiably claim that their health service "was without doubt the best in the whole tropical world." The mortality rate dropped from 30 to 40 per thousand in the interwar period to 20 per thousand in 1957.

Paradoxically, however, rather than stimulating decolonization (which was the hope of many Europeans), these improvements inspired many young Europeans to come to the Congo and seek their fortunes. One Swiss agronomist, still living in Zaire today, told me that in 1956 there were eight coffee plantations at Mungbere (70 km. south of Malembi), whereas by the time of independence in 1960 there were forty-five. Between 1911 and 1960 the European population in the Congo rose considerably.

The older Lese men I interviewed in Zaire, who entered adulthood and established their families at this time of florescence, tend, in retrospect, to idealize colonialism as a time of prosperity and health; they describe the world of the 1950s as a virtual welfare state, with high wages at plantations, increased market activity, and an active road with hundreds of trucks, as well as cars and motorcycles, passing every month. This traffic meant extensive trading and interaction between people living hundreds of kilometers from one another. At Ngbongupanda there was a dispensary stocked with European medicines (such as penicillin and antimalarial tablets) that, the Lese hoped, would cure them of infertility. New teachers in a growing school system easily persuaded the Lese that education promised *health* and *money*—the two things which, for the Lese, were synonymous with *children* and *wives*. The wider road, no small advance for the Ituri forest, meant greater availability of goods such as blankets, shirts, and pants. Catholic hospitals and dispensaries were built near Nduye, and by the time of independence, the Lese were engaged in markets and were attending mission-sponsored primary and secondary schools. The missions thrived during the 1950s, and most Lese were converted, either to Catholicism or to Protestantism. The missions also served as commercial centers; Catholic priests began sending cultivated foods and ivory into markets, and they hired many people in and around Nduye to live and work on the mission stations. The legacy of the missions is that the Lese of Malembi consider themselves to be Christians. Although the vast majority of the Lese do not understand French, Lingala, or Swahili, the languages used by the Zairian preachers who come to give their sermons, many Lese attend either the Protestant or Catholic churches now situated near Malembi.

The elder Lese living at Malembi in the 1980s were ambivalent about these developments. They seem to have welcomed health care and greater access to Western goods, but they remained fearful, cautious, and concerned. About health care, they seemed particularly uncertain and ambivalent, for they wanted to be cured of illness and infertility and went to the hospitals to seek treatment, but they were afraid of the unknown and were often terrified at having Belgian physicians treat them. A few Lese men and women traveled to Belgian hospitals for hernia operations, but they preferred the hospitals of the Italians or Americans, since it was the Belgians primarily who were believed to be cannibals. One elder Lese woman recalled three men from her clan who traveled to Irumu for medical treatment: "Tumu, Malangu, and Mutoembi went to the Belgian doctors at Irumu, where [the Belgians] killed people. They killed Tumu, and the others on the same day. Later, Selimani of Andisopi went to die there. They cut him open, and his wife saw everything. They took out his muscles. One doctor said, 'This part is mine,' and another said, 'This part is mine,' and they cut him all up, and served him on plates—there were all the pieces of our elders."

For most people, the desire for treatment outweighed the terror of hospitals as "places where people die." The Lese suffered, and continue to suffer, high infant mortality and low fertility and sometimes extreme hunger. Those who went to hospitals had undoubtedly been given indigenous medical treatment first, or were on the brink of death, and they accepted Western medical care as a last resort. It is for these reasons that some Lese men and women now say that they were better off thirty years ago than they are today. Yet many people blame their suffering on the Europeans and argue that before relocation, they were more mobile, and therefore more prolific, and much less hungry. Schebesta, writing in 1933, some ten years before relocation, offers some evidence to reject the Lese notion that relocation was to blame for their infertility and hunger. He notes that the Lese were by the turn of the century a "dying stock." And the high rate of infertility and infant mortality was, according to a Belgian report Schebesta cites, the result of venereal diseases introduced by the Arabisés.

The Lese are today bewildered about their decreasing numbers. At a Lese funeral in 1987, a well-respected Lese man summed up many of the Lese's concerns:

> The Dese used to be numerous, and Andisopi were many. Now, since Baltusi [Baltus] brought them out to the road, they are few. The Europeans said we would sleep here for only seven years, and then would sleep another seven at Wamba. They cut a tree at Andoka village at Dingbo to mark the place where the road would go, from Dingbo to Wamba. My friend Asakba told me this forest here is bad, and that his forest was good only until the land of the Karo past Andili, and you see we have begun to die here. We don't know what it is that is killing us here.

THE SIMBA REBELLION AND THE ROAD TO ISOLATION

For a time, it appeared that the Lese were becoming more and more enmeshed in European enterprises, whether at hospitals, plantations, or missions; much of that involvement would end with the chaos that followed independence. The disorder of the First Republic of Zaire sparked a breakdown in central authority, the fragmentation of provinces and districts from the nation-state, and a series of violent rebellions in 1964 and 1965. The most severe political conflict occurred in the northeast, beginning in Stanleyville (now Kisangani). Along the north-south road cutting through Malembi, guerrilla fighters of the *Armée Populaire de Libération,* popularly known as Simbas (lions), formed a corridor of violence that extended as far north as Isiro (Vanderstraeten 1985). The Simbas were commanded by Nicholas Olenga, Christopher Gbenye, and Antoine Gizenga. Neither their ideological basis nor their motivation is well understood, even by the most knowledgeable historians of Zaire (Young 1965), but we do know that Olenga was closely tied to Patrice Lumumba (the founder of the first political party in the Congo, the Mouvement National Congolais, or MNC, and later prime minister before his execution in 1961 under General Joseph Mobutu's first regime) and that the Simbas' anger was directed against wealth and privilege, and against anyone whose political views conflicted with those of Lumumba. Their quarrel was with the centralized Zairian authority, and they sought to control the region of Haut Zaire, with the goal of secession. The Simba rebellion was not dominated particularly by an antiwhite ideology, and yet hundreds of Europeans fled the country, and many were executed.

The Simbas made no exceptions for the Lese, many of whom probably did not even recognize the name of Lumumba. In October of 1964, at Nduye, the Simbas executed two local chiefs, Lupao and Angoba, both of the Lese-Karo group. News traveled quickly to the Malembi area, and within a few days soldiers passed by Malembi. According to the Lese with whom I lived, the Simbas arrested, tortured, and murdered some Lese and Efe men, raped Lese and Efe women, pillaged the Lese gardens, and established a temporary post at Dingbo. All of the Lese of Malembi ran from the roadside to escape the dangers, and took refuge in the forest to the east and west of the road. Nekubai, then chief of the Lese-Dese, narrowly escaped. Most of the Lese, Karo, and Dese sought shelter east of the road, an area that they had rarely occupied, and many others returned to their sapu, or pre-1940 villages; those who did not escape were killed. There are no accurate figures on how many persons were killed during the Simba rebellion, and there is no strong evidence to suggest that many of the Lese-Dese in my study area died as a direct result from Simba occupation. However, at one Lese-Dese village that, for reasons unknown to me, did not relocate in the 1940s—the Andituba village—and that stood directly on the path of the Simbas on the road toward Kisangani, nearly every man living there was killed. Today only one Andituba man remains, as compared with twenty-seven men in 1947 (census of the Belgian colonial administration, District du Kibuli-Ituri Historical Papers).

Many Lese did not flee immediately from the roadside. They were afraid of what might happen to them if they were caught escaping, and they did not know how they would survive in the deep forest, far from their gardens. For a short time, the Simba rebellion gave many Lese the chance to punish people with whom they had disputes. For example, when an Efe man from the Andisamba band, associated with the Masa, allegedly stole repeatedly from the gardens of a young Lese man at Andingbana village, the Lese man reported the thefts to the Simba commander stationed at Dingbo. The members of Andingbana and the Masa had never seen eye to eye, since the Andingbana occupied the territory of the Masa; they had fought frequently and violently over rights to land and to the palm oil trees that the Masa had previously planted there. The Andingbana man saw an opportunity to damage the Masa and their Efe. The Simba commander behaved as he was expected to, and arrested and executed the accused Efe. In other matters, such as bridewealth disputes and adultery, the Simbas offered swift adjudication and harsh measures. Many women whose bridewealth had not been paid were taken as concubines of Simba soldiers, and some of my informants told of a few people who were accused of adultery and then were executed.

Several people from Malembi were tortured by the Simbas. According to my informants, the Simbas from Dingbo murdered a man from the Andingire clan, and then mutilated his wife's genitals with a burning log; some were beaten severely, sentenced to death, and then released, while others joined the Simba army in order to avoid execution. Some of these actions appear to have been unprovoked, but many may have been prompted by charges such as the one made by Andingbana, mentioned above.

But most Lese evaded extensive interaction with the Simbas by escaping with the Efe into the forest and remaining there until the rebellion had been quelled. Generally, the Lese spent about one year in remote upland forest, living either in occupied or in abandoned Efe camps. Some Lese went deep enough in the forest to reach their sapu, where they were safely beyond the Simba guerrillas. Many people, including many small children, died while in hiding, few women became pregnant, and very few babies were born. Without the Efe, who, despite the dangers, were willing to travel from these distant camps to the Lese villages they had abandoned in order to get food, many more Lese might have died. Many Lese remember this time as one of extreme fear, but also, as in the period of rubber collecting, of closer association with the Efe. Efe and Lese men hunted together, and Efe and Lese women fished and gathered food together. The Efe and the Lese rarely slept together at the same residence, but their camps were almost always within hearing distance. As during the period of rubber exploitation, the Lese were reminded of how important the Efe could be to their survival in a dangerous world.

By 1965, the Simbas had disbanded, the local colonel had been arrested by European and South African mercenaries (with the help of some Efe men), and, although minor skirmishes continued for two years, the Lese were able to end their seclusion in the forest. Within a few months after the rebellion had ended, international aid organizations, primarily the Red Cross, traveled through the region and gave cooking oil and sacks of rice, beans, and flour to the Lese villages of the Andisopi phratry.

One of the most important consequences of the Simba rebellion was the coup of General Joseph Mobutu (now President Mobutu Sese Seko), the chief of the Congolese army and leader of the Congolese government for a short time in 1961, who took advantage of the disruption to seize power for a second time. The Lese of Malembi think of Mobutu as a heroic peacemaker. Even though the last Simba commander was not captured until late in 1970 (Wilkie 1987; Hart and Hart 1984; Waehle 1985), peace came to the north-south road in 1965, and many of the Lese returned to the roadside.

Some of those who came out of the forest to return to the roadside have in recent years moved back to the sapu—some because of conflicts with fellow clan and phratry members or with government officials, others in response to the illness and mortality attributed to the roadside villages. Mobutu's peace did not bring prosperity. Even before he took power, the road had begun to deteriorate, and the market economy, fueled by Europeans, had diminished; dispensaries now contained few medicines, and, importantly, the Lese were hesitant to invest in the cash crops—cotton, rice, tobacco, and peanuts—that had been pillaged during the rebellion. Many Lese worked at coffee plantations near Malembi, Dingbo, Nepoko, and Njaro, but the success of these plantations was short-lived. Mobutu's seizure of power in 1965 began a decade of uncertainty and lack of direction throughout the country, during which agricultural production fell by more than 50 percent (McDonald 1971; Wilkie 1987).

Mobutu's desire to rid the country of "neo-colonials" and achieve economic independence for Zaire was ambitious but disastrous. On November 30, 1973, in a speech to the National Legislative Council of

Zaire, he promised that farms, ranches, plantations, concessions, commerce, and real estate agencies would be handed over to Zairians. Under this policy, Europeans left most of the plantations near Malembi, and Zairian politicians, businessmen, and civil servants, most of whom maintained close connections to the central government, applied to the government as "acquirers." But the process was so slow that many plantations became overrun with vegetation before they could be allocated to new owners and managers, and even those Zairians who acquired plantations quickly had little capital with which to pay workers. (Some Europeans, especially Greeks and Portuguese, were able to hold on to their businesses by having their Zairian wives apply to the government as acquirers.) Along with uncontrolled government spending, there were empty shelves at plantation stores, high inflation, and exorbitant prices. The government developed huge deficits because the new acquirers did not pay their taxes. Thus Zairianization actually benefited only a small number of Zairians; for the majority, it meant the loss of employment, and, for the Lese and others, the loss of one of their primary sources of cash. After 1976, when the policy was finally abandoned, former non-Zairian plantation owners were invited back into the country, but many plantations, including those near Malembi, were never revitalized, and those near Dingbo never became as large as they had been under colonial rule.

ECONOMIC CONTEXT OF LESE ISOLATION IN THE 1980s

Given these circumstances, it is not surprising that the Lese are ambivalent about their participation in the Zairian economy. With every step they have encountered a new form of domination and new risks to their ability to choose their own history. The Belgian administration of the Congo was, by all accounts, severe and violent. With independence came the Simbas, and the Lese were forced once again to relocate, literally running for their lives. Yet, there were always the Efe. The Efe helped the Lese achieve their rubber quota, helped them to flee the post-independence rebellion, and nourished them while they were in hiding from the Simbas. The Lese of Malembi would be the first to say that their relations with the Efe have changed over the years, with periods of greater and lesser intimacy. They would also say that the Efe have helped them in the past, and may help them in the future. A young Lese man with perhaps more insight than any of my other informants explained to me:

The road near Malembi, August 1986. *Photograph by R. R. Grinker.*

> A long time ago, everyone killed everyone else: today you are alive, tomorrow you are dead. If you had Efe, they could kill your killers. They would take revenge if they did not save you. I don't like Efe. I don't know how to live with them. But I give them things. I will never do badly to an Efe. He might help me if there is a war. He might give me meat, or bring me food from my garden. He will see witches and kill them.

The relationship between the Lese and the Efe thus has a meaning, quite apart from the economy, that is embedded in the history of conquest, colonialism, and the beginnings of the Zairian nation. Today, some twenty-five years since the new nation was established, the Lese interact with few non-Lese. Forty years ago, truckers passed by frequently to pick up loads of cotton, coffee, and other crops grown by the Lese; tourists came to stay at Camp Putnam near Epulu (a hotel founded by Patrick Putnam, a Ph.D. candidate in social anthropology at Harvard), traveling up and down the Ituri from Stanleyville (Kisangani) to Paulis (Isiro); government workers regulated and managed the recruitment of local labor for the construction and maintenance of roads; they measured gardens and established health care facilities as near as Ngbongupanda; coffee plantations were scattered throughout the Lese area, some within a few kilometers of Malembi. The Lese seem to have prospered to some extent under these associations, whether or not they actually enjoyed them. Turnbull (1983a) notes of the Bila that they have never welcomed strangers, and they have encouraged the deterioration of the road. He also says that some Bila, like some Lese I have observed, dig holes and trenches across the road to trap passing trucks and hold them up (1983a:61). But Turnbull relates such behavior *only* to the Bila tendency toward isolation (as an enduring cultural disposition) and not to the more practical and historically situated disposition to avoid the brutality and invasiveness of the state.

The isolation of the present-day Lese is both economic and social. Two large coffee plantation settlements, one thirty-five kilometers to the south of Malembi, the other eighteen kilometers north of Malembi, serve as end points for two truck routes, but plantation owners have little reason to enter the Lese area. Once a year, in November or December, plantation owners from another plantation center (30 km to the north of Malembi) send a truck or two to transport Efe men to the plantations in order to harvest coffee, but few Lese are recruited for coffee harvesting because the harvest occurs at the time when the Lese are beginning to clear their gardens and harvest rice. The few Lese men who do go to the plantations are usually bachelors who have no gardens and are attracted by the chance to get food and some cash in payment for work. The Efe enjoy these two-to-six-week periods away from their Lese partners as a break in their routine and also for the opportunity to earn enough money to buy cloth for their wives; they can also establish ties of friendship with the Lese-Dese from Dingbo. After their work period, they sometimes spend another week or two living at the plantations, making new acquaintances, and they sometimes return to Dingbo in times of crisis to find shelter, food, or other forms of assistance, from these Dingbo Lese.

Only the sisters from the Catholic mission at Nduye use the road south from Malembi, and they do so less often than once a month. In July of 1987, and again in September of that year, the bridge that serves as the northern boundary of the *Collectivité* Lese-Dese (the unit administered by the Lese-Dese chief) and connects the Lese village area with the Dingbo plantation area, collapsed.[5] The local chiefs attempted to mobilize villagers to repair the bridge, but they were, for the most part, unsuccessful. Nearly three weeks passed before any construction began. People lazily made some gesture of helping by bringing a few small trees

5. The major Zairian administrative units include, from smallest to largest, the *localité* (several villages headed by a *chef de groupement*), the *collectivité* (several *localités* headed by a *chef de collectivité* and often named for the dominant ethnic group living in those *localités*), the *zone*, the *sous-région*, the *région* (all headed by *commissaires*), and finally the *République du Zaire*.

to place over the gap in the road, but that was more to avoid being fined or beaten or imprisoned than to offer real help. Only when plantation owners from Dingbo agreed to use their trucks to transport large rocks to the bridge site did anyone agree to cooperate to repair the bridge. Those who lived near the bridge complained that they were doing all of the work for the benefit of those who lived far from the bridge. The rebuilt bridge was very weak, and about a month later it collapsed again; this time it was repaired with a few trees and wooden planks. The Lese who talked with me about the matter said that they saw no reason to repair the bridge, since they benefited so seldom from it. Word of the bridge's condition, and the Lese's apathy, spread rapidly to plantation owners farther away, and this of course reinforced their stereotype of the Lese as poor workers and confirmed their belief that the Lese villages are inaccessible.

In the past, the Lese occasionally sold peanuts, rice, cotton, and coffee to outside buyers, primarily Greek owners of plantations 30 to 100 kilometers away. Since Zairianization, there are few buyers, and those who continue to work in Zaire are now reluctant to bring their large trucks onto the dilapidated bridges and poor roads. During the years 1980–83, nearly all Lese farmers obtained the bulk of their yearly cash income from the sale of peanuts and rice to traders coming north from Mambasa (R. C. Bailey, personal communication). To my knowledge, between 1985 and 1987, not one Lese individual sold peanuts or rice at a market. The Lese say that they cannot take their goods to market by foot because the loads are too heavy to carry, but the weight of the crops provides the Lese with an excuse for economic isolation and is not a real barrier to trade. Were there sufficient goods and a hospitable trading environment, traders from the north and south would hire carriers and use motorcycles and bicycles for transport. Zairian buyers told me that they are reluctant to enter the area because they are afraid of becoming trapped in a place where there is so little food, and where, if they were caught in the ditches, or stopped by a mechnical failure, they could not easily get help at mission stations, or find car parts and fuel. They also fear the Efe because the Efe carry bows and arrows and are reputed to have short and violent tempers. These buyers also know that the Lese are among the poorest farmers in the region of Haut Zaire, and that probably they would not be able to buy enough food to make the trip into Lese territory worth their while. Outsiders, like the traders, for the most part think of the area where the Lese live as a deep and wild forest, a place not to enter without good reason.

In consequence, most of the Lese trading with outsiders takes place at Lese villages with Nande, Zande, and Mangbetu men who occasionally ride bicycles, and very rarely motorcycles, into the area. This is how Lese normally obtain the cloth they purchase for their wives, children, and Efe partners. These traders bring their goods with the hope of obtaining meat in exchange. Nepoko and other plantation towns are known to be rich in dried, salted fish and palm oil but poor in meat. Traders I spoke with in Mungbere firmly believe that meat is abundant farther in the "interior," as they call the Malembi area, and they are usually disappointed to find that the Lese and Efe most often kill only what meat they need to feed their families. The traders try to sell trapping wire to the Lese, hoping the wire will help the Lese to kill more animals; some traders even advance the wire to the Lese on condition that they receive a return of meat captured in the future. I have known only one Lese man to pay off such a debt. The chances that the trader will return to the area at the same time that meat is available, and that the Lese trapper will admit to having obtained meat, are very low. The result is that the Lese acquire trapping wire, and the traders acquire very little meat, if any at all.

Since October 1985, a weekly market has been held in the town of Dingbo, a ninety-minute walk north of Malembi. The market has been successful in stimulating many Lese men to produce more meat by hunting or trapping it themselves with metal trapping wire. The brother of the *Chef de collectivité* arranged for a market shelter to be constructed in an open area in Dingbo. This involved clearing a small portion of land and building six stands on which merchants could place their goods. Market data presented here show that most of the persons in my study area do not participate often in the market, as buyers, sellers, or observers. During nearly two years of observations, I observed Efe men or women at the market only four times (once to drink alcohol and sell bananas, once to sell honey, once to sell meat and *opi* fruit, and once to buy honey). After the first few months of the market, during which time some Lese purchased palm oil, bananas, soap, and salt, people noticed more traders coming to the market from Nepoko or Mungbere in search of meat. Many Lese men quickly obtained nylon or metal trapping wire and began to set traps that were much less fragile than standard Lese traps made of cord from *kinga* trees. By the summer of 1986, several men were traveling to the market regularly with large quantities of meat, sometimes selling up to six animals (usually duikers) in one day. They attributed their success to the ready supply of metal

TABLE 1

ETHNIC COMPOSITION OF SELLERS AT THE DINGBO MARKET, 1986–1987

Date	Lese	Longo	Azande	Budu	Mamvu/ Mangutu	Other	Total
1986							
Sept. 19	10	6	5	3	1	1	26
26	10	8	5	5	1	1	30
Oct. 3	12	3	2	2	2	0	21
10	12	5	1	3	4	1*	26
17	14	7	2	8	1	1	33
24	10	3	1	6	1	0	21
Nov. 7	1	3	1	3	2	0	10
14	13	2	2	2	2	0	21
21	3	1	1	3	2	1	11
28	6	2	4	0	2	1	15
Dec. 5	8	0	2	5	2	2	19
12	2	1	1	1	0	1	6
19	7	2	1	3	2	2	17
26	1	0	1	3	0	0	5
1987							
Jan. 9	6	4	1	1	0	0	12
16	2	0	1	2	0	1	6
30	5	1	0	5	4	0	15
Feb. 13	4	0	2	2	0	1	9
20	6	3	1	4	0	1	15
27	6	2	2	2	0	0	12
Mar. 6	4	4	1	4	2	2	17
13	4	2	3	4	1	4	18
20	9	2	3	7	1	1	23
27	3	1	2	2	1	0	9
Apr. 17	5	1	1	2	0	1	10
24	4	0	1	2	0	2	9
May 6	11	1	2	3	2	0	19
20	8	2	2	2	2	1	17
27	3	2	2	0	0	2	9
Jun. 5	6	2	1	0	1	1	11
12	11	3	3	2	3	0	22
19	8	2	2	3	2	0	17
26	3	2	1	4	0	2*	12

TABLE 1 (*continued*)

Date	Lese	Longo	Azande	Budu	Mamvu/ Mangutu	Other	Total
Jul. 3	6	2	1	4	1	2	16
24	10	0	2	4	1	1	18
Aug. 7	2	0	1	1	0	1*	5
14	7	1	0	2	0	1	11
21	6	1	1	2	2	0	12
28	12	2	2	4	1	0	21
Average	6.62	2.13	1.69	2.95	1.82	0.97	15.49

*These sellers were Efe men. On Oct. 10, 1986, one Efe man sold elephant meat and opi fruit; on June 26, 1987, two men sold sweet bananas (kitika), and on Aug. 7, 1987, an Efe man sold honey. All sold their goods for cash.

wire. One Lese man reported earning more than two thousand zaires in one day, approximately one-third of the average total per capita income per year for Lese men (approximately $50 U.S.).[6] Although kinga cord is widely available in the forest, many Lese are unwilling to employ the cord as trapping wire; they say such traps require too much effort, are more easily broken by large animals such as forest hog, and are the "traps of our ancestors," not of the educated and modern youth.

The ethnic composition of sellers demonstrates the localism of market sales (see table 1). Lese men and women, mostly those from the Dingbo area, are by far the most common sellers. Along with the Mangbetu and Mamvu, the Lese who live at Dingbo sell cassava, bananas, salt, and other foods. Longo, Zande, and Budu men and women primarily sell palm oil. Market observations show huge fluctuations in numbers of buyers. I found some of these fluctuations to be unexplainable, but most appear to be due to military and police activities in various areas. When the police are visiting Nepoko, which is about thirty kilometers north of Malembi, the Longo, Zande, and Budu who live there choose not to particpate in the market. Any money these traders make at the market would likely be extorted by the police for fines,

6. The figure of $50 U.S. was derived by Richard Wrangham and Elizabeth Ross (personal communication, Ituri Project Notes at Ngodi Ngodi, Zaire) according to cash income generated from the sale of peanuts and rice. Since few peanuts and rice have been sold after 1983, the average yearly income has probably decreased considerably below $50 U.S. As comparison, an average piece of Zairian printed cloth cost approximately $6 U.S. at the time of this study; an average leg of duiker cost about $1 U.S.

food, or alcohol. When the police are visiting the Dingbo area, the Lese merchants stay at home and wait until the next week to sell their goods, if they have not spoiled by that time.

The Lese interaction with the market is significant because it is recent and because it is one of the only opportunities they have to meet people who are neither Lese nor Efe. While they often go to the market to buy things that they do not themselves produce, they also seem to buy many goods simply to paticipate in the market exchange. Mostly they buy plantains, soap, salt, and palm oil (see table 2). Soap is not produced locally, and indigenous salt is extremely bitter and difficult to find. Palm oil is scarce because so few Lese plant palm oil trees, which require up to seven years to produce the fruit from which oil can be extracted (processing is labor intensive). Though the Masa appear to have planted some palm oil trees, the Lese chose not to, believing that they would never live at one village for more than about seven years.

TABLE 2

TOTAL NUMBER OF PURCHASES MADE ON TWENTY-ONE CONSECUTIVE MARKET DAYS (MARCH–AUGUST 1987)
(112 individuals in sample)

Item	*Number of Purchases*
Palm oil	52
Plantains	38
Soap	28
Salt	18
Tobacco	14
Cassava	13
Peanuts	5
Kerosene	4
Beans	3
Earrings	2
Bread	2
Underwear	2
Metal drinking cup	2
Matches	2
Rice	2
Necklace	1
Candy	1

TABLE 2 (*continued*)

Item	*Number of Purchases*
Candles	1
Marbles	1
Sugar	1
Safety pins	1
Cloth	1
Razor	1
Tetracycline	1

Other items purchased during the 1985–87 markets observed that do appear in this sample included meat, potatoes, honey, scarves, hammers, dried and salted fish, sodium bicarbonate, pens, notebooks, thread, sewing needles, and alcohol.

On the other hand, plantains, cassava, and tobacco, which were bought by many Lese at the market, are grown in almost every Lese garden and were available during the period of my observations. Since the purchases I recorded were not made during a time of hunger or drought, other reasons than urgent need were obviously at work. It appears that the foods were not purchased as an attempt to display wealth and achieve status in the public arena, since the purchase of staple foods signifies that one has a poor and unproductive garden, a reflection of an unskilled or lazy farmer. Nor were they bought because of immediate demands of guests, or police and military. A more plausible reason is the lack of availability and limited storage time of cultivated goods. Plantains are not always available even in large gardens, of course, and many Lese gardens contain only a handful of plantain plants, so at times when the plant is not bearing one may have to buy at the market, probably from someone who has a large crop that cannot be stored for very long. Aside from some maize and peanuts, usually stored for future planting, most crops are too perishable to be stored for future consumption. Peanuts can be stored for up to six months, rice for a few months, plantains, bananas, cassava, and potatoes for only a few weeks, and even peanuts and rice may be destroyed by fungi and other organisms within a matter of weeks. Indeed, one reason the Lese do not plant larger gardens is that surplus foods will rot.

One of the most important reasons for Lese to buy foods they already have is that they want to *spend* any money they have earned, and they prefer to spend money on items that are perishable. Two men stated that, although they had plantains in their gardens, they had few that were ready to be eaten during that particular week, and they added that if they did not spend the money, then others would—meaning, I inferred, that their cash would be lost to kin or to the military, for when kin ask for money and soldiers or police demand payments of fines, it is better to refuse honestly by admitting your true poverty than to lie or have to give up on demand.

The principle can be stated: *what you don't have, you don't lose.* Most Lese men and women can tell of times when they carefully saved money and bought a radio or a bicycle, only to lose it to state officials. If the items are not taken by officials, they are taken by borrowers. The items are then overused, mishandled, and frequently ruined. The younger Lese men still like to buy watches, shoes, and radios, but they frankly admit that the risks of such purchases are great. When people do save money for a long period, meaning over about three months, they save it not for long-term goals such as sending a child to a mission school but for buying specific items, particularly cloth, the purchase of which is seen by women and wives, especially, as a gauge of a man's ability to care for his house.

My records of purchases made at the Dingbo market do not show any cloth purchases, however, because the price of cloth there was very high, twice that of the market at the city of Isiro (over 200 km. away), and the people in my study area could not afford to buy cloth. The Longo traders, for example, were demanding around 1,300 zaires for three pieces, whereas at Isiro the price was three pieces for 600 zaires. Many of the Lese of Malembi got their cloth from the anthropologists who traveled to Isiro every six weeks for supplies, and pieces of cloth were also the most common gift given to the Lese by Ituri project members upon their departure from the field.

However, though the Lese would seem to have few ways of obtaining cash, I have never known a man to be without some money. Lese men can sometimes sell tobacco or meat for cash to people traveling from outside the study area, and they also can get cash through bridewealth and through death, childbirth, and umbilical cord payments. It is not uncommon, too, for plantation owners to pay not only with food, but with zaires; plantation workers in 1987 earned, on average, 30 to 35 zaires a day (about 25 cents, U.S.). Occasionally, goods at the market are sold for cash, and once in a while a trucker comes into the area to buy coffee. This happened only once in 1987, and he bought coffee at prices well below the national coffee price. The Lese who did not sell to him had a very difficult time transporting their sacks of coffee by bicycle to the Dingbo plantations. As of March 7, 1987 (near the end of the coffee selling season), 18 out of the 58 men living along the stretch of road between Malembi and Dingbo had produced coffee (31.1% of men), but only 13 of the 18 producers (22%), representing 11 out of the 19 villages sampled (57.8%), sold their coffee. Tabulated according to village income rather than personal income, about half (47.3%) of all of the villages received some cash from coffee production in 1987.

Another important source of cash in recent years for Malembi has been the foreign research team of anthropologists who have hired both Efe and Lese to build houses for them, cut firewood, and serve as guides and informants. Archaeologists paid entire Efe groups large sums of money for their help as guides and workers on extended field trips. Anthropologists bought meat and souvenirs and often hired regular informants and cooks. Two women who were hired as cooks prepared food and maintained the research camp; they were paid 240 zaires a week (per cook, for an entire year), totaling 12,480 zaires a year (about $110 U.S., double the average Lese yearly income). Two Lese men, hired to build a house for the anthropologists, received 700 zaires each over a six-week period (about $6 U.S.). One of the most interesting facts relating to the market data is the contribution that our cooks and two informants made to the total number of purchases made at the Dingbo market. Because they earned so much money, the two cooks and my two regular informants traveled to the market regularly; of the 227 purchases I recorded between March and August 1987, the purchases of the two cooks alone (50 separate purchases) account for 22.1 percent of the total market purchases and 30.9 percent of the total purchases made by women.

But money is rarely saved, in part, as I have said, because the police demand payments in cash and so there is little point in having too much, but also for the very practical reason that money is truly a perishable good. Money is liable to be eaten away not simply by variations in currency values but by the ever-present fungi growing in the rain forest. The fungi attack the bills, sometimes seeming to prefer the serial numbers to any other part, and soon make the notes worthless; this is especially true of the Efe's money because there are so few dry places at Efe camps where they can store money safely. Until 1987 there were no Zairian coins, and the paper money, especially the smaller five and ten zaire notes, are in poor condition in all parts of the country. More than once, the Republic of Zaire has declared all circulating money to be void until new money with new designs and values is printed. A few years ago the chief of the *collectivité* heard on his radio that the president of Zaire had issued such a *démonétisation,* several days before the Lese of the Malembi area heard that news. The chief quickly paid off the bridewealth payments due to his wife's family at Andingbana village, and Andingbana discovered within a few days that the cash was worthless. A dispute ensued, but Andingbana was not able to recover its loss.

SWISS ARMY BUTTONS: A NEW CURRENCY

Recently, the actions of Catholic missionaries at Nduye have had much to do with Lese fears about the instability of the Zairian currency. The missionaries at Nduye believe that the Lese hold the Efe in "slavery"; they say that the Efe work hard for the Lese, and in return receive only marijuana and tobacco, and they have therefore told the Efe that they may bring to the mission any kind of handicraft, such as bows and arrows and bark cloth, and receive Swiss army uniform buttons in return. These buttons have now become currency. The small ones are worth one or five zaires, the larger ones are worth 25 to 100 zaires. Only the Efe are allowed to use this system. The sisters expect the Efe to use these buttons to buy foods cultivated in the gardens of the mission and put on sale at the mission store, rather than to seek foods in the gardens of the Lese, for whom, since they are excluded from the mission trade system, the buttons are presumably worthless.

So far the plan has backfired, however, mainly because many Lese-Karo, who have suffered under the fluctuating currency, have decided that buttons from the Efe are good payment. They accept the buttons for cultivated foods, tobacco, or marijuana and use them in turn to hire Efe labor or to buy meat from Efe hunters. Instead of disrupting the Lese-Efe exchange system, these Catholic missionaries have simply fueled it with a new exchange item, a new currency that, at least for the moment, is far more stable than the national currency.

POLICE AND MILITARY

Although the Lese participate in the market rarely, they do manage to utilize it for minor purchases, and as a way to sell meat and obtain cash. Cash is consistently used not only for purchases but for negotiations with military, police, and other state officials. The Lese must pay taxes and the fines leveled against them for minor infractions. They are frequently arrested and beaten, and many live with continuous dread that they will be affected by hostile and manipulative officials. The state jeopardizes their insularity, and threatens to remove (by arrest) people from their families and gardens. Some Lese say that their troubles with the state are one reason they do not invest in developing more food than they need for basic subsistence.

The shifting of authority in Zaire following independence did not involve a comprehensive overhaul of the colonial administrative structure. Following independence, Chief Nekubai continued in his chiefdom more or less as he had formerly done. He died in 1968 after developing gangrene in his foot. He was succeeded by Sukari, and after Sukari became ill with hypertension and other ailments, his eldest son, Joachim, assumed the chiefdom. Within two years, Joachim developed tuberculosis and infectious hepatitis. He died in December of 1986, at which time Faustin, Sukari's middle son, became chief.

Although Faustin, together with his younger brother Francois, has been instrumental in developing the Dingbo market, his administration has been plagued by inadequate communication and much disorganization. In many ways, Faustin's administration resembles that of Chief Mbula in the 1920s. Like Mbula, Faustin has been unable to collect taxes—and therefore he has been unable to provide funding for his superiors at the zone and subregion levels. Nor has he been able to mobilize the labor needed to maintain the roads and bridges of the *collectivité*. In striking similarity to the Belgian authorities during Mbula's administration, many of Faustin's superiors have considered removing him from power and consolidating the Lese-Dese and the Lese-Karo chiefdoms into a single administrative *collectivité*. The bad state of the road, which has kept the Lese isolated from outside markets and has also kept buyers from plantations and mission health-care workers from coming into the area, is largely responsible for increasing poverty and poor health. Even if the Lese can produce agricultural surpluses, they often have to travel long distances to obtain cash and to receive any sort of Western-style medical care. The poverty of the Lese who live in the Lese-Dese *collectivité* frustrates the chief, if only because his own wealth and position in the government depend upon what he can extract from the population. Administrators at the level of the zone are under the impression that Faustin is lazy and has little control over his area, and this impression has led the military to become more active in dispute settlement and in the general administration of the Lese-Dese chiefdom.

The chiefdom is situated within the *Collectivité Lese-Dese*. The administrative headquarters of the *collectivité* is maintained at Ngbongupanda, eighteen kilometers north of Malembi, where the *chef de collectivité,* his family, police, and secretaries live. The police (all of them unarmed) are, for the most part, criminals who were sentenced to posts as policemen—being a policeman is considered to be highly undesirable and is therefore a punishment—and they are badly paid. In 1987, a policeman for the *collectivité* earned 300 zaires per month (about $2.50 U.S.), about one-third the salary of a plantation laborer. The police accompany the chief on his travels and help him to collect taxes, impose fines, and detain and arrest anyone believed to have violated the law. Any Lese villager can complain to the chief that someone has committed an unlawful act, and the police will arrest, and sometimes beat and torture, the accused before any trial.

To supplement their low pay, the police seek to gain in whatever way they can. They impose fines without the chief's knowledge, threaten to beat or arrest people if they are not given food or money, and take, as their own, goods such as bicycles, radios, and shoes, claiming that they might be stolen goods, or at least that they are unaccounted for by receipts. All Lese must have receipts for material goods and must have paid a garden tax, cultivated a garden, and paid taxes on all the material goods (including chickens and goats) contained within their household; they must possess a valid *carte de résidence* and *carte d'identification,* and they must give food and shelter to any state official who requests it. If they fail to do any of these things, fines are imposed and arrests are made. Many persons are fined and/or arrested for refusing to give food to policemen, and many are detained and beaten for not "giving respect" to the officials. On one occasion, a state census taker observed an Efe man and a Lese women fighting. The census taker's only legitimate task is to write down names and numbers, yet I watched as he held a trial and imposed a heavy fine on the Efe man. The Efe man told the census taker, "Pardon me, you are the state (*l'état*), and I did badly." The Efe man's Lese partner, alarmed by what might happen to him, and to his agnates, treated the census taker as a judge, acquiesced, and paid the fine for his Efe. I should point out, however, that the military and police are much more active in Malembi today than they were before 1985. Other Ituri project members report that between 1980 and 1985, neither they nor the Lese of Malembi encountered many problems that resulted in torture, or in any other kind of physical abuse of the local population.

A small group of soldiers (all non-Lese), armed with rifles and two machine guns, is posted at Nduye, sixty-six kilometers south of Malembi. This post was established during the Simba rebellion in 1963 to protect the local population from the Simbas who occupied the north-south road, and it has remained there ever since. Like the police, these soldiers must supplement their low pay by fines and extortion. They are reputed to be far more brutal and violent than the police, and gossip tells of soldiers murdering innocent civilians. Moreover, unlike the police and the chief, the soldiers come from Mambasa and Bunia, the towns that are reputed to have the most horrendous prisons. Most Lese believe that people imprisoned at Bunia are executed there. Many of my informants contend that the severity of prison life increases with the distance of the prison from the *collectivité.*

The chief of the military post, the *adjudant,* has the authority to arrest both the chief and the police, and to replace the chief as the principal investigator in cases of homicide. As a result, past chiefs and *adjudants* have engaged in bitter rivalries, with each side attempting to slander the other before the *commissaires de zone* and other state officials. Both recognize that they are competing for the same resource. During my stay in Zaire, the *chef de collectivité Lese-Dese* consistently tried to shield his criminal investigations from the military, and the military consistently ignored the fact that the Zairian law books allow chiefs to impose and collect fines and prohibit soldiers from doing so.

The chief walks from Ngbongupanda to the Malembi area regularly to collect taxes, to hunt, and to discuss with the local *chefs de groupement* and *capitas* the news from the *zone* or *sous région.* Occasionally, the *governeur de région* requests money from the *commissaires de sous région,* who in turn requests money from the *commissaires de zone,* and so on, until the chief is compelled to look for money from among the villagers. In addition, the chief consistently tries to mobilize workers to clear trees and repair ditches on the sides of the road, to help foster trade or prepare for visits from his superiors. When the chief receives word that officials from Bunia or Mambasa will be arriving at his home at Ngbongupanda, he orders his police to take chickens, potatoes, squash, meat, cassava, and rice from the local populations; he orders them also to arrest a number of persons on various minor or fabricated charges—from working in the garden without carrying a *carte de résidence* to having cleared a garden smaller than is legally required by every citizen—and transport them by foot to the prison at Ngbongupanda. While at Ngbongupanda, the prisoners pay their fines and prepare for the arrival of guests by clearing and weeding the village, repairing the road, digging up cassava, potatoes, and other foods, and repairing the roofs of the houses. Unmarried female prisoners are intended to be sexual partners of visiting police or military, and to be *animatrices* (dancers) for songs praising the president and the government of Zaire. Several times a year unmarried girls, who have committed no crime, are ordered to be *animatrices* at Ngbongupanda. If people resist going to Ngbongupanda, as is often the case, they may be beaten severely and receive fines or prison sentences. Fathers and brothers fight, to no avail, to keep their daughters from going to Ngbongupanda, where, it is said, the girls have no choice but to engage in sexual activity with the police or soldiers.

Soldiers and police do not enjoy trekking into the *collectivité*, because they know that the Lese have few chickens or goats, and little food. Several soldiers told me that they believe the Lese to be "worthless" (*sans valeur*) and therefore feel little compunction in beating them. Still, the soldiers and police say, they can always find some food and money. Many officials view the Efe as being subhuman, "like the monkeys," and so are quick to beat them. One violent fight that I witnessed began when the chief, drunk on palm wine, became angry at an Efe man because that man's son had refused to travel as a messenger for the state. The chief struck the Efe man in the face, and then called the police to his side, saying that the Efe man had struck him in the face. The police beat the Efe man severely by kicking him and hitting him on the chest and back with a stick. The Efe man insulted the chief, and stated that, as a *premier citoyen,* he was independent (*indépendant*) of the state (*l'état*). Within an hour, the police hung him from a tree by his wrists. They beat him on the legs and back, and yelled, "Here is your independence!" After about fifteen minutes, the police lowered him and proceeded to his camp, where they took every chicken.

Fortunately for the Lese, the police do not carry guns. But the military do have guns, and they use them not for shooting but for beating the local population. In December 1986, after three people died from eating poisonous wild yams, five soldiers entered the area and remained for six days, eating Lese foods and taking large bags of cultivated food with them on their return. They accused the local population of murder, beat several people, took four goats, twelve chickens, and about two thousand zaires. They moved on toward Dingbo, where they accused the residents of selling coffee illegally to coffee smugglers from the Sudan. They pointed their guns at people and beat several people severely. Villagers eventually surrounded the soldiers, engaged in a lengthy hand-to-hand fight, and took the guns from them. One man carried a weapon seventy kilometers to a military headquarters and informed the officers that the military were being unusually violent in the Lese-Dese chiefdom. The chief military officer traveled to Dingbo and ordered the military to return to Nduye, but not before more goats and chickens were taken.

The police and military thus have a profound effect on the way the Lese go about their lives. Economically marginal, socially and politically isolated, the Lese and the Efe live on the edge of subsistence. To a great extent, this subsistence economy is a response to exogenous historical forces, which have taught the Lese to produce very little food and to engage in few relations of exchange as a way to protect themselves from an oppressive outer world. It may also be true that the neat conceptual separations—for example, between the inside Lese/Efe world and the outside foreign world, between Lese and Efe, between farmer and hunter-gatherer—are a result of repeated threats to choice and autonomy of cultural and social practice. As A. Gupta and J. Ferguson remark on the tendency for identities and localities to be fused in contexts of deterritorialization among refugees or migrants, "Territoriality is thus reinscribed at just the point it threatens to be erased" (1992:11). But, as I discovered, the groundwork for social and economic insulation can also be found within the village itself, in a Lese image of themselves as an isolated society, as well as in a history of domination. A spirit of autonomy and insulation may predate the turmoil of recent years, and it may well be that the Lese have found the pressures exerted by those labeled "outsiders" to be consonant with a culturally valued goal of insulation. Historical and cultural experience may, indeed, have resonated with one another and worked together to produce an ethnographic situation in which isolation has become so important an aspect of ethnicity that it comes not solely from either exogenous or endogenous forces, which are analytically distinct but experientially indivisible, but from a dialectic between the two.

CHAPTER III

Gender and Ethnicity

"We [the Lese] gained our independence from the Belgians in 1960, but the Efe have not gained their independence from us."

A Lese man at the funeral of his Efe partner

At night in the Lese villages, men sit outside their houses in their *pasa,* the roofed meeting places in the village plaza, and tell stories. At the center of the pasa is a fire. The nights are chilly in the rain forest and children may come to warm themselves by the fire while their mothers sit on makeshift chairs on the edge of the pasa. At these times, men and women will talk about the forest, of its dangers and darkness, and of the tricksters and other spirits that harass and torment the farmers who try to enter. It seemed to me that the stories were directed toward the children and even intended to frighten them. One story tells of a man who goes to the forest and is seduced by a female forest spirit. She forces her way into his body and rips open his skin, disemboweling and killing him. Another story tells of a farmer who goes to the forest to set an animal trap. He meets a female forest spirit with leprosy who tells him that he can pass by only if he licks the blood and pus from her lesions. Even after he agrees, she transforms herself into a knife and impales him. A third story tells of an Efe spirit named Befe who comes from the forest into the village, exhumes and rapes the corpse of a Lese girl, and then rapes the village houses by penetrating the doors with his large phallus.

This chapter is about the the village and the forest. But it is more generally about the opposition between the Lese and the Efe. It is difficult to imagine oppositions that are more sharp and fundamental than those which the Lese make between themselves and the Efe: village versus forest, culture versus nature, the civilized versus the savage, male versus female, white versus red, light versus dark. The Lese hold that they are civilized and cultural, because, among other things, they live in villages, cultivate food crops, and go to school and church, whereas the Efe are savages who live in the forest, hunt and gather, have only temporary settlements, and know nothing of God, mathematics, and the French language. Through metaphor, the Lese seek both to define themselves and to denigrate the Efe.

Gender is perhaps the most salient metaphor for characterizing the Efe; Lese men and women frequently characterize the Efe, and the forest in which the Efe live, as female.[1] The Lese, in contrast, characterize themselves, and the villages in which they live, as male. In fact, the distinctions they make between themselves and the Efe, as groups, can be seen to parallel those between men and women in general, and between Lese men and their wives in particular. The Lese see the Lese-Efe relationship as part of a series of male-female oppositions, which, by implication, puts the Efe in the subordinate female position. The metaphor also implies a more specific relationship between the Efe and Lese men's wives and draws an analogic equivalence between them. In the Lese house, these two groups of people are subordinate to Lese men, and are thus culturally represented in similar ways. The central argument of this chapter is that the symbolic incorporation of the Efe into the Lese house is made possible by a particular Lese discourse about Lese-Efe differences.

The data presented in this chapter, in which I explore the ways gender constructs can be appropriated as a means of structuring relations of inequality, are directly relevant to anthropological discussions of the relation between domestic and political/public domains, and the metaphors through which male/female relations of power and domination are established (Modjeska 1982; Ortner and Whitehead 1981; Schlegel 1977; A. Strathern 1982). Considerable research has been conducted on the ways in which gender can be constitutive of perceptions of inequality in general, and of inequality between men in particular (especially in Melanesia; see M. Strathern 1987:15). However, as M. Strathern notes for the Melanesia context, differences between men and women are not constitutive of differences between categories such as

1. Feminizing the subordinate or subordinating by feminizing is extremely common. Two of the most compelling examples are Jean and John Comaroff's discussion of the feminization of Africa and Africans by nineteenth-century Europeans (Comaroff and Comaroff 1991) and Jean Jackson's description of the Tukanoan denigration of the Maku in the central Northwest Amazon (1983:227–239).

ethnic groups or classes (1987:15). One of the categories to be described later in this chapter, that of the *aku-dole,* or man-woman, will demonstrate how inequalities between Lese men are framed in terms of gender. But that same idiom is employed to distinguish between ethnic groups. The more general significance of this ethnographic case is to confound and betray the inaccuracies of the conventional opposition between the public and private, between the relationships that obtain in the larger political structures of society and the relationships that obtain in the house. Ethnicity in Malembi depends very much on the definition of relationships in the house.

I must be clear about the extent to which the representations I shall discuss are conscious or unconscious. I do not intend to argue that all Lese men and women consciously draw a comparison between Lese men's wives and the Efe. I am only attempting to explicate certain affinities and parallels that are analytically discernible in a number of contexts, even though my informants did not, and perhaps could not, articulate them in the abstract.

I should also point out that I am not concerned here with power relations or authority, in an individual sense, or with specific cases of domination or subordination in particular fields of social action. I am concerned here with inequality as a function of the social evaluation of human differences (see Berreman 1975)—with the images of domination and the discourse of hierarchy through which perceived relations of inequality are constituted. Hierarchy refers here to a "conceptual system which ranks a set of entities in relation to each other so that they are not all equal" (Rousseau 1990:163). Hierarchy thus does not refer to social stratification, which, as Rousseau notes, is but one kind of hierarchy.

Hierarchies have integrative functions: the very differences that are discernible between the Lese and the Efe are precisely those that make the Efe complementary to the Lese. The incorporation of the Efe into Lese village life is formed largely by Lese representations of differentiation, particularly because distinctions between the Lese and the Efe, as groups, parallel those between Lese men and their wives. Louis Dumont's remarks about India (1970:191) are relevant to the Lese-Efe context: "in the hierarchical scheme a group's acknowledged differentness whereby it is contrasted with other groups becomes the very principle whereby it is integrated into society."

In the discussion that follows, I address the denigrating representations of the Efe in different contexts. I begin with explicit denigrations of the Efe made by my Lese informants in everyday conversation and then go on to show how these denigrations are constituted in legend; in beliefs about color oppositions that bring out symbolic affinities between the Efe and gender relations, primarily in the context of the Lese theory of conception; in the Lese-Efe relationship as revealed by interactional and linguistic evidence; and finally in the images of the Efe that have been appropriated directly from the engagement between the Lese and European administrators and missionaries.

THE FOREST AND THE VILLAGE

Although both the Lese and the Efe live in the Ituri forest, the Lese of Malembi with whom I lived deny that they themselves live in the forest. They say they live in the village and the Efe live in the forest. This dichotomy, repeated time and time again in Turnbull's work, is as fundamental to the Lese as was the opposition between Europe and the "dark continent," the white and the black. The forest for the Lese is analogous to the "jungle" for the European, conceived as impenetrable, dark, and dangerous. Stanley's description of the "green hell" (Vansina 1990a:39) he traveled through while crossing the Ituri forest is echoed in the experience of other explorers, missionaries, and administrators in the Congo. And the Lese of Malembi, recalling the missionaries and other Europeans, are proud that they are "of the village," whereas the Efe are "of the forest." The forest is the place where the hostile ancestral spirits of the Lese dwell, spirits the Lese call *tore,* and translate into Swahili as *shaitani* (Satan), and the attributes associated with the forest—darkness, wetness, danger, and uncertainty, among other things—are therefore also associated with the Efe. The construction of ethnic boundaries goes hand in hand with the construction of inequality, in which the village is made to represent everything good, while the forest represents everything bad. This division of the world is echoed by Bahuchet and Guillaume (1982) in their account of Aka-Bantu relations, as well as by E. Waehle (1985:392), who writes: "The Efe are savages and sub-humans (likened to chimpanzees or forest hogs); they are thieves; the forest is the contradiction to the village (almost as nature to culture)."

The two worlds are diametrically opposed, and the difference between them represents one of the most significant and basic markers of ethnic distinction. For example, when an Efe woman marries a Lese man, and moves, as she must, to the village, the Efe and the Lese say that she has married the village (*anga-ni ubo-ke*); the groom is said to have "married [a girl] of the forest" (*anga-ni meli-ba*). Lese men insult other Lese men who engage in extensive hunting with the term "forest people," and any man who behaves in a manner believed by the Lese to be stereotypical of the Efe will be referred to by the Lese, disparagingly, as either a "forest person" or an "Efe."

For both the Lese and the Efe, the forest begins and ends with areas cleared for Lese houses and pasa. The forest is where the cleared land surrounding the village becomes wild and overgrown. Even a small patch of wild foliage creeping into the village area will be called forest, and the Lese may say that the forest "is coming closer." With the exception of forest paths, any area in which trees and shrubs have not been cut down and weeds and vines have not been removed will be considered forest. Every village will contain houses, cooking areas, and one or more pasa (the number of pasa depends upon the number of houses and the degree to which those houses have friendly relations with one another and can share the same public meeting space). At their best, the villages are free of foliage, weeds, and grasses, but they may contain banana and coffee plants, and they are regarded as tended, so that even when people go just a few meters outside of the village and away from the road, they say they have gone to the forest. Efe camps, even when they are situated only a few hundred meters from the village, sometimes within the garden of their Lese partners, are said to be in the forest.

Even with this close proximity, there is a noticeable difference between Lese and Efe settlements. Though the Efe usually cut down some trees and vines, their camps are not cleared of all plant life, as are the Lese villages. The borders of Efe camps form a circle, or at least a highly curved and ambiguously defined domain. The huts are hemispherical, made of leaves and sticks, and the land of the camp area is black, brown, green, moist, and full of plant and insect life. Because the land is rarely weeded and so many trees are left standing, the sun cannot penetrate the canopy of the forest, and the land on which the Efe live remains damp and soft. The Lese villages, in addition to being well-defined and impeccably cleared areas of land, contain square or rectangular houses that are placed symmetrically in relation to the road and to other houses.

The Efe also find the opposition between the forest and the village to be significant. During my fieldwork, the Efe complained, in particular, about the insects in the village. Echoing Turnbull's reports of the Mbuti attitude toward the village (1965b:18), Efe told me that the mosquitoes are far more common in the villages, and that when Efe live in the villages for a long time they become ill. Indeed, outside the villages mosquitoes remain in the higher levels of the forest, where the trees have not been cut, and because the mosquitoes feed upon the monkeys and other arborial organisms, they are less irritating to human beings. In addition, when Efe camps become polluted with refuse and begin to attract fleas, the Efe can abandon the camp and quickly build another one nearby. The Efe would surely agree with Turnbull's characterization:

> Where in the villages, and in the plantations that surround them, the midday temperatures soar well into the nineties, and the ground is covered with a dry, choking dust that quickly turns to mud, in the shade of the forest the world is cool and fresh, with only rare places, such as along river banks or at salt licks, where sunlight reaches the ground without first being filtered through a leafy roof. Also from the point of view of comfort, and of health, where village conditions lead to gatherings of flies and mosquitoes, these disease bearers are seldom if ever seen in the depths of the forest, except at such sites as are easily avoided. The Mbuti frequently compare their lot, in these respects, with that of the villagers, who in turn grudgingly admit to some advantages of forest life. (1965b:18)

Yet Lese men, women, and children asserted that they could not live in the forest, that they would be cold, hungry, wet, and prone to disease; they might be bitten by snakes or insects, or, worse, they might encounter trouble from supernatural forces. The Lese often complained about the insects of the forest, namely, fleas and other creatures that are attracted by the garbage that collects in Efe camps.

LESE REPRESENTATIONS: HYGIENE AND SEXUALITY

For the Lese, then, Efe camps represent a whole set of ideas about dirt, health, bodily odors, and secretions. Lese children were particularly illuminating about these ideas. Once when I accompanied a Lese family through an area of forest to check on a fish trap in a river, we found ourselves in an Efe camp that had been abandoned for about a year. One hut was still standing, and I held the hand of a six-year-old boy to whom I was especially close as I went to look inside it. He pulled away from me suddenly, and when I asked him why he was afraid, he said that he did not want to go inside the hut. I told him I only wanted to look inside, and he said that he did not even want to look, that he might get lice or fleas or become sick and die. The huts, his father explained, still contain body products, "things of their bodies," as he put it. The same little boy once shrieked with disgust after he smelled the scent of my shaving cream; he said that it smelled like the Efe, and that the odor "made [his] stomach unhappy." Lese adults, especially women, spoke to me about Efe hygiene, and cited Efe body odor as one of the main reasons why they would not engage in sexual intercourse with Efe men (indeed, I know of no cases, and only a few rumors, of this). Moreover, though under special circumstances some Lese may eat food out of the same cooking pot as an Efe, they will not eat food off the same plate, or banana leaf, as the Efe. This is more than a simple display of inequality. Serving food on the same plate is considered to be an unclean and unsafe act.

Lese women noted that whereas Lese men wash their hands and bodies frequently, sometimes once a day, the Efe may bathe only once a week and do not use soap. Many Efe also live with open skin ulcers that go untreated, whereas the Lese are more likely to attend to their cuts and sores by seeking medical care from a local healer, an anthropologist, or a missionary. One man stated,

> They say they will go to a hospital, but they do not. They don't feel pain. They continue with their sores, and maybe they die, but it is nothing for them. They sit in the dirt with their sores touching the ground, and there are flies all over the sore, and their cloths are soiled with its [the sore's] water. The customs of the Efe are different, they know only dirt.

When I asked one woman whether she "liked" Efe, her answer moved from comments about manners and habits to comments about cleanliness and dirt:

> I like Efe. No problem if they steal from me. I will not beat them. I get angry just to frighten them. They are not like *muto* (people). They have no *akiri* (intelligence, in KiSwahili). Our heart is the same, but their akiri is not the same. Their thoughts are different. They forget quickly, like conflicts with other people, they forget them quickly. But their eyes are the same as the eyes of people. They have the same sweat, but it smells different. It is pungent (*ikochi*). They sleep [live] for two months sometimes without bathing, or maybe they don't bathe for two weeks. Their underarms smell and they sleep on old banana leaves, and the old leaves smell too. They do not like to wash; they are used to old things—it is their custom (*desturi,* in KiSwahili). And their chests get very dirty, and if you give them soap, they do not wash their bodies, they will only wash their clothes.

Finally, the Lese of Malembi often spoke among themselves about how Efe defecate. Lese build outhouses, but the Efe do not, and, according to my informants, Efe will defecate anywhere in the forest. One Lese legend tells of an Efe girl who drowns in her own relative's diarrhea, and many other legends about the Efe incorporate excremental or anal themes. Two Lese men tried to help their Efe partners build outhouses, but said their attempts were in vain because the Efe are not "civilized" (*civilizé*), that they still live like "animals" (*ura*).

The excremental theme is used primarily to characterize the Efe, but it can be used by the Lese self-referentially in joking contexts. One joke concerning the physical differences between the Lese and the Efe asks: When someone defecates the feces falls and can be heard hitting the ground, but when someone urinates, the urine falls lightly onto the ground, and is silent—what am I talking about? The answer is: the Lese and the Efe. The Lese are fatter, taller, and heavier; the Efe are leaner, shorter, and lighter. But whereas height may be the most significant difference for American or European observers, the Lese pay closer attention to weight, skin color, the *shape* of the body, odor, the hair, and the eyebrows. The joke itself concerns the differences between the weight of Efe and Lese. One aspect of the joke that is not obvious is the analogy of color between the pair's feces-urine, and Lese-Efe. Both the Efe and urine are considered to be red in color, since Efe skin color is lighter and more reddish than Lese skin color, and urine is also red (there is no word in either the Lese or Efe dialects for yellow). Likewise, both feces and Lese skin color are considered to be black. The Lese admire the Efe's lighter skin color, find it more beautiful, and value highly reddish skin color among themselves.

Lese also note the variation in muscle tone and fatness. Whereas the Efe have little body fat and are very muscular, the Lese are fatter and appear less robust. The Efe are light-footed, an advantage for hunters, whereas the Lese are heavy-footed and make noise that frightens off the animals. In addition, the Efe are more hirsute. Their eyebrows are much fuller than those of the Lese, and the Lese say that when they travel in areas where there has been extensive intermarriage between Efe and Lese, where some of the physical distinctions are thus blurred, and where differences between the Lese and Efe dialects are not as clear, they can distinguish between Efe and Lese by looking first at the eyebrows. Moreover, Efe women have more chest hair than Lese women. Another joke told by Lese to refer to body hair as well as duplicity and shiftiness is the following: Efe have hairy chests—what am I talking about? The answer is: an *ene* animal trap, a large trap hole covered and hidden by leaves, sticks, vines, and other wild plants.

Lese men are extremely attracted to their stereotypical characterization of Efe women, specifically Efe women's body hair. Thirty-three out of forty men I interviewed (83%) on the subject of sexual attraction reported that during their lives they had engaged in sexual intercourse with an Efe woman; only five (12.5%), the youngest men in the sample, had never had sex with an Efe woman (two men did not wish to answer my question). In fact, the one physical attribute of the Efe women that the Lese men consistently reported as the most distinctive, attractive, and sexually arousing was body hair. Lese men speak among themselves of how exciting *torumbaka* (or pubic hair) is to them. *Torumbaka* literally means "hair from the crotch," but it is used specifically to refer to hair around the navel, or between the breasts; it is said to be unique to the Efe and is also said to have the power to produce instant erections in men.

CONTROLLING NATURE AND CULTURE

Lese men project their own anxiety about control of their sexual desires for Efe women onto the Efe, whom they perceive to be sexually wild—like the forest in which they live. Indeed, the issue of control is central to Lese conceptions of the Efe and of themselves. From the Lese point of view, the Efe are uncontrolled, unrestrained; they act without planning or meditation, and their social organization is turbulent and disorderly and permits sexual relationships that the Lese consider incestuous. Efe men, according to Lese men, are addicted to sex and must engage in intercourse at least once a day. Lese men also say that the Efe's desire for marijuana predisposes the Efe toward violence and disorder. Lese men place a high value on their own self-control and for this reason very seldom smoke marijuana in adulthood. In addition, the Lese want to control the Efe. What Turnbull writes of the Bila and the Mbuti (1965b:42, 83–84) applies somewhat to the Lese and the Efe, since the Lese do not use physical force and rarely go into the forest to control the Efe: "The villagers themselves admit their inability to exert physical force to bend the Mbuti to their will, for the Mbuti always have the ultimate escape of flight to the sanctuary of the forest. The villagers are completely unequipped to pursue the Mbuti into the forest and never attempt it" (1965b:84). On one occasion when I was traveling to an Efe camp, an excited Lese villager named Filipe gave me a note he had written in Swahili ordering his Efe partner, Abdala, to come to the villages. The Efe who live near Malembi do not know how to read, so I read the note to them. Abdala then asked me to tell Filipe that he would come soon. When I returned to the village and reported Abdala's reply, Filipe became irate and asked, "But when? When will he come? I do not know where he is." In fact, Filipe knew very well where Abdala was, but he was perhaps expressing outrage at being unable to control his Efe's movements. Indeed, the desire to control the Efe seems to be not a desire for political domination so much as an expression of anxiety about Efe mobility. Lese men and women often seemed disturbed when they heard, sometimes by word of mouth, that their Efe partner had moved from one camp to another or had gone to a plantation to sign up for wage labor. They also seemed worried when they learned that their Efe were traveling or living near the Lese gardens—partly because of the unpredictability of their Efe's whereabouts, partly, too, because they were afraid the Efe would steal their cultivated food. Like the forest growth that encroaches upon the swept earth of the village, the Lese say the Efe encroach upon the village gardens and threaten to ruin the carefully tended fields of cultivated food.

The notion of control occurs in legend also, as in the following story told to me by an elderly Lese woman, Maruokbe, of the Andingire clan, about the origin of the Lese relationship with the Efe. The relation between this woman's husband and his Efe partner has been rather more turbulent than most. There has been no violence, but there have been periods, sometimes of several years, during which they have not given foods to one another. Maruokbe was quite willing to talk about the Efe:

> There was Andimoi [clan] at Nduye. They took an Efe out of the *Ndau* tree. It was thick, it had holes in it, and Efe families lived in it. They spoke from within. One day the muto had an idea at Andimoi to cut down this tree, and they went and cut it and the Efe yelled, "Do not cut me, do not cut my stomach! My head! They poured out of the tree." We returned with them to near the village. They are Andindau Efe. Every Andindau Efe knows this story. They were our Efe because we took them out of the tree. Later they left us to go to Andibuku of Andape. They have stayed there since.

Some Lese use this story to support their contentions that the Efe were in the past monkeys who came down from the trees to live with the Lese. I interpret the cutting down of the tree as equivalent to harnessing the Efe; the Efe exist as a part of the forest and must be removed from it by the Lese. While the Efe live *with* the forest, the Lese live *against* it.

In contrast to the Efe, the Lese consider themselves to be predictable

In a Lese village, a Lese man (left) teases his Efe partner. *Photograph by R. R. Grinker.*

and stable, controlled, restrained, organized, and thoughtful. They also believe that they have a greater akiri (intelligence) than the Efe. For the Lese, someone with akiri is educated, speaks several languages, can offer advice, can be trusted, is dependable, and is not self-destructive. At one Efe funeral, a Lese man simultaneously criticized and complimented the Efe in my presence by saying, "The Efe of before had no akiri, but now they do. Look at this white person [the author] who doesn't go to the forest everyday, but resides more often with the Lese. He has akiri. To go to the forest every day is bad and without akiri." In addition to being more sedentary, someone with akiri is also well-liked and diplomatic: "Someone with akiri doesn't say what he wants very quickly; he waits, and when he thinks that the person he is with likes him, and is calm, he will say what he wants." In contrast, the Efe are unwilling to "soothe" (*iruka*) their partners, and will let their desires be known at the start of a conversation with an exchange partner.

The notion of intelligence is used to denigrate the Efe as children, just as Europeans denigrated Africans. Like children, my informants say, the Efe have to be taught language and custom; they have to be nourished and nurtured. If left to their own devices, my informants argued, the Efe would act only according to their instincts, and this might involve both destructive and self-destructive behavior.

One of the most common and explicit ways that the Lese disparage the Efe is to accuse them of stealing ("like baboons") foods out of their garden and destroying (*ima-ni*) the garden, even after they have been given food by the Lese partner. Lese make a connection between the Efe, a specific kind of insect, and rainbows, all three of which are believed to damage or destroy the Lese crops. Efe are frequently called *kongu,* the name for a species of large flies that can always be seen buzzing near the prized *njeru* variety of bananas, and that, in legend, inhabits the far end of rainbows (*raba*—for the Lese, an extremely dangerous phenomenon) and helps the rainbow to enter into the village from outside and destroy cultivated foods. The Lese also speak of the Efe as gluttonous in their appetite for food, tobacco and marijuana, and sex. The Efe, the Lese say, cannot farm for themselves because they have no *sibosibo* (patience), and because they lack the capacity to engage in a productive activity that does not offer immediate gratification.

Because of their lack of patience, my informants insisted, Efe men do not save food or money. Yet many Lese also consider the Efe to be careful observers of the quantities of Lese food, who even urge the Lese to save food. One woman stated that several times an Efe man stopped her from giving him too much salt because he was concerned that she save some to give to him later:

> The Efe will refuse you to give too much and he will say stop, that is enough, like for salt, with tobacco, and salt, it is true. He is nervous that you will finish your supply. He wants to come back the next day, and if you give him a lot, he will have to split a greater quantity with his brothers. Efe cannot eat alone. If an Efe comes to stay alone at the village, and you give him food for himself, he will not eat well. He wants to eat a little bit of a lot of people's food over a long period of time. They eat ten times a day, a little bit at a time.

She went on to say that if he had gone to his camp with a great deal of salt or tobacco, he would have been obliged to give most of it to the other people in his camp. By asking his Lese partner's wife to save, he believed he could minimize the goods he would have to share back at camp.

As noted earlier, the Efe and the Lese speak differently. In addition to some differences in vocabulary, where the Lese use glottal consonants, the Efe instead place faucial gaps. But many Lese say that the difference is not so much in the words and grammar as in the organization of ideas. The Lese said that Efe speech is often incoherent and babbling, that when they speak they jump from one idea to the next, that their "ideas have no straight path" (*ide-ba todi a upu kikikiko embi-ani*). Paralleling what some Lese seem to think is an attention deficiency, Efe men are also said to have short and violent tempers and to murder without much provocation. These perceptions have their basis in the angry and sometimes violent fights that punctuate the daily life of many Efe camps, but actual murders are extremely rare. In addition, the Efe are the most fierce and frenzied actors at funerals. The fact that Efe always carry their bow and arrows and/or spear also contributes to the perception of the Efe as wild or savage.

Many Lese think that the Efe are forgetful, have no desire to go to school and learn to read and write, are unable to subsist without agricultural foods because they are lazy, and are addicted to marijuana. Yet it is not clear whether the Lese believe the Efe to be innately deficient, or whether they simply believe the Efe have a skewed and incorrect ranking of values. Except in the case of an argumentative confrontation with Efe, the Lese will never refer to the Efe as animals, or monkeys, and they firmly believe that the Efe are a type of human being. On several occasions my informants told me that the two groups *iradi-ni* (surpass one another), a term that also implies noncomparability.

In terms of the classification of living things, in both the Efe and the Lese dialects, the Lese are called *muto* and the Efe are called *Efe. Muto* means "person," as I was called a *mutotufe* (white person), and Africans are in general called *mutokosa* (black person). In terms of the classification of ethnicity, the Lese are called *Lese* or *Dese,* and the Efe are called *Efe.* Thus, while the Lese have three terms, one to distinguish themselves from the Efe and animals (*muto*), one to distinguish themselves from other groups (*Lese*), and another to distinguish themselves from other Lese (*Dese*), the Efe have only one term. The term *Efe* thus denotes nothing other than the archer Pygmies, and, unlike the word *muto,* has no other usage. The term *Efe* is not subsumed within the term *muto.* Linguistically, then, one might think that the Efe are not considered to be people. However, there is little uniformity regarding the location of the Efe in humanity; in the Lese language, Efe are under no circumstances called *muto,* nor do Efe refer to themselves as *muto.* In the KiNgwana form of Swahili, however, I was told, "yes the Efe are *watu* ['people,' in Swahili] but they are not muto ['people,' in Lese]." It is entirely possible that the Lese word for person, *muto,* also means "farmer."

At any rate, the Efe are not granted the same humanity as the Lese, and this form of denigration (and ambivalence) is common in interethnic relationships (Barth 1969). Jean Jackson's superb ethnography of the Tukanoans, for example, includes discussion of "servant-master" relations between Tukanoans and the forest-dwelling Maku (Jackson 1983). Long-term economic relationships are forged as one Maku group attaches itself to one Tukanoan longhouse. For many reasons—one of which is that the Maku do not build houses—Tukanoans hold that Maku are not *true* "people." So we should not be surprised that the Lese hold an ambiguous belief that the Efe are simultaneously human and less than human. In fact, I echo Jackson's confusion about how to describe the symbolic represention of the subordinate. Are they dehumanized or simply culturally differentiated? She writes:

> When Tukanoans are discussing human nature in general, the tendency is to include all people—whites and Maku—in the discussion. In this framework Maku are not seen as categorically and eternally excluded from the status of "true people" but potentially as members of the human race in good standing if and when they start to comply with certain rules and regulations. (1983:162)

For both the Lese and the Tukanoans, hierarchy is accompanied by a well-elaborated ideology to explain and legitimize it (Jackson 1983:163). The ideology imputes primordial cultural and biological traits to the subordinate, but the characterization is not necessarily neat and clean.

Nonetheless, the extent to which the Lese hope to surpass the Efe in terms of status cannot be overemphasized because this ideology of inequality bears directly on the argument that the two groups must be considered as one. It is easy enough to simply record denigrations. The Lese are quick to say that they believe the Efe should be *amu-ba-ni karu-ta* (under our feet) as the Efe have always been *amu kondu-ni karu-ta* (under our ancestor's feet). The more difficult task is to analyze the various denigrations of distinct contexts for symbolic patterns and associations. Indeed, analysis of the characterizations tells us something more general, something central to the very fabric of Lese identity. What all these characterizations of inequality suggest is that the Efe are not wholly "other" to the Lese because they are such a strong component and defining characteristic of Lese representations of themselves. For example, for the Lese, the dirtiness of the Efe is paired with their own cleanliness, the wildness of the Efe is paired with their own wish for self-control. The Lese and the Efe are thus less in conflict than they are mutually constitutive. According to the Lese, Efe men and women act according to physical instincts involving food, sex, and aggression, and they are driven primarily by somatic influences. They are unable to harness their anger and are not capable of logical or rational thinking; they live with the forest rather than against it and, as represented in mythology, are closer to nature. The Lese believe themselves to be capable of mediating between their drives and the exigencies of proper and ordered social life. They represent rationality and reason, whereas the Efe stand for untamed passions. The Lese and the Efe are two interrelated organizations, and the Lese find meaning in their contrasts.

The contrast between the Lese as cultural and the Efe as natural is highlighted in a story that can serve as an introduction to the way in which the Lese establish unconscious symbolic oppositions about themselves and the Efe. This is one of many stories about the origin of Lese-Efe contact; every Lese phratry preserves a legend about the first meeting. Here, the narrator tells of how the Efe taught the Lese the difference between male and female genitals, and how to have sexual intercourse; the Lese in turn taught the Efe ingenuity and the value of tool use.

The Efe of long ago were Andisamba, my Efe. Andisamba's great grandfather was named Abeki. He was the Efe of Andali, of all the Lese-Dese. His wife's name was Matutobo. His grandmother's name was also Matutobo. Abeki went to the forest and returned. His grandmother came to rub her anus on the top of his thigh. Abeki had many children, a boy here, a girl there. One day, Abeki took off to the forest, and arrived at a garden where there were ripe bananas. Efe ruin [deplete] our gardens, so the Efe went to take the bananas. He thought a lot about what his grandmother did to him, and so he thought a lot about the feces on his thigh. He had never seen bananas before, and he tried one, and he liked it. So he took bananas for his children. He now returned to the garden a third time. The villager left his village and saw footprints. The man saw the Efe sitting there, and then they saw each other. The man called out "ungbatue!" and the Efe said "ungbatue!" and the man asked the Efe to come to his village. "Do not be afraid! I will not hurt you!" They went together.

The man was named Aupa. The Efe said again "ungbatue! See it is stupid, the feces on my thigh, it is by the hand of my grandmother [*andu*]. Every day she does this." The man said, "Soon we will sharpen my knife [to kill the woman]." The man said he would rip open [*ataba*] the Efe's thigh and insert the knife inside it. Then her anus would rip, and the corpse would fall to the ground. The Efe returned until he reached his camp, and his grandmother said to Abeki's wife, "So your man returns?" The children said yes. Then she came to ask him to straighten out [*itesi*] his leg. She wiped herself, and the knife cut her. Corpse. They destroyed her house, and then the Efe moved with his wife to the villager's garden.[2]

From there, the Efe man came to the village woman, and her man was waiting there. "She is ill my woman." The Efe asked "Where is she?" "She is lying down in the pasa." The man went to get some alcohol, and with the Efe, the two of them drank together. The Efe asked, "Am I not able to see

2. The content of the story, in which the Efe and Lese partner collude to murder the Efe's grandmother, deserves some attention. The term *andu,* used for the grandmother, is a term of reference and address for any woman of a given Ego's grandparents' generation reckoned either matrilineally or patrilineally (including the biological grandmothers). Here, *andu* may refer simply to an elderly woman living in the same residence as the Efe man, Abeki. We can assume coresidence, since the man and woman have frequent and intimate contact. Most of the listeners to this story believed that the woman was unmarried, or widowed. Elderly women, especially widows, are not enjoyed by the Lese, and they are rarely encouraged to remain with their children. Widows whose children have died are encouraged even more strongly to leave the affinal village and return to their natal village. They are thought to be dangerous as witches and to be needy and unproductive drains on the economy. Infertile widows are psychologically abused, and sometimes physically abused, until they pack their belongings and return to their natal village. Thus, listeners to this story did not consider Abeki and his Lese partner's murder of the grandmother to be unmotivated. She offers the Lese and Efe partners a common task: for the Efe, the removal of a nuisance and an unproductive consumer; for the Lese, the removal of someone who would be unable to reciprocate his gifts of food. The story is essentially about the ideal relationship between Lese and Efe partners, a relationship that can be enjoyed when the partners are free of intragroup burdens and responsibilities, potential competition, and the envy of others.

> this illness?" The man told the Efe to go and look. He said, "My wife has no penis or testicles, only a wound in her crotch, and every month she bleeds from it, and I cannot stop the bleeding for several days."[3] The Efe said, "I will teach you." So he had sex with the village woman, and she became pregnant, and a child came, the first child. Later he gave her another pregnancy. The villager got mad at the Efe and said, "You will have sex with my woman? I will try myself." From there the Efe and Lese were together."[4]

By illustrating sex between a Lese woman and an Efe man, the characters reverse the conditions of the present day, in which intercourse between Lese women and Efe men is prohibited. But the origin story dramatizes the fact that it is the Efe who symbolically contribute knowledge of the natural world, while it is the Lese who contribute knowledge of the cultural world, to the Lese-Efe relationship. The forest, and the Efe who inhabit it, represent the wild and uncontrollable aspects of humanity, while the village, and the Lese who inhabit it, represent the civilized and controlled aspects of humanity. The Lese-Efe relationship binds the Efe to the Lese village. Conceptually, the villager's power lies in his exclusive knowledge of farming technique, and in the Efe's intractable and gluttonous desire for cultivated foods. The production of these foods attracts the Efe to the village and thereby controls them.

The nature/culture dichotomy so pronounced in this story appears to parallel the distinctions between men and women noted by S. B. Ortner (1974) in her well-known essay on the universal subordination of women. Through their social roles and reproductive function, women are identified with the natural world, while men are identified with the cultural world. Correspondingly, sexual ideologies hold that women's creativity is expressed through childbirth while men's creativity is expressed through the development of technology. Ortner's dichotomy has been subject to criticism, primarily on the grounds that it is not universal, and that conceptions of nature and culture are Western cate-

3. Blood is equated with being wounded, and young Lese children will often make the mistake of saying "I'm bleeded" (*be kutu*) or "the knife bleeded me" instead of using the proper verb for "to wound."

4. Joset (1949) reports a similar story among the Lese-Obi. "The origin of this friendship between the Mambuti and the WaLese is given to us by a known legend: One day, a MoLese was in the forest. On the trail, he met a Mambuti who was walking with his daughter. In honor of this meeting the Mambuti gave his daughter as a gift. However, [the MoLese] did not know what to do. For him, the sexual parts of the woman were a wound, which he tried, in vain, to cure with medicines. Some years later the Mambuti returned and asked his son-in-law where were the children. The MoLese [sic] declared to his father-in-law that he didn't know what to do to have them. The Mambuti stopped the medication, and fornicated with the woman. Nine months later, the first child was born" (my translation from French).

gories whose relevance in ethnographic analysis is limited (H. Moore 1988, MacCormack and Strathern 1980; Mathieu 1978). More precise and meaningful criticisms emerge from the analysis of gender in detailed ethnographic studies (MacCormack and Strathern 1980). Do the Lese pair Efe and women together as representations of nature? If so, what is the nature of the relationship between these two categories of person? The Lese and Efe case appears to support the applicability of such a dichotomy to male-female relations in general, but it does not. For, as we shall see, the idiom of gender used to denigrate the Efe does not derive from women qua woman, but from wives. And wives are denigrated not because they are women but because they are outsiders.

To answer the questions posed in the preceding paragraph, let us now look more deeply into the construction of Lese identity to examine the symbolic organization of the images of the Efe as women. We will find not only that Lese identity is formed through the conjunction of gender and ethnicity but also that the house is a basic locus of the gender and ethnic differentiation that encompasses many of the symbolic representations.

THE FEMINIZATION OF OUTSIDERS IN LEGEND

A complicated and intriguing legend introduces us to a social structural equivalence between Lese men's wives and the Efe. In particular, the use of names in the legend suggests that Lese men's wives and the Efe are conceptually linked in terms of their integration into Lese villages, and in terms of the rules of sexual intercourse.

> Life without Efe? Life without Efe is bad. For a long time we have been with them. There was once a man who had a wife and children. One child walked away, and came back, and found his mother peeling bananas. "I am hungry," he said, "burn [cook] me some bananas fast." "No, look how I am cooking, this way, why does hunger take you like alcohol? You should marry a woman, and she will cook for you, like your brothers' wives cook for them." He was sad, so he went to his garden and cut Masirongo bananas [one of four types: Afoka, Masirongo, Akbandoro, Alambi]. He had an arrow. On his return he saw an Asaba monkey and he shot it, and he took the banana and the monkey and returned.
>
> He went near a river and wanted to burn the hair off the animal at the river. He started to roast the animal, but it split open. He was upset, and he threw the banana into the water, and threw the monkey into the water, and followed the goods as they drifted downstream. A man had a fish trap downstream. This boy we are talking about was named Mandeu ako. The

man with the trap had the very same name. He arrived at the trap. The man saw him and said, "Who are you?" "I am Mandeu ako." "Oh, you are my *atu* [namesake]—come here. Cross over the trap!" The man had *aibo* [a disease with sores on the nose, or near the genitals; often includes a deep sore that extends into the sinuses; possibly syphilis].

He gave the boy a chair. The boy said, "I cannot sit on a chair alone." "You are my atu, you and I shall sit on one chair." He said he was going to look at a trap. He went. Inside was a monkey and a banana and fish, and he said to his wife, and all the girls to whom he had given birth, if someone does you well, you do him well. This boy killed a monkey, it must be him. They gave him some water to wash with. The boy said, "Put the water in the pot my atu uses, and put the pot where he washes and nowhere else." He washed, ate fish. At night, the man said, "You will sleep in the house where my girls sleep." He slept on some logs for two days. Later, the girls' mother said to the girls: "How was it? How did you sleep?" They answered: "We slept like he was our brother. Our bodies never touched." The mother said, "That is good."

Later, the father asked the boy: "How was it that you got to this place?" He said, "I came with sadness because my mother said I eat all the food, and I won't get married, so I left with sadness and came here." The man told his wife to get the singbe horn and she got it and the man took it and gave it to the boy. "Go out there till you see a gbongo tree, hit this horn to its body, then go to a rofo tree and do the same." "O.K. I have gone!" "Just do it!" He came to the gbongo tree and beat the horn. Efe came out of the tree, and he beat the rofo tree, and village people came out of that tree. They all came out of the tree with their women. A wife for this boy came out of the tree too. The Efe came out. He did not have his own Efe. No one did; this is the story of where the Efe came from. Had he slept with the man's daughters the man would have killed the boy; he had killed boys before. The boy made his village there where the *rofo* tree was, and his wife said, "Where did you come from?" "I came from a village." She said, "Let us go there."

He went with her there. Bad hunger was there, and so he saw his mother again. He said, "Mother you said I could not marry a woman. Here she is. I am married." "What will you do about this hunger?" she asked. He took two boys and took them to his village near the rofo tree to feed them and help them. The man had the boy's name and face; he was not a tore [malevolent spirit]. Efe came from a tree. This is the first story to say that Efe were in trees.

Several aspects of this legend require further explanation. A Lese man may have one or more Efe partners only if he is married, but although a married man should ideally have an Efe partner, he does not have to have a partner in order to get married. The reason for this is, as the Efe and Lese say, that it is the Lese women who grow food and who circulate it; Lese women often mediate economic interactions between Lese men and Efe men, and more often the women are the ones who actually carry out the distribution of goods. Partly for this reason, the boy's mother encourages him to find a wife. There is no doubt that the Lese boy depicted in the legend is a true villager because he is portrayed as an incompetent hunter. Although the Lese are active hunters and trappers, they do not believe themselves to be skilled at monkey hunting. The man, Mandeu ako, whom the boy meets in the forest, is a representation of the Efe. His body is covered with sores—Lese frequently characterize the Efe as covered with open sores that go untreated—that extend to the sinuses. This alteration of the sinuses changes the sound of the voice considerably. Frequently in stories such as this some reference is made to the fact that the Lese and Efe speak different dialects: Lese meet up with Efe and are struck by the fact that the previously unknown Efe man speaks a language that is different from the village language. Mandeu ako's voice is most likely altered, as the disease aibo would indicate.

Names are an important part of most Lese legends, and they illustrate the structural equivalence of Lese men's wives and the Efe. Most legends concerning the first meeting of the Efe and the Lese contain an event in which the members of these groups realize that they have an atu relationship—that each possesses the other's name. The atu is itself a name held in common between two or more people, as well as a relationship between the namesakes. The atu refers, however, only to Lese names *abe mani* ("real names"), and not to the Swahili or French names *abe ika* ("other names") that most Lese acquire at some point in their lives. In the following myth, an atu relationship is established when two men discover that their sons are namesakes:

> Makoro were the Efe of Andisengi phratry, and there was a villager [Lese], and his son was named Aupa. There was also an Efe with a son named Aupa. Enemies killed the villager Aupa with an arrow. Aupa's father sat to cry, "Aupa! Aupa! Aupa!" Efe traveled near the periphery of the village and heard this crying every day. The man who cried was Andikose, and the Efe was Makoro group, Andosa clan, the Efe of Andisengi. "Ungabtu! Why are you crying?" "I am crying for my child, his name was Aupa; they killed him with an arrow!" "Ah! That is my son's name also!" So the villager gave the Efe bananas, and they ate together. The Efe man said, "We will go to war for your child's problem [*ude-pu-ni-ba ugu-ba olu*] and get revenge [*uki ere-ini*]. First go and wash your child's corpse." They went and killed. Then the Efe said they would move to Andisopi. The man who went to wash his child said, "There are too many Efe for just one Lese village. The Efe that have moved here should divide among their new relatives [*Efe gawa-ba edenungu-ini-ni*]." This happened when my ancestors left to move to Mount Menda.

The namesake relationship links the Efe to the village. They leave their former residence and move to their new partners, just as the other important group of outsiders, wives, leave their natal village for an affinal one. In fact, the term *atu* is used in two instances: (1) as a term of reference and address for one's namesake, and (2) as a term of reference and address for a specific set of affines: men call their brothers' wives, and women call their husband's brothers, atu. Namesake relationships are formed by the exchange of names in which a Lese partner gives a Lese name to a newborn of his Efe partner's clan (Efe do not give names to Lese). Once the naming has taken place, the two groups are said to be namesakes. The two instances—the Lese-Efe atu relationship, and the relationship between a woman and her husband's brothers, and between a man and his brothers' wives—are related. Both kinds of atu possess spouses who, as spouses, are nonrelatives and therefore potential sexual partners with whom sexual intercourse is nonetheless forbidden. First, men should ideally never have intercourse with their brothers' wives, and conversely, of course, women should never have intercourse with their husband's brothers. Secondly, men should never have intercourse with the women of the Efe group with which their partner is affiliated. In the latter of the two cases, because of classificatory kinship between associated Lese and Efe groups, Lese men reckon Efe women of the clan to which their partners belong to be related to them. The inverse is also true. Efe women should never have intercourse with Lese men of the clans to which they and their consanguines are associated because they are classificatory siblings, and Efe wives should never have intercourse with those men because they are related to them affinally. In both sets of atu relationships the participants may have daily interactions with one another (especially in the atu relationship between men and their brothers' wives, in which the atu are coresidents), and the designation of this very specific relationship accompanies the greater opportunity and potential that exists for sexual intercourse between them. Sexual restrictions of the Efe and wives parallel one another, and are expressed in the use of the term *atu*.

METAPHOR AND THE HOUSE

We can discern an analogy whereby Lese is to male as Efe is to Lese men's wives. But this does not mean that wives and Efe have sexual similarities. The analogy juxtaposes village insiders (Lese men) and village outsiders (wives and Efe); wives and Efe are structurally similar as village outsiders. More specifically, gender symbolism creates an analogic equivalence between the Lese men's wives and the Efe by stressing the parallels between the relationship the Efe have to the residences of their Lese partners, and the relationships wives have to their husband's residences. There is a paradoxical usage of the gender idiom by Lese women; Lese women denigrate Efe women in the same way as they denigrate Efe men—as "female." This usage highlights the point that the most culturally salient aspect of the idiom is not differentiation between male and female, but differentiation between "outsiders" and "insiders." The Lese feminization of the Efe arises not out of perceived similarities between women and Efe, but rather out of the structural similarities established by the use of gender as a metaphor of denigration.

The gender metaphor is an "external" or "analogic" metaphor which, as defined by Aristotle in the *Poetics,* is "when one thing is in the same relationship to another as a third is to a fourth" (Sapir 1977:22–23). Metaphor is ordinarily conceived as the juxtaposition of two terms from separate domains, such that they share certain features. To use Sapir's example, "George is a lion," conveys the sense that, although George is not really a lion, he and the lion are alike because they share courage or ferociousness (1977:23). Efe and women are not alike but are arranged in metonymic juxtaposition. As Sapir phrases it, "The similarity now derives from the relationship each term has to its proper domain" (1977:23). In the case of the Lese denigration of the Efe, the two terms "woman" (which we have already seen is more accurately defined as "wife") and "Efe" are linked not because they are similar but because they share a common link to a third domain: the Lese village and house.

What appears to be the characterization of the Efe as women is actually the characterization of the Efe as Lese men's wives. Both the Efe and wives are outsiders in relation to any Lese house or village. The Efe, as I have already described, come from the forest and symbolically enter the house of the Lese. Lese men's wives come to live in their husband's houses, often from villages more than two days' walk away, and they feel like outsiders as well. Imatokuni (literally "the mother of Tokuni") was an outsider. She lived in a small village and had daily contact with only two or three other wives of her generation, one of whom was an Efe woman. She was able to leave her village every day for washing and other chores, to visit friends, to have a stylist braid her hair, but for the most part she, like all women, remained in the village or in the garden. In the Andimokbe village, Imatokuni's main difficulty, in addition to the isolation and initial loneliness, was her silent mother-in-law, who would not allow her to prepare her husband's food for a period of about a month because she was afraid Imatokuni would poison his food—a common fear among the Lese. Moreover, Imatokuni did not feel free to walk openly in the center of the village. She was conspicuous, and so she hid in the kitchen area (*mafika,* Swahili). In addition, she received a name that could be spoken in public only after the birth of her first child, when she was named "the mother of" her first child.

Conceptually, Efe partners and wives are brought further together in the Lese house. Marriage and the Lese-Efe relationship are the basic constituents of the house, and ideally they are formed at the same time. A man sets up a house only after he is married, and all married Lese men should have Efe partners that they inherited following the marriage.[5] In a man's first marriage, the arrival of his wife should be within a year or two of the inheritance and establishment of a partnership with an Efe man.[6] In fact, on a few occasions, Lese men described their relationship to their Efe partners with the term *anga-ni,* which means "marriage" but also refers to the joining together of two separate things. Marriages and houses, like husbands and wives, Lese and Efe, go hand in hand in social life. Houses are thus places for the coming together of things from the outside and things from the inside.

Marriage is considered to be in process from the earliest negotiations of bridewealth or classificatory sister exchange, but the union is not fully legitimized until the bride actually comes to the husband's village to stay in a house with him. Children born to a woman not living in the house of the father are thus frequently the subject of custody disputes

5. Maurice Bloch (1991) makes a similar point for the Zafimaniry of Madagascar: "Marriage without a house is a contradiction in terms, simply because the Zafimaniry notion which I choose to translate as 'marriage' is distinguished from other forms of sexual union precisely by the existence of a house, and because the normal way of asking the question corresponding to our 'are you married?' is phrased, literally, to mean 'Have you obtained a house with a hearth?' (p. 3).

6. All of the Lese of Malembi claimed to have Efe partners. Although most men inherit their Efe partners from their fathers, variations in demography prevent every man from inheriting in this way. A man's father's Efe may be childless, or he may have fathered girls only. Still more problematic, a Lese man may have more brothers than his father's Efe has sons. As a result, older sons inherit partners, and the other sons must try to establsh partnerships elsewhere, usually by inheriting a partner from a patrilineally related man, such as a father's brother, or, as in a few cases, by reaching a partnership agreement with an Efe man who was not inherited, or whose *muto* died. These partnerships, far from the ideal, lack the trust and permanency of those that are inherited.

between the families of the future bride and groom. The house is also the symbol of the dissolution of marriage. When a woman arrives at her husband's house she brings with her a *membo,* the collection of materials also called "things of the house"—such things as utensils for food gathering, processing, and cooking, and blankets, baskets, combs. The presence of the membo in the house represents the continuity of the union. A woman who wishes to leave her husband permanently will collect her membo and leave with it, thus "destroying" (*ima*) the house, and therefore the marriage. A woman who wishes to frighten her husband will take her membo and hide it in another place in the village, and a woman who simply wishes to separate from her husband for a short time will leave her membo intact, thus assuring her husband that the separation, even if carried out in the wake of a fight, is not permanent. Similarly, an Efe man identifies himself with a particular house by aligning himself specifically with his partner, rather than with other men in the village. Before the actual inheritance of the partnership, Efe men and women will perform services and provide goods for a number of Lese within a village, but once the Efe man is "shown," he is expected to limit his village interactions to the house of his partner. One way that the alliance is expressed is by the giving of products designated as "forest goods" to his Lese partner. These include things such as arrows designed for monkey hunting, termites, and fruits. The Lese partner may in turn give his partner the dog from the house, to be used by him when hunting. The Lese partner will also give his Efe kitchen items, such as metal pots and pans for cooking. Just as a marriage dissolves with the removal of kitchen items from the Lese house, the Lese-Efe partnership is seen to dissolve when the Efe man returns kitchen items to the Lese house. While these two actions may seem to be the opposite of one another, the difference between taking and returning the goods reflects differences in residence. Efe men are members of the house, although they do not actually live in the house. They are incorporated, in part, by possessing "goods of the house." The return of these goods separates the Efe partner from the house, just as the removal of the goods by wives separates women from the house.

The terminology used to characterize marriage parallels the terminology used at the onset of the Lese-Efe relationship. A Lese man may establish a relation with an Efe partner by inheritance or by some other sort of arrangement. But even in the case of a direct inheritance passing from father to son, the recipient must have been "shown" the Efe either by his father or by another Lese in his own village. The term for "to

At an occasional dance, an Efe man dances in front of two Lese women. *Photograph by R. R. Grinker.*

show" is *itadu,* a word that is used to describe personal interactions in only two other contexts: that is, the "showing" of a wife to her future husband, and the "showing" of an unmarried woman to a man as a real or classificatory sister to exchange for a wife. The person who "shows" someone either a wife, or an Efe partner, is called *lakadu,* and the use of this term in Lese-Efe society is exclusive to these two contexts. This points to an equivalence, from the Lese man's perspective, between relationships with Efe men and relationships with wives. "Showing" establishes the dominance of Lese men in both marriage and ethnic relations. I should also add that, just as some few Lese men marry polygynously, so too is it possible (although it is rare) for a Lese man to be shown and to maintain partnerships with more than one Efe.

Efe are further linked to wives during the honey season. Between June and September, the Efe leave their camps located near the Lese villages to collect honey in more distant areas of the forest. It is customary for a Lese man or woman to lend an Efe man a cooking pot. The Efe man will use the pot to collect honey for both his family and the family of the woman to whose membo the pot belongs. Cooking utensils are entirely women's items, owned and used by them. When the Efe returns to the village with honey, he presents the honey in that pot, and his Lese partner is expected to give him a cloth in return, at some time in the near future. The husband's primary responsibility to his wife is to provide her and her children with meat and with printed cloth. Cloth is designated to be a woman's item, and even those Lese men who may, on rare occasions, wish to wear a cloth in place of shorts or pants use their wive's cloths. Most Efe men wear printed cloths, and in the Lese role as the providers of Efe men, the cloth serves to differentiate the Lese as cloth-givers, and the Efe as cloth-takers.

In the village, whereas Lese men spent most of their time in the *pasa,* Lese women, Efe men and women, and Efe and Lese children spend the majority of their time in the mafika, or kitchen. Efe men do not ordinarily enter the pasa of any Lese man without being invited to do so. Lese women almost never sit in the pasa. As a result, when Efe men, from any camp whatsoever, enter the village they head for the kitchen, or women's area, and seat themselves on a log or a chair, if one is offered to them. In contrast, when Lese men enter the village they are free to enter the pasa and sit down on a bamboo chair. In the kitchen, Efe men may help the Lese women, play with children, and pass on gossip and other information. Lese women ask the Efe men to help them with women's work, fetch water, cut firewood, sweep or weed the village, and for the Efe this is not unusual work; in their own camp life, they customarily take care of children and prepare and cook food, while their wives are away gathering food or working in the Lese gardens. These are tasks that Lese men, however, do not ordinarily perform.

While Efe men are engaged in these activities, Lese women and children frequently tease them. For example, Lese women, married and unmarried, may pretend to steal an Efe man's bow and arrow, or anything else he has carried with him, and they frequently refer to the Efe by nicknames, or by kin terms. Efe with watches, shoes, or hats, are particularly susceptible to teasing, but taking away the bow and arrow is the most humiliating. Efe boys carry bows and arrows almost as soon as they can walk, and Efe men are rarely seen without them. The bow and arrow are the obvious symbols of Efe maleness, the items that distinguish Efe men and identify Efe men as hunters. When an Efe man's bow and arrow are taken from him, and especially when they are taken by a woman, he is symbolically emasculated in the eyes of the Lese.

AKU-DOLE: THE DENIGRATION OF LESE MEN

Lese men who are outsiders are also frequently denigrated in the form of "feminization." Lese men, women, and children who come to villages as visitors are not explicitly denigrated, but Lese men who have come from far away to live in a particular village to which they are distantly related are often treated badly. They are asked to help wives in some of their chores, a humiliating task for most men, because, they say, they are asked to behave like Efe men and like Lese men's wives, sitting and working with women in the kitchen. These men are then criticized for doing precisely what they are asked to do and are referred to pejoratively as *aku-dole,* literally "man-woman"—that is, a man who is like a woman (or like an Efe man). Village agnates also refer to such immigrants as *meremere,* a pejorative term meaning specifically someone who has come to the village but is not a direct patrilineal descendant. Thus, outsider Lese men are denigrated with the same idiom used to denigrate Efe men and Lese men's wives.

RED AND WHITE, FEMALE AND MALE

Having demonstrated the saliency of gender as a metaphor for relationships between insiders and outsiders, we can now explore the metaphors of "red" and "white." Both "red" and "white" are open-ended in that they have a variety of different meanings. But the meanings together constitute a specific pattern of metaphoric relationships. The colors red and white are related to one another in the same way as female and male; wives (as a gender) and the Efe (as an ethnic group) are symbolized by redness, whereas men (as a gender) and the Lese (as an ethnic group) are symbolized by whiteness. Red, white, Efe, Lese, female, male are all of a piece, as we shall see in the symbolic constitution of human bodies, the Lese-Efe partnership, and house construction.

Lese relate lack of control, wildness, anger, and violence directly to the color red (*ikomba*), and more specifically to blood (*kutu*). Someone who is angry has hot blood (*kutukemu*); he is "with blood" or his blood is "traveling fast." Anger stimulates the circulation of blood within the internal organs and promotes a loss of control. When Lese describe the internal organs, they say that the heart should ideally be without blood, that blood should remain in the stomach; a heart that is filled with blood will cause death. Blood is also a life-giving substance. The patriline, as a life-giving force, passes to its members the same blood. Long ago, opposing clans fused and became "brothers" after the leaders of the two clans made incisions in their palms and then shook their hands, thus "mixing the blood." When an elderly man was on his deathbed in 1987, members of his clan reported to me that he confessed to murdering seven Lese witches during the 1950s after he administered *sambasa* poison to them at a witchcraft ordeal. He was reported as feeling remorseful and saying, "Their blood made our clan strong, but blocked my path to God."

The colors are also related to fertility. Menstrual blood is said to be the *tisi,* or semen, of the woman. Women are thought to be most fecund during, and just after, menstruation because the blood has begun to flow and can mix with the *tisi,* or semen, of the men. The theory of conception is thus encompassed within the red (*ikomba*)–white (*itufe*) categories. When a child is born, its white aspects, the bones, bone marrow, and brain, are attributed to the contribution of the father's *tisi,* while its red aspects, the organs and blood, are attributed to the contribution of the mother's *tisi.* The bones are said to protect the organs, as a man protects a woman, as a Lese protects his Efe partner by feeding him and raising his children within the structure of the Lese partner's house.

J. W. Fernandez (1982:122–23) notes a nearly identical theory of conception for the Fang of central Africa and similarly describes how Fang women's symbolic role in house building parallels the Fang theory of conception: "The extension and replication of corporeal experience which was involved in the older procedure [of traditional house building] lay in the Fang belief that in the creation of the infant the red drop of female blood containing the homunculus was surrounded by the protective and fostering shell of white male semen. In the adult person the male element was the skeletal structure and tissues and tendons, all white, within which the sources of vitality—the blood and bloody organs—carried on their primary activity." Turner (1967) has also written of the red-white dichotomy, stating that, for the Ndembu, red is directly related to women's blood, the blood of murdering or stabbing, the blood of circumcision, and, in general, to power, anger, and danger. White, on the other hand, relates to semen, life, goodness, fertility, health, and good fortune. In addition, Turner notes that although the colors red and white are not always sex-linked, the incorporation of the two colors in ritual contexts often stands for the opposition of the sexes. The main contrast with the Ndembu is that, for the Lese, red and white together, *as opposed to white on its own,* represent fertility.

Blood flow signifies life, but the excessive flow of blood can lead to death and must be stopped with white bark powder. In the most common Lese origin myth, the story of Hara, the creator (see chapter 4), the deceased are brought back to life when white bark powder is placed on their bleeding sores; in the Hara story, the main character Akireche starts life by first causing a man's tongue to bleed, and then stopping the flow of blood with white bark powder, thus separating him as a human being distinct from the trees and plants of the forest; finally, in the origin myth presented above, the Lese man fears that his wife will bleed to death, and the Efe man stops the woman from menstruating by inseminating her with semen (white *tisi*).

The symbolism extends to house building. When Lese build houses, men travel into the forest, or recruit their Efe to travel there, to find the appropriate small trees and vines for building material. Lese men take the trees and build the walls (*ai-ba*) and doors (*ai-ti*) of the house (*ai*). After the walls are complete, Lese men and women and Efe men begin digging up the reddish iron-rich earth at the edge of the village, arrange barrels or pots with which to collect water, and wait for a rainy day. The water or rain turns the earth into mud, and, on the day of mudding, women and children begin to mud the walls. Mudding is considered to be women's work. Men contribute the sticks—the skeleton—while the women contribute the mud. The mud is wet and red, as opposed to the dry, hard, light-colored trees, and must be supported by the structure of the walls. The notion that one element supports the other resembles the statements of the earliest observers of the Lese and the Efe (Schweinfurth in 1918 and Schebesta in 1938–1948) that their relations were characterized by dependency (Waehle 1985:391). Indeed, the dependency relations of both conception and the construction of the house parallel the relations between the two ethnic groups. The mud and the organs depend on (*ogbi*) the structure, as the Lese say that the Efe depend on (*ogbi*) them for their subsistence.[7] The house is thus a combination of the male and the female, in which the female depends upon and is encompassed by the male, just as the Efe depend upon and are encompassed by the Lese.

The Efe are indeed described as being red in color, and their habitat is described as being dark and wet and dirty. In contrast, the sunny village is bright, dry, and clean. The goods that the Efe are supposed to give to the Lese (meat and honey) are called red; these are, of course, also wet goods—bloody, sticky, moist. Thus meat and honey are red like the Efe who acquire those goods, and wet and dark, like the forest. The village, and the Lese, represent the production and accumulation of white, dry goods—cassava, potatoes, corn—which are cultivated, cultural products. Iron, also given by the Lese to the Efe, is referred to as white. I would even suggest that the red-white dichotomy also includes sexual relations and intermarriage between the Efe and the Lese: Lese men give white *tisi* to the Efe women, who contribute red *tisi* to the production of a child within the village context.

I suspect I would have found other expressions of the color pattern in Lese ritual had there been more rituals performed during my fieldwork. The *ima* ritual, for instance, celebrates a girl's maturity, more specifically the beginning of menstruation. When the first-born daughter of any man reaches menarche, usually at about age sixteen, she is ordinarily secluded in an *ima* hut (*elima,* in Turnbull 1965a, 1965b) for approximately six months to a year. The hut looks very much like an Efe hut except that it is square and flat roofed instead of hemispherical. During the time she is in the hut, she remains in a liminal state; her feet cannot touch the ground and so must be wrapped in leaves if she is to walk inside the hut; she cannot look up toward the roof or sky. The

7. Curiously, the term *ogbi* is rarely used, and I have heard it used only with reference to contexts of dependence, including any situation in which someone cannot carry out a task without the help of someone else, on whom he/she therefore depends. It follows, then, that the symbolic meanings Lese attach to the Efe parallel those attached to the ideas of dependence inherent in conception and house building.

distinction between light and dark is not difficult to discern. She stays in darkness, and when she must urinate or defecate she is carried to an outhouse by her Efe or Lese helpers (girls about eight to fourteen years old) and is covered with palm leaves so that light does not reach her body. She is secluded within the small hut and prevented from doing anything more physically demanding than walking about the hut. While in the hut she is supposed to become fat, and she is encouraged to consume as much palm oil and meat as possible. The palm oil is a bright red color, and this oil, and oil in general, is linked to life force; both Lese and Efe believe that an animal is not fully dead until its oil has been removed and the blood has completely drained from the body. The helpers (*ima kanja*) of a girl who has reached menarche and is in ritual seclusion anoint her body with palm oil, just as women anoint their newborns daily with palm oil for several months after birth. During the seclusion, the helpers do not rub their own bodies with palm oil, but instead paint their faces and bodies with white clay. On the day of the girl's departure from the hut, a day that ideally should coincide with her marriage, women and Efe perform an extensive series of dances. I have never witnessed these dances at Malembi (I have witnessed them at Baitepi, among the Mamvu and the Efe), but I am told that, like the Mamvu *ima* rituals, all the participants rub palm oil over their bodies so that the audience glistens with red color. The new woman is said to have "ripened" (*itabo*), a term that also means "to become red" (as when a person blushes, his skin becomes sunburned, or a papaya or pineapple turns reddish in color). In addition, although the Lese-Dese have no indigenous circumcision ritual, I was able to observe a Lese-Karo circumcision ritual; the Lese surgeon spread white clay on the boy's body, and asked me if I could provide him with a white-colored antibiotic to put on the bleeding penis. He said that he preferred the white penicillin to the yellow (*ikomba,* or red) tetracycline because white substances promote coagulation.

The red-white dichotomy contains within it symbolic oppositions of social relations, sexual relations, house building, and exchange relations, and constitutes a specific pattern of meaning. The Efe, as (1) red, (2) hot-blooded partners contributing (3) red and bloody goods are integrated symbolically into a pattern of Lese beliefs. Moreover, each of the oppositions presented above (Efe-Lese, fertile-infertile, dark-light, red-white, meat-cultivated foods, wet-dry, wet goods-dry goods, dirty-clean, natural-cultural) are functions of the ideas about the differences between the inside and outside of the village, and between men and women. The oppositions also bring us back to the symbolic material out of which ethnic relations are constructed. We can imagine a series of nesting structures, each encompassing and encompassed by another. Blood is encompassed by semen, organs by the skeleton, the body by the house, female and Efe by Lese and male.

EUROPEAN IMAGES

The consistent use of metaphors of gender to differentiate between the two ethnic groups is striking in its similarity to the use of metaphors of gender in European constructions of Africans and Africa. In an eloquent description of the place of Africa and Africans in the European scientific and religious discourse of the eighteenth and nineteenth centuries, Comaroff and Comaroff note that the "thrust into the African interior likened the continent to a female body" (1991:98). Gender was as salient a category as race, a lens through which domination at home could be projected onto domination abroad; as the Comaroffs put it, "In late eighteenth century images of Africa, the feminization of the black 'other' was a potent trope of devaluation. The non-European was to be made as peripheral to the global axes of reason and production as women had become at home" (Comaroff and Comaroff 1991:105). Africa was imagined as female in a number of ways: as a body to be penetrated by Europe, as mysterious and erotic, deprived of power, natural rather than cultural, and irrational and labile rather than rational and stable. These characterizations grew out of fundamental changes in gender ideology in Europe; whereas in the eighteenth century, maleness and femaleness were often thought of as fluid and imprecise categories, nineteenth-century scientific discourse held that a single sex could be discovered (Comaroff and Comaroff 1991:106). The scientist's challenge was to discover the true nature of women, which, it was imagined, was embedded in the body in general, and the uterus in particular. The uterus became the center and cause of emotional and neurological disorders (Sulloway 1979:23–69), such as hysteria (from the Greek word for womb or uterus, *hystera*). Men, in contrast, were driven not by their organs or sexual nature but by reason, sensibility, and rationality. As we saw above, Lese distinctions between male and female are grounded upon distinctions in mental capacity, and between culture and nature.

I would not argue that the Lese appropriated the European metaphor; there are no data to support such an argument. But Europeans and the Lese may have formed similar characterizations because they use the same cultural material for their symbolic representations of the denigrated other. "Female," a meaningful category of domination in both local European and Lese contexts, becomes the basis for domination in other areas as well. The category served both colonists and the Lese as a way to define and maintain both difference and social boundaries (see Cooper and Stoler 1989:610).

Certainly there is some similarity between the Lese dehumanization of the Efe and the European dehumanization of all Africans and of foragers such as the Efe in particular. In an early example, the physician Edward Tyson presented the body of a chimpanzee as the body of a "Pygmy." Chimpanzees were not named until 1816, so Tyson believed that his chimp specimen was an ancient dwarf, not quite monkey and not quite human. Tyson's title placed the Pygmies squarely within the animal kingdom: *The Anatomy of a Pygmy Compared with that of a Monkey, an Ape, and a Man, with an Essay concerning the Pygmies of the Antients. Wherein it will appear that they are all either Apes or Monkies, and not Men, as formerly pretended, to which is added the Anatomy and Description of a Rattlesnake: also of the Musk-hog. With a Discourse upon the Jointed and Round-Worm* (Tyson 1751 [1699]). But if Africans were not human, then the missionaries had their work cut out for them; they were in the business of saving souls, and only human beings had souls. However, nineteenth-century scientists appreciated the idea of a chain of being, within which a variety of different kinds of human beings were organized hierarchically (Comaroff and Comaroff 1991:98). Biologists were mapping the mind of God, and every new discovery of different, and supposedly inferior, human beings led to further knowledge of the greatness of Western civilization, and the intricacies of God's creations (DeVore 1989). Thus, even when it was concluded that Africans, including Pygmies, were human, writers continued to describe these peoples using nonhuman images. Sir Harry H. Johnston, for example, reported to the Smithsonian Institution (1903) that the "Pygmies of the Great Congo Basin" were "ape-like negroes" (p. 481) with "baboon-like adroitness" (p. 482) reminiscent of the "gnomes and fairies of German and Celtic tradition" (p. 482).

The metaphor of the Efe as children also echoes the way that Europeans denigrated Africans. Alongside the popular European image of the noble savage ran the arrogant and patronizing image of Africans as children—children who were pure and unadulterated by an existence outside the Western world, and childlike in their naïveté. The Comaroffs note of the Tswana (1991:117),

> By the time our missionaries encountered the Tswana and began to write their own texts, the infantilization of Africans was firmly established. Adult black males were the "boys" whom the civilizing mission hoped one day to usher into "moral manhood." And "boys" they would remain well into the age of apartheid, whether or not they actually became Christian. Even at their most subtle and well meaning, the various discourses on the nature of the savage pressed his immaturity upon European consciousness, adding to his race and symbolic gender yet a third trope of devaluation. This was no less true of the abolitionist movement, the most self-consciously compassionate voice of the age.

If adults were seen as children, one wonders what African children were likened to. In his report on the "dwarfs" of the Congo, Johnston described "a survival in the adult of that hair which appears in the fetus in all human races, a soft brownish down" (1903:488). Martin Johnson (1931), in his popular account of the Pygmies of the Ituri, *Congorilla: Adventures with Pygmies and Gorillas in Africa,* continued the image:

> The pygmies lead happy lives of carefree slavery in their Utopian forest homeland. They are mere children mentally as well as physically, always ready to sing, dance and make merry. They spend their days like youngsters at an endless picnic and there is nothing mean or malicious about them. They are truly unspoiled children of nature. (1931:62).[8]

Even today, the image of Africans as children runs through much of the literature on the Pygmies, such as K. Duffy's recent book, *Children of the Rainforest* (1984), and Turnbull's romantic depiction of the Mbuti as carefree, happy, and playful (1961).

METAPHORS OF DENIGRATION IN THE LESE HOUSE

The Lese view of the Efe as children extends beyond the level of everyday discourse to the symbolic representation of Lese houses, into which the Efe are symbolically incorporated as children. This view is directly connected with Lese conceptions of the house as a reproductive domain.

Lese clans present a contradiction. One's membership in a clan depends on one's descent as reckoned patrilineally, and though every

8. To these images one might add that of Ota Benga, the African Pygmy man, from Kasai, Congo Free State, brought to the United States in 1904 by Dr. Samuel P. Verner. Ota Benga was displayed at the 1904 St. Louis World's Fair, and later, in the Monkey House at the Bronx Zoo (Bradford and Blume 1992).

woman is a member of a clan, clans are idealized as groups of men. But social relationships reckoned through the mother are just as important to every Lese man or woman. Like clans, houses are constituted by both males and females, despite the fact that it is men who found and give identity to the house. Clans and houses are, in fact, conceived in a way that mediates the contradiction between their character and composition. They are both personified as mothers, and are said to be *ochi-ani,* to contain birth potential, or more literally, a uterus or womb (*ochi*). Clans and houses are reproductive organs. Marriage creates the uterus for the house and therefore also for the clan. Conflicts within the house, from dispute to divorce, disturb the uterus and produce infertility. To increase the fertility of the uterus, the Lese bury the placentas of the live births of Lese men's wives and sometimes Efe partner's wives inside the house into which the child was born. Stillbirths, the placentas of stillbirths, and the remains of miscarriages are all buried outside the house. The house is also said to contain a specifically Efe uterus, meaning that the house can produce Efe children and eventually Efe partners for one's family.

In addition to making children from adults, houses also make adults out of children. As one informant phrased the ideal, "most people in a village are either parents or children." People are "children" until they marry and have their own house, at which time they should become parents. The few Lese men who are thirty to forty years old but still unmarried and childless are in fact considered to be children. Although Lese men refer to their Efe partners and others of his generation as *imamungu,* literally, "my mother's child," or "sister/brother," Efe partners are considered to be the "children" of a particular house and, as in the Lese kitchen, are frequently denigrated by forms of teasing reserved for children. Many Efe partners at some time during their childhood lived in their father's Lese partner's houses, and are then said to be the children of the village, and to have been "raised" (*ire*) by the Lese. Even Lese children tease Efe men. One three-year-old boy was chasing a chicken around the periphery of the kitchen when he looked up and said to a member of his father's Efe's camp, "I won't let you take care of my chicken because it would get sick and die." It was a childlishly innocent remark, perhaps, but an insult nonetheless. Children also denigrate Efe children as objects for manipulation and control. In children's play, Lese girls treat Efe girls as if they were dolls, braiding their hair and adorning them with beads, earrings, and other forms of ornamentation.

Are the Europeans who came to the Ituri forest ultimately to blame for the Lese treatment of the Efe as children? The Lese were likely introduced to some of the European images of denigration, and, I would suggest, the Lese were often the ones denigrated. But where the Lese were treated like children, they in turn treated the Efe like children. By using images provided by Europeans, the Lese may have been able to construct a more positive image of themselves. Frequently during my stay in Zaire, my Lese informants justified their denigration of the Efe by referring to their experiences with colonial administrators, and it seemed to me more than just an attempt to speak to me in a language they thought I might find meaningful; in several contexts in which I was a distant observer, I heard that the Lese had "colonized" (*colonisé*) the Efe, that the Efe were "savage" (*sauvage*) and needed to be tamed. One informant said, "We [Lese] gained our independence from the Belgians in 1960, but the Efe have not gained their independence from us." To some extent, these Lese are merely saying that the Efe cannot live without the Lese because they are culturally and materially deficient. Informants cited the fact that the Efe do not speak French and speak Swahili poorly; in situations that demand communication with state authorities, such as the settlement of disputes, the paying of taxes, and participation in state-organized work groups, Lese men represent their Efe before the authorities. The Lese also say that although the Efe work for them in their gardens, they know little or nothing about horticultural techniques and cannot even feed themselves; the Efe can become independent, according to these informants, but only after they learn to govern themselves.

The Efe's inability to govern themselves is shown, my informants say, in the absence of Efe houses. While the Lese stay put in village houses, the Efe do not have houses and may move their residence many times a year. Houses, my Lese informants said, could bring the Efe into civilization, but the Efe refuse to build them. Permanent settlements, they insisted, could also "civilize" the Efe, but again the Efe refuse. The Lese themselves were, of course, very mobile until they were relocated by the Belgians, who hoped the Lese would remain in their villages at least seven years, and did their best to restrict mobility by allotting strictly delimited areas of land to each clan within a chiefdom. Today, the Lese say that the Efe need to be settled, and one of the best ways to do that is to make sure they are integrated into Lese life. If the Efe ever separate from the Lese, my informants said, the Efe would be in a situation of chaos or disorder (*ovio*). The integration into the Lese social world gives the Efe a "place" (*fazi*).

The question of independence raises two other issues: the relation between the Efe and humanity, and the relation between the Lese as the saved, and the Efe as the heathen. It is commonplace in Africa for intergroup comparisons to involve mythical representations of one group as nonhuman, or else descended from the nonhuman. Lese origin stories tell of how the Lese came from a mountainous region ravaged by wars and famine, to find the Efe already living in the forest; other stories tell of the Efe's relation to nature. The story in which the Lese free the Efe from a life in trees is a story of liberation from savage ways. The missionaries under the colonial administration, like the Lese today, argued that membership in a civilized community like a mission was dependent not only on conversion to Christianity but also on the formation of permanent houses and gardens. Savages are accepted as mobile, but the civilized are always permanent. In the Lese language, a church is "God's House" (*mungu-ba ai*): heaven is called the "giant house" (*ai-tudu*), echoing another Lese notion that in ancient times all Lese lived in one house and the men gathered under one pasa. The Efe are thus the heathen (*paien*) who have not been admitted to the house of God and therefore have little hope of attaining salvation and humanity.

CHAPTER IV

The House and the Economy

"The most that one can say about the economic aspect of the relationship is that it appears to be one of mutual convenience."

Colin Turnbull, Wayward Servants,
on the Mbuti-Bila partnerships

Part One: The House

In a creative study of the local Colombian economy, Stephen Gudeman (1990) suggests the house as an alternative to the model of the corporation. He argues that Colombian peasants use a model of the house to organize their social and economic lives, and he defines the house primarily in opposition to the model of the corporation, which he believes coexists in dialectical tension with the house. Gudeman holds that the house economy is an institution of such long standing that it preceded historically the development of the market and its corporate organization (1990:9). He also contends that the notion of a house economy has widespread applicability and relevance and thus asks whether, in rethinking the corporation as a model for local forms of organization, we might modify the use of that model in African studies as well.

The corporate model upon which lineage theory is based is a specifically Western model that has been imposed on others at the expense of their folk models. The house, in contrast, seems to represent the way that many people conceive of and model their own economies. In fact, one of the ancestors of descent theory, Evans-Pritchard (1940), reveals that the Nuer do not conceive of their social world in terms of a lineage model. For example, in 1933, Evans-Pritchard posed the question: "What exactly is meant by lineage and clan? One thing is fairly certain, namely, that the Nuer do not think in group abstractions called clans. In fact, as far as I am aware, he has no word meaning clan and you cannot ask a man an equivalent of 'What is your clan' " (1933, part 1:28). In *The Nuer,* Evans-Pritchard offered a definition of lineage that has little to do with corporate or descent groups: "A lineage is *thok mac,* the hearth, or *thok dwiel,* the entrance to the hut" (1940:195). For Evans-Pritchard, then, lineage was the model for the hearth and home. But might the hearth and home, rather than the descent group and lineage, be the Nuer models for political opposition? Might the lineage be an imposition of a European corporate model? Or might there be, as I argue for the Lese, two or more coexisting models—say, a descent model for one set of social processes, a house model for another set? Gudeman notes,

> One can only wonder how the history of descent theory might have appeared had theorists of the 1940's, instead of exporting their own market experience, used a model of the home and the hearth, as Evans-Pritchard's own foundational work suggested (1940:192, 195, 204, 222, 247; 1951:6, 7, 21, 127, 141), or the local imagery of kin groupings. We might never have established such trust in the existence of the corporate descent group or even, for that matter, the lineage. (1990:184)

Gudeman's emphasis on the house helps us to find models that reflect local conceptions of social organization rather than those tendentiously formulated by anthropologists. But if a house model is to advance our ethnographic understanding, we have first to distinguish our use of the term "house" from other uses.

The importance of the house as a primary unit of social organization, or even as a model for the larger social order, has never been questioned in anthropology. Not only have ethnographers clearly pointed out that the architecture of the house is related directly to both cosmology and social organization (see Morgan 1881; Bourdieu 1971; Fernandez 1976; Feeley-Harnik 1980; J. Comaroff 1984; Blier 1987; J. Comaroff and J. L. Comaroff 1991), but also there is a strong interest in reconceptualizing the organization of some societies, especially Indonesian and Indo-European societies, as being of the "House" type (Lévi-Strauss 1979; Errington 1987; Pak 1986; Schloss 1988), or what Lévi-Strauss calls "Société à Maisons." In addition, there is a rich and extensive literature on households and their economic functions (see, for example, Guyer 1981; Wilk 1989, Heald 1991).

Lévi-Strauss notes the existence of societies throughout the world whose units of social organization are not easily defined by terms such as "family," "lineage," or "clan," as they have been used conventionally in anthropology. Unfortunately, the anthropology of Boas and

Kroeber, he says, "did not offer the concept of the house in addition to that of tribe, village, clan and lineage" (1979:174). Lévi-Strauss sees in the house an institutional form for the mediation of conflicting social structural principles, such as patrilineal and matrilineal descent, filiation and residence, hypergamy and hypogamy. This view has been followed by S. Errington (1987) in her study of how the house resolves contradictions between brothers and sisters in Indonesia, and by J. A. Boon (1990) in his study of Balinese twins.

It is clear that the "house," as developed in this literature, is suited to the characteristic kinship contradictions in island Southeast Asia, many of which are managed or reunited at the level of the house. But the concept of the house, in whatever context it is elaborated as a unit of social analysis, can help repair some of the problems associated with the preoccupation with descent rules, and it can illuminate new aspects of social organization and its symbolic representation. In Indonesia, for example, whereas a focus on descent would emphasize the differences between societies with distinct kinship patterns, a focus on the house reveals important continuities between unilineal and nonunilineal and exogamous and endogamous societies—according to Boon (1990), these may be transformations of one another. For the Lese, the conception of the house, as we shall see, leads us to consider social relationships and ideas obscured by descent; namely, the role of gender and inequality in constituting ethnic differentiation within the economy.

Despite the centrality of the household in the economic anthropology of Africa, a house *model* has not been systematized, and where it has appeared as a central metaphor it is usually employed as a component of descent organization (see Schloss 1988; Jones 1963; Mitchell 1956; Lloyd 1957). M. R. Schloss (1988) views the houses of the Ehing of West Africa as constituting distinct descent groups, and G. I. Jones (1963) and J. C. Mitchell (1956) analyze houses as constituted by unilineal extended families. In these cases, the house is not a local model for the society and the economy but rather an institution, a component of social structural systems, such as lineages and descent groups, whose relevance is to be found "on the ground" rather than in the realm of cultural modeling. The Lese house is relevant to both contexts. For the Lese and the Efe, the Lese house is where production, consumption, and distribution take place. Indeed, the house is the physical locus of economic interaction between the Lese and the Efe. But the house is also the locus of the symbolic organization of relations of inequality, including relations of ethnicity and gender. The house, then, is not only a component of larger sets of social relations but a *model* that has to do with the conceptual organization of relations of difference as well as the organization of social practices. My treatment of the house and descent falls more in line with a few exceptional works in African anthropology: Enid Schildkrout's analysis of the domestic context of multiethnic communities in urban Ghana (1975, 1978), Jan Vansina's and Curtis Keim's political histories of the equatorial rain forest in central Africa (Vansina1982, 1990a, 1990b; Schildkrout and Keim 1990), and M. Saul's recent study of the Bobo house in Burkina Faso (1991). Schildkrout finds that, in Ghana, social and cultural integration of ethnically diverse persons takes place in a domestic context, and Vansina and Keim both find that a house model of social organization among central African forest peoples made possible two contrasting ideological principles: the lineal and egalitarian groupings on the one hand, household and hierarchical groupings on the other. I will discuss these authors in more detail below. For Saul, the house, like descent, is a metaphor, a way of "expressing the idea of regroupment in space" (1991:78); for the Bobo, social behavior and political and economic rights are shaped by the house metaphor, but also by a number of other organizational principles, including descent and other patrilineal associations. For the Lese, too, the house is not the only conceptual system for social organization and classification, but the Lese restrict the organization of certain relationships (gender and ethnic) to the house, and others (those between Lese agnates and Lese men) to the clan, phratry, or lineage. These restrictions contrast with the social organization of the Bobo, for whom, as Saul notes, ritual and land associations, among others, can be based on any of a variety of organizational principles—as he calls it, "a kind of political game" (1991:97).

The house, as I shall use it, is also distinct from "family" or "household" in the sense in which these terms are generally understood—that is, the two terms are frequently distinguished, with the former referring to genealogically defined relationships, the latter referring to coresidence or propinquity (Yanagisako 1979). In the Lese-Efe case, however, houses are not defined by coresidence so much as by membership, with membership founded on common participation in the production and distribution of cultivated foods. Indeed, Efe men seldom reside or even sleep in their Lese partner's houses, but they are still considered house members. Because the partnership, and therefore house membership, is defined through individual Lese and Efe men, the children of Efe partners are not considered members of the house. Yet, at the same time,

Efe children often live in their father's Lese partner's house. Thus, neither lineage, propinquity, nor the family defines the Lese house.

One further point: it is frequently assumed that households have well-defined functions and have easily definable boundaries, yet the functions, activities, and organizations of households vary widely. In spite of all this cultural variation, "household" is still generally taken to be a uniform concept across cultures. S. J. Yanagisako, for example (1979:165), says: "Generally, [household] refers to a set of individuals who share not only a living space but also some set of activities. These activities, moreover, are usually related to food production and consumption or to sexual reproduction and childrearing, all of which are glossed under the somewhat impenetrable label of 'domestic' activities." And she points out that, because "all the activities implicitly or explicitly associated with the term 'household' are sometimes engaged in by sets of people who do not live together" (p.165), several anthropologists have suggested using alternative terms—such as "domestic group" (Bulmer 1960)—to refer to persons who acknowledge a common domestic authority: "co-residential groups" (Bender 1967) to designate propinquity, more specifically, and "budget unit" (Seddon 1976) to distinguish economic functions from coresidence.

I use an alternative term, "house," for a number of reasons. First, and most importantly, this is the best translation of the term *ai*, which the Lese use to describe the actual structure within which people live and within which economic activities are organized. Second, given the assumptions of coresidence inherent in the conventional use of the term "household," "house" is a less confusing term. Third, I do not wish to dichotomize a coresidential or domestic unit from a politico-jural domain. The house integrates entire ethnic groups and so has to be seen as part and parcel of the political and economic structures of society. Yanagisako (1979) and H. Moore (1988) note that anthropologists have only recently begun to explore relations of inequality within households as constitutive of domestic organization. Since the Lese house contains within it members of different ethnic groups, ages, and genders, it goes even further to draw our sights toward relations of social and political inequality at the level of the ethnic group.

Finally, although the term "house" as I use it in this study refers to an actual structure, it also refers to a model that has to do with the conceptual organization of ethnic and gender relations, as well as the organization of social practices. As I suggested in the Introduction, it is a source of core symbols as well as an arena for interactions structured by them. As for Gudeman, the model is a "detailed working out or application" of a series of metaphors. A wide range of societies may model their society and economy after the house, but the house still remains a local model that we should not expect to find duplicated exactly in other contexts. The anthropologist should understand the "cultural sense" of each house model, for each will vary in meaning and function across cultures. Rural Colombians and the Lese both model their world on the house, but they use very different metaphors and images.

As we saw in chapter 3, the Lese house is the chief component of Lese life and thought. Built upon metaphors of the body and gender, the house becomes the center of relations of inequality between men and women, children and adults, Lese and Efe. As we also saw in the previous chapter, the relations between men and women are modeled upon the actual structure of the house (in which sticks support mud as men support women), and Lese-Efe relations are, in turn, modeled upon gender relations (in which the Efe, as a group, are feminized). In other words, the symbolic material out of which the Lese form an image of the Efe, and thereby a contrasting image of themselves, has its origin in perhaps their most basic social space: the home and the hearth. What could be a better source for cultural representations of inequality than that most fundamental form of domination and subordination, male-female relations?

One of the central arguments of this book is that Lese-Efe ethnicity and the forms of inequality associated with it are discernible in the Lese house. In addition to integrating the Lese and the Efe into a common function—the production, consumption, and circulation of foods—the Lese house is a means of grouping together and culturally structuring relations of ethnicity and inequality. This chapter explores two sides of the house: its symbolic representation, partly as revealed in Lese myths, and its role in the Lese-Efe economy. We will begin to see how Lese ideas about the house ramify to the production and circulation of foods and to the organization of the Lese and the Efe. In the myths, we find embodied a number of basic ideas about the house that are not explicitly brought out either in everyday discourse or in social and economic life.

THE HOUSE IN MYTHOLOGY

Both the Lese and the Efe cosmologies include stories about an Efe ancestor, named Befe, who became an evil spirit, who still exists and continually plays tricks and carries out violent acts in Efe camps and

Lese villages. Befe is described as having the physical appearance of an Efe man, although he has a gargantuan penis several feet long. One Lese story about Befe explicitly represents the penetration of the Efe into Lese villages. The story tells of a Lese girl named Uetato who tries to find a place to sleep among her siblings, but because the house is so crowded, she has to lie down on a small area of ground inside the house. During the night, Uetato's brothers and sisters have diarrhea, in fact, so much diarrhea that it eventually chokes and kills Uetato. After she is buried, Befe comes into the village and uses his large penis to exhume her body. He first rapes Uetato's corpse and then goes on to rape each of the village houses by penetrating the doors.

Befe is especially dangerous because he comes from the forest and because he is sexually powerful. In everyday life, Lese men fear both that Lese women will be sexually attracted to the Efe and that Efe men will attempt to engage Lese women in sex. Befe is a projection of that fear, and Befe's physique and character are shaped by the Lese notion that Efe men have strong and uncontrollable desires for sex. It should have struck the reader by now that the "masculinization" of the Efe in this story stands in contradiction to the "feminization" of the Efe described in the previous chapter. As I shall elaborate later, the two characterizations are not contradictory, for just as Europeans managed their fear of Africans by infantilizing them, so do the Lese manage their fear of Efe male sexuality by feminizing them. Befe represents the Lese image of Efe sexuality in its most raw and unrevised form.

Perhaps the most important element of the story is the rape of Lese houses, for these are not only penetrable by the Efe, they are already penetrated, since the Efe are members of Lese houses. Another story, presented earlier in chapter 3, highlights the suggestion that Befe represents the incorporation of the Efe into Lese houses, and, indeed, that the Efe are essential to the formation of the Lese house. Recall that an Efe man teaches a Lese man that his wife bleeds every month not because she has a wound where there used to be genitals but because she is menstruating. The Efe man teaches the Lese about sexual differences, and, through a reversal of normative roles, produces the first Lese man: a child fathered by an Efe and mothered by a Lese. This story illustrates the bringing together of both nature and culture, sexual and cultural knowledge, as well as the establishment of the house, for all houses ideally contain a married couple with children and are defined as basic reproductive and economic units. The story also informs our analysis of the house through two reversals: in the first, the Efe man and Lese woman engage in sexual intercourse, a reversal from everyday affairs in Lese-Efe life in which sexual intercourse between Lese women and Efe men is considered by the Lese to be a most heinous crime; the second reversal revolves around the pasa. The Lese woman lies in the pasa, yet the pasa is a meeting place for men only and is not an appropriate place for someone who is ill. Women should very rarely be in the pasa, and when they are ill they should be inside the house. Of course, there is no indication that these people lived in a house, and indeed my informants stated that the characters had not yet been given a house by God.

In the third Lese story, one that is widespread among the Lese of Malembi, relations between Lese women and Efe men are represented in a more subtle and complex fashion. The story begins with the myth of the first man, who had few human features. His body was vaguely like that of a man, but he had crops growing out of his hair folicles, and out of each of his orifices. His eyes, testicles, and heart were fruit. He could not eat, speak, defecate, or engage in sexual intercourse. As one informant put it, the first man "was a tree." But soon woman was sent by the Creator, Hara, to give man speech and human bodily functions. Once man had learned to eat and eliminate food, and had shed his treelike appearance, Hara built the man and woman a house and told them to have sexual intercourse. It is in the house that man became a complete biological and social adult. In the most complete version I heard, the myth was elaborated as follows:

> Hara was his name. He was also called Bapili [*Ba* = already, *ipili* = turned upside down]; we black people also call him *mungu* [Swahili for God]. His son was Mutengulendu (literally, man all by himself a long time ago), also called Ngochalipilipi. Hara "put" [created] Mutengulendu, and then chased him away. Mutengulendu stayed in the forest and wandered around the forest. The girl Akireche discovered him in the forest. Hara also "put" Akireche. Hara put only girls. Her work was to dam water to get *titi* fish. Akireche went to the water, and she remembered something. Hara had told her, "Look for someone who is in the forest."
>
> She said, "Today we are going to dam water farther down the stream than we usually go." When Mutengulendu heard voices he went down to the water. The day when the women went to the water, the other women said, "Today we will go really far downstream." The woman who went ahead went to find the man, and she said to her sisters, "There is a man here!" Akireche said, "This is my man, not yours." They began their return home, and Akireche said to her father, "I found a husband today." "Where?" "At this place in the forest." "Did he say anything?" "No. He had a lot of hair. There were yams and bananas and roots coming out of his

> head. He is not like a person" [*muto*]. This river was the Apukarumoi. The man was drinking this water. He wandered in the forest without a house. The father said, "Where did you see him?" "At this place in the forest." Hara was happy.

The name of God, it should be noted here, also means "turned upside down." Might we also expect other reversals to occur in the story? This first Lese man appears to be represented as his opposite, an Efe man. The first man is not like a muto. He is hirsute, a quality never attributed to Lese men, but which, for Lese, is a hallmark of Efe physical appearance. The story also introduces a forest/village dichotomy and gives the impression that the village area has boundaries, for it is only from a bounded area that the woman can go "farther" in search of the man. In addition, the man is said to wander in the forest, just as the Efe are said to wander in the forest, living in temporary huts and never building houses.

The story thus suggests a sexual association between Lese women and Efe men. Woman finds this man when she travels to the river. In Lese stories, women characters who go to the river go there to engage in sex or in acts specific to women, such as washing one's vagina or navel, or digging for shellfish. In a few stories, women who travel too far downstream actually lose their vagina or navel when it becomes detached from their bodies. In this origin story, woman is explicitly looking for a husband. And if we are to believe that the first man is a symbol for the Efe, the impending sexual relationship between the two people reverses the natural Lese order in which Lese women and Efe men are forbidden to engage in sexual intercourse with one another. The story continues:

> Day broke. Hara gave white *riga* [weeds] to the girl, and said, "When you find him, cut his head hair, and when it falls down, put it in the mud, bury it in the mud. This hair will change into *eji* [liana cord used for constructing houses]. When you travel to the forest, you will use this to build a house." Then tell him to stick out his tongue. When he puts it out cut it down the middle. You will draw blood. Put the weeds on his tongue to stop the blood.

The Efe, of course, provide house-building materials for the Lese; they bring the liana cord and trees from the forest that the Lese use for the skeleton of the house. In this case, the integration of the first man, or shall we say, Efe, into the human world depends upon altering him severely, including cutting off his hair. Given what we know about the feminization of the Efe, it does not seem farfetched to interpret the cutting of the hair as a symbolic act of castration. By cutting the hair, and presumably the crops growing out of his orifices, woman also begins to bring him into the realm of the farmer, making culture out of nature, incorporating nature into culture. The hair of the first man, like the rest of his body, is material to be cultivated (cf. Gudeman 1986:142–157 on the body as an economic metaphor). When it is planted in the mud, it grows, as the seeds of last year's harvest grow when replanted in the soil. The body is a metaphor for the composition of the world, as expressed in everyday life when Lese farmers refer to the first sprouts of their crops as "its hair." Woman is thus the farmer; she takes the forager out of the forest, away from foraging, and into village life.

The cutting of the tongue has to be seen as a sexual drama, in which the woman, having altered the first man, repeats the act of reproduction. Menstrual blood is drawn from the man but its flow is halted by the white substance. The process is identical to that found in the myths and rituals outlined in the preceding chapter, in which white substances, in the form of bark powder, or semen, stop the flow of blood and create life. Furthermore:

> The girl came to find Mutengulendu and she said, "Stick out your tongue." When he stuck out his tongue she sliced it down the center, and began to cut his hair. She cut it all off and put it in the mud. She placed white riga leaves on his wound. When she put the leaves on it, she also put medicine on it, and he stopped bleeding. Right away he started to speak. Akireche returned alone to her father and said, "I cut his hair and his tongue, and he started to speak." The father said, "Go and build a *gburukutu* [Efe house], and then take the man inside." She went and built the house, and they came inside. Night came, and Hara gave them sleep. A lot of sleep. A machine came at night and cleared a huge area for the village, machines sent by Hara. The big village had big houses, without people, side to side, facing each other. But for all the houses there was only one pasa. They slept and slept and slept until midday. The woman woke up and said, "Open the door, night is over." When they left the house, they saw the big village, and they were surprised. The woman went to look, and so did the man. They thought there were people, but there were none. They went and saw good houses, and found a good one in which to sleep. They moved there. Night came, they went inside. They slept, and his penis would not stand up. Night came again and the penis would not stand up. The woman said, "I am going to Hara." Hara asked the girl if he urinated. "No. He vomits everything. He vomits his feces too. And his stomach is huge." Hara said, "It is good that you spoke to me. Go back. Return."

At this point, the first man is about to realize full adulthood in the Lese house. He has been removed from the forest and has made the transition from living without a house, to living in an Efe hut, to living in a Lese house. Those with psychoanalytic concerns will be interested to note that his changes parallel the developmental phases outlined by Freud, from the oral, to the anal, to the phallic. From here:

> Akireche returned, and Hara came to the periphery of the village to break *mabondo* [cut down a palm wine tree]. They all asked, "Who's cutting something?" He told her, "I am going to look." Mutengulendu arrived at the place. "Hey friend! *Banai!* Wait! Let us drink!" When he drank he began to vomit. Hara asked, "Why are you vomiting?" "My stomach does not like a lot of things inside of it." So Mutengulendu said, "I am returning." Hara said, "Come in the morning!" Hara returned as well. In the morning Hara arrived. Ngochalipilipi said, "My friend came." The woman said, "He is not your friend, he is your father." "No!" Ngochalipilipi said, "He is my friend, not my father."

The confusion over how the first man should address his father parallels the confusion over how Lese and Efe men should speak to each other. Most partners call each other either "my Efe" and "my Lese" or *ungbatu,* which means "partner" and is used exclusively to refer to the relationship between Lese and Efe partners. Often, however, kin terms are used because the Lese and the Efe adopt their partner's kinship universes as their own. The kin terms they choose to employ have connotations of both equality and inequality. For example, partners will address and refer to one another with the term *imamungu,* meaning "sibling" or "my mother's child." *Imamungu* indicates friendship and equality. The same is true of *banai,* as used in this story, a form of address that literally means "friend." Inequality also has its terms. Efe men may express their subordination to their partners by calling them *afa,* meaning "my father," and Lese men can refer to their Efe partners as *maia ugu,* meaning "my child." The difficulty of finding terms of address, as expressed in the myth, arises out of the contradiction between the dual idealized relations between the Lese and the Efe: inequality, on the one hand, intimacy and loyalty, on the other. Every Lese and Efe partner has to face the confusion of how to conceive of the other in terms of equality and inequality. Hara, as the one who brings Ngochalipilipi into the village and gives him a house, is no exception. Next, we see that Hara successfully completes the transformation of the first man, and, at long last, Lese society begins:

> He came and found Hara and he saw that Hara had placed a board across a large gorge at the river. He became afraid. Hara said, "Climb up." "No. I will fall." Ngochalipilipi climbed up, and when he got to the center, Hara

> said, "Now stop, and lie down." "I can't!" He lay down. "Turn your buttocks so it faces downstream." Hara came, cut an anus in Nogochalipilipi's buttocks, and feces came shooting out. Everything came out. Hara took the *riga* and placed them on the anus, and the sore healed. Hara told him to descend. One thing was left. He gave him palm wine, and he drank, and he gave more, and he drank more. He wanted to urinate. Hara said "take this *riga* and place them on your penis." He urinated right away. They returned to the homestead. In the morning she went to Hara and he asked her, "How did you sleep?" "His body has not moved mine, and his penis will not stand up." Hara told her to sleep naked. That night she slept naked. It was futile. Hara told the woman to tell her man to come to him. In the morning he went to Hara, and received medicine to place on his penis in case he wanted to urinate. When he returned, and he wanted to urinate, he placed the medicine on his penis, and urinated. The father said, "Give this medicine to your woman when you arrive at the homestead." When the woman took it she put it under her [in her vagina] for a moment, took it off, and put it in Mutengulendu's hand. Right away a fetus appeared there, and she had it many months, and gave birth to a boy.

Other stories concerning the origin of Lese people or clans do not include the Efe as central characters, but the plots are nonetheless linked to Lese-Efe relations. With only a few exceptions, these stories relate incidents of social fragmentation in which the Lese of a single clan split into smaller clans, which then split into smaller villages that may contain as few as one or two houses. According to my informants, the original clan in history was, like all clans, a single village, and this village constituted the whole of the Lese people. When I asked how many houses were contained in this immense village, my informants gave different answers. Some said that the Lese all lived in one giant house linked to a single pasa, and others said that they all lived in separate houses, but that they shared a single pasa. The disagreement is irrelevant, however, because the pasa is the symbol of the house, and since no house is complete without a pasa, the myths tell us that the Lese consider their ancestors to have been members of one house.

It is to more concrete concerns that I now turn, to examine the role of the house in political organization, and to address the question of how the house informs aspects of Lese everyday life not informed by the lineage or descent. The house and the actual terms of the economy provide the cultural foundation for the Lese-Efe partnerships and for the mythology just presented. Together each of these aspects of Lese society and culture will demonstrate that the Lese and Efe economy is a cultural economy right from the start, culturally modeled and represented. The economy is not founded on a command of resources or of the power of one group to dictate economic knowledge or practice. Yes, there is a group that has more power than the other, but neither group inhibits the economic practices of the other. Before proceeding to the cultural model of the economy, we shall consider the Lese in light of some specific observations made by other anthropologists in central Africa.

ISOLATION AND POLITICAL ORGANIZATION IN ANTHROPOLOGICAL REPORTS

One of the more striking characteristics of Lese village life is the absence of collective activities. Rather than encourage group activities, Lese society makes a distinct effort to isolate groups from one another. The smallest social unit is the house (*ai*). In the Lese language, those social units more inclusive than the house are identified by one word, *gili*. *Gili* is a relative term of reference, and whether it refers to the clan or to the ethnic group is determined by context. *Gili* is an oppositional term with variations in meaning that are due, as Evans-Pritchard put it in the context of the overarching Nuer term *cieng,* not to "inconsistencies of language, but to the relativity of the group-values to which it refers" (1940:136). *Gili,* when appropriated, implies specific degrees of structural distance. Yet, for analytic purposes it is important to note that each of the social units considered gili has a definite empirical status. These units may be classified into the phratry (political alliances of intermarrying clans), the clan and the village (groups of people who may or not be genealogically related, although they believe they are descended from an unknown common ancestor), and the ethnic group (Lese or Efe).[1] According to my informants, the Lese have always wanted their population, phratries, clans, villages, and houses to remain physically distinct from all others. For both the Lese and the Efe, phratries are opposed to other phratries, both politically and spatially. Not all Lese settlements are arranged in the same pattern, but an attempt is usually made to place clans next to other clans of the same phratry, with a greater distance maintained between phratries than between the clans of the same phratry. Before resettlement at the roadside, clans of the same phratry were usually located as much as several kilometers

1. The Greek *phratria,* or clan, was in fact a subdivision of the *phyle,* or tribe, but in anthropological literature phratry has come to represent a collection of clans allied by marriage, and I use it in that sense out of convention.

from one another, and some phratries were located as far as a day's walk from one another.

Lese, the elders say, should live apart from non-Lese, and members of different Lese phratries should meet rarely, and then only for war or marriage. Even members of different clans, though they should meet occasionally to drink palm wine, should live apart. (Some younger men told me that for the sake of the Republic, the Lese should live together with members of other ethnic groups, like the Azande or Mangbetu, but these same men also expressed fear that in a village with Lese of different clans and phratries life would be marked by violence and death.) On the next level, too—that of houses—the ideal is privacy, not communality: the members of different houses should neither cultivate, circulate, nor eat foods with one another. It is all right for meat to be shared between members of the same village, and sometimes between members of different villages, but cultivated foods should not be shared with other houses. The distribution of cultivated foods creates inequalities between givers and receivers, and all the Lese living in a given village should be socially and economically equal to one another. It is common, of course, and permissible, for the Lese to give cultivated foods to the Efe, because the Lese and the Efe are not intended to be equals.

Nearly every ethnographer and explorer to encounter the Lese, Efe, or other farmers and foragers of the Ituri has remarked that the farmer inhabitants tended to interact rarely with other ethnic groups (with the exception of the various Pygmy groups), and that they had no extensive political organization but sought to separate, rather than link, various social units from one another. Jan Vansina, for example, notes that southern central Sudanic culture, and Proto-Mamvu and Proto-Ubangian societies in particular, maintained house-centered political traditions. He points out that although marriage, ritual, and age grades among Proto-Mamvu societies established intervillage linkages, "the original southern central Sudanic culture had been one of herders and farmers living in dispersed settlements, where each household lived by itself without territorial leadership beyond the household. . . . There was therefore very little organization in Proto-Mamvu society beyond the extended household. There were Houses but no villages, no districts, and no big men" (1990a:171).[2]

2. In my own usage, I do not capitalize the word "house." However, when citing or discussing Vansina, who capitalizes the word, I shall respect his usage.

Paul Joset (1949), Helena Geluwe (1957), Edward Winter (n.d.), and Colin Turnbull (1983a), all of whom have conducted research on Ituri forest societies, have each commented on the tendency for villages to fragment into insular households, and on the infrequency of social and economic relations between houses, villages, and groups of villages. In his "Notes Ethnographique sur la Sous-Tribu des Walese-Abfunkotu," Joset describes the way in which villages feuded with one another, and houses feuded with houses, and how the feuds strengthened the internal stability of each of these social units and separated them further.

> The Lese offer to our eyes a model of the tribal family, each community composed only, in effect, of one family, in the extended sense. Scattered throughout the immensity of the forest, living by themselves, without significant relations with others, engaged in chronic wars, these communities gave to their members an independent spirit which, having been conserved nearly intact, inhibited the unification of political organization. (1949:5, my translation)

Of the Bila farmers with whom the Mbuti Pygmies live, Colin Turnbull (1983a: 62) wrote:

> A few villages offered a warm and friendly welcome to visitors, though even there, and even in the smallest of villages, there would always be some who voiced suspicions that the visitor was in truth some malevolent force seeking to destroy the village. And against all those who passed through, on foot or by car or truck, most houses had medicine hanging from the eaves to ward off the evil carried by "others," even kin from a nearby village.
>
> The larger villages, consisting perhaps of thirty or so houses, showed the same manifestation of suspicion and concern with supernatural forces within themselves. Families, lineages, and clans clustered together in clearly recognizable units, each with its own meeting place, or *baraza* [the Swahili term for pasa], each with its own protective medicine. And as often as not, a single house could be found isolated on the outskirts of the village, or, sometimes, boldly established in its own special space right in the middle of the village. In the latter case it was most likely a blacksmith, always associated with the power to manipulate supernatural forces. Those isolated on the edges of a village were generally considered witches or sorcerers, though in the first instance they may actually have chosen to build their house there because they had no close kin or friends in that village. Even that in itself would be suspect, as would any preference for privacy.
>
> Just as each tribe considered neighboring tribes to be masters of the craft of evil, accusing them of all manner of barbarity, including cannibalism, so each village suspected the next, and each household its neighbor.

As much as I am inclined to distinguish myself from these kinds of generalizations, one point became clear to me as my fieldwork proceeded: that many Lese, young and old, want to be disconnected, inaccessible, and remote, and that they want these separations to demarcate a variety of different levels of society. One way the Lese conceptualize their social organization is in terms of membership—in the house, the clan, and the phratry. As will become clear later on in this chapter, with the exception of the house, the members of each of these social units wish to have as little to do with one another as possible. Phratries oppose one another, as do villages and houses. Ideas about malevolence (a subject I shall take up in chapter 5), conspicuous in Turnbull's and Winter's work, are one expression of this opposition.

THE AMBA

The absence of indigenous political organization raises the question of whether a descent or corporate model is applicable to the ethnographic description of the farmers of the Ituri. Fortunately, we have an account, Winter's *Bwamba: A Structural-Functional Analysis of a Patrilineal Society,* which seeks to fit the Amba of the eastern Ituri in a structural-functional and corporate model. Because of numerous similarities between the two groups, Winter's work on the Amba is especially useful for analysis of isolation and the role of the house in Lese society. Amba witchcraft beliefs, marriage patterns, family structure, domestic economy, and even much of their language, in many ways resemble those of the Lese of Malembi. Winter and I studied very similar societies but we saw very different things. My criticism of Winter is that his structural-functional blinders led him to emphasize clans and egalitarianism among the Amba and to de-emphasize, even ignore, the relations between the Amba and the Pygmies with whom they lived.

"Amba" is, in fact, a large category that includes a group of people who call themselves the Lese-Mvuba. The Amba live in a section of the Ituri that, at the time of Winter's research, was the eastern border of the Belgian Congo, and today extends into western Uganda. Winter (n.d.:137) uses the term *Amba* to encompass a variety of linguistic groups: the Buli Buli; the Bwezi, who speak Bantu languages, and the Lese-Mvuba, who speak a Sudanic language. Importantly, the Amba maintain relations with Pygmy groups who speak the language of the Buli Buli. Though Winter pays little attention to the Pygmies, his oversight, which perhaps was due to his theoretical concerns, will inform our larger argument that a corporate model does not apply to the Amba and does not take into account interethnic relations.

Winter fits his data neatly within a structural-functional model of corporate descent groups and minimal and maximal lineages, and describes the Amba as having corporate groups. He defines the corporate group according to A. R. Radcliffe-Brown's criteria: (1) adult male members come together for collective action, (2) there are group representatives such as chiefs, and (3) groups such as a clan or lineage possess or control property collectively. Winter concludes that the lineage system based on patrilineal principles of descent organizes all of Amba life.

It is undoubtedly true that the Amba organize much of their life around descent. However, given the criteria appropriated from Radcliffe-Brown, there is little evidence to suggest that the Amba have corporate groups. While the Amba reckon descent, as do people everywhere, there are few forms of collective action among descent groups. Winter discusses the "blood feud" as a form of collective action, but he presents few data to support the contention that blood feuds exist, or existed at a historical period before his fieldwork. The only evidence he cites of a blood feud is a story (apparently told to him) about a woman who murders her husband and is then beaten by the husband's brothers (n.d.:110). Regarding the subject of authority, Winter states that, "at most, a person may excercise authority over a group composed of himself, his own children, his brothers and their children," that there is no authority above the level of the village (n.d.:102). Elders exert influence, but they do not form a separate body within the community.

Usufructuary rights to land are limited to those who live in villages situated adjacent to the land, but these rights last only as long as the village (about seven years). Winter notes that land is so plentiful there is a "lack of interest in land" on the part of the Amba (n.d.:107). Rights to land are inherited solely from father to son, as is any other wealth. If there are no children, the land may be claimed by anyone, regardless of connection with the deceased's minimal or maximal lineages. Witchcraft beliefs pit houses, rather than clans or lineages, against one another so that there is considerable fission and very little fusion of clan members. In fact, farming is carried out at the level of the house:

> The village does not function as a unit of production. As will be seen . . . agricultural production is carried out almost entirely within the immediate family. Even the polygynous family breaks down into its component parts for this purpose. There are no village working parties. In fact, each man and his wife carry out their agricultural activities by themselves (n.d.:85).

Winter goes on to note that consumption of cultivated foods and meat is also limited to the house. And beyond the level of the village, which ideally consists of single clans, and which is identified by a single clan name, Winter finds no overarching sets of political alliances: the area occupied by the Amba is simply "a series of villages," the "villages are completely independent of one another," and "the village is the largest corporate group to be found in the traditional system" (n.d.:85).

For the Lese, as for the Amba, I would suggest that collective action is rare; nor is there much evidence to suggest the existence of corporate groups. Each village represents a single clan and contains from as few as two to as many as sixty residents. The Lese have no indigenous authority position beyond ritual elder of the village, and inheritance of property does not usually occur. When a man dies, his house is usually destroyed along with his property, and land is not inheritable. It is true, however, that clans, rather than lineages, are vital to Lese social life. Social identity and organization are reckoned according to clan membership, as are preferred and prohibited marriage alliances, and clans unite against other clans in cases of dispute, illness, and warfare. The Lese do not have groups we can easily define as lineages, nor do the Lese use lineal descent to organize social or ritual practices.[3] There is little evidence to suggest that either the Lese or the Amba make sense of their world by applying a corporate model, in Radcliffe-Brown's sense, and there is much evidence to suggest that a more central organizing model is the house.

Yet no author, including Turnbull, has related this political organization, or lack of it, to the partnerships between farmers and Pygmies. Winter notes that the Amba and the Pygmies "have always lived in the closest association with each other" (n.d.:8); the Pygmies are made fictive kin of the Amba, and there is a forager-farmer relationship in which the Pygmies give meat to the Amba in return for cultivated foods and iron. But Winter takes his analysis no further—perhaps, in part, owing to his (and Turnbull's) concern with illustrating egalitarianism and solidarity. At the level of the clan, everyone is idealized to be alike, even interchangeable; the clan is conceived of as a group of adult males, and so there is a great sense of likeness among its members. Clans unite in opposition to other clans and can mobilize for collective action in the case of dispute or illness. Inequality is shunned at the level of the clan;

3. W. D. Hammond-Tooke (1985) makes a similar point about the Cape Nguni in South Africa: "In fact, the important descent groups among the Cape Nguni would appear to be clans, rather than lineages. It is the common possession of the same clan name which gives certainty of common origin and place in the social structure. It is by virtue of clan membership that exogamic rules are defined and the (clan) ancestors invoked on the occasion of a ritual feast, despite the fact that the clan is widely dispersed and its members never come together as a clan. Thus the 'transformation' in descent

at one funeral, a Lese man proclaimed, "We are all Andisopi clan, we are all Zairians, we are all black people, we are all dying." At the same funeral a group of women shouted out, "On this day we are all the Andisopi clan, there are no foreigners here, we are all of one clan; on this day, we all have penises, we are one clan, one large clan." The clan, then, mutes relationships of difference, whether ethnic or gender.

MANGBETU-MEJE HOUSES OF NORTHEASTERN ZAIRE

There is an important distinction that must be made between the Lese clans/villages and houses and those of other societies in the Ituri. In Jan Vansina's historical construction, the villages in the Mangbetu and Budu region, near the Lese, consisted of a single house (Vansina 1990a: 172; 1990b: 78). He states that "Village communities were thought of as a single family whose father was the village headman, and the big men of each House were his brothers. The village was thus perceived as a House on a higher level" (1990a: 81). The Lese house, in contrast, is not a figuration of village or clan relations (the village being synonymous with the clan) but the model of a particular set of social processes that are not modeled by the clan.

Vansina's work on kinship organization is especially relevant to this study of interethnic institutions, however, because he suggests that different ethnic groups and clusters within the rain forest share a common tradition and are the product of complex interethnic interactions. Vansina argues that by the eighteenth century there were several different types of social organization related to the different historical traditions of three immigrant groups: the Ubangian ancestors of the Azande and Mayogo, the ancestors of Bantu speakers, and the Eastern Central Sudanic speakers—the ancestors of the Mamvu, Lese, and Mangbetu. The Ubangians did not maintain a strong political organization with chiefs, headmen, or war leaders, and their settlements were temporary and dispersed (Vansina 1990b:76). The Bantu speakers maintained three distinct levels of social organization: the House, the village, and the district. The Bantu House, in this case, was essentially an extended household that could incorporate members of a number of different lineages. Finally, the Mangbetu had a flexible and dispersed social orga-

group theory from clan theory to lineage theory (Kuper 1982) has been a retrograde step for Cape Nguni studies" (p. 90).

nization (Vansina 1990b:77) with little leadership above the extended household. As these loosely organized groups met, they mixed their customs and social organizations, and they developed a common House-centered organization that provided the cohesion and hierarchy that had been absent from any one of these groups. The interethnic mixing about which Vansina writes echoes Evans-Pritchard's earlier historical account of the very complex ethnic composition of Zande society (1971:22–43). Precisely because the house is the locus of interethnic integration, it is a dynamic and historical social institution.

The similarities and differences between Mangbetu-Meje and Lese houses also help us understand the structuring of Lese houses. In contrast to the Lese house, the Mangbetu-Meje house, in the early colonial period, was structured around a core of members of a patrilineage (Schildkrout and Keim 1990:89). Whereas Lese houses resemble nuclear families with the addition of the Efe, Mangbetu-Meje houses could contain from one hundred to two thousand members. Although, like the Lese house, the Mangbetu-Meje house was not constituted by the clan or lineage, it often included as its members many nonlineage and nonclan individuals: in the Mangbetu-Meje case, this included wives, sisters, sisters' children for whom childwealth or bridewealth payments had not been made, slaves, and clients.

Despite these profound differences between the houses, it would seem that there are some fundamental similarities in the principles underlying Mangbetu-Meje and Lese houses: namely, the structuring of the house illustrates two complementary but opposing models. Schildkrout and Keim write: "Overall leadership of the Mangbetu-Meje House was determined according to two sets of principles. One set reflected the ideals of the lineage; the other attitudes towards the individual" (1990:89). In addition, paraphrasing Vansina, the authors describe contrasting ideologies: "The first set posited unequal categories of House membership such as elder-younger, patron-client, master-slave, male-female, and controlling lineage-junior lineage. . . . The second set assumed equality between the members of the dominant lineage and allowed the lineage to choose the most capable leader" (1990:90). For the Lese, in contrast, I have stressed that activities and leadership are not organized according to lineages or corporate groups, although clans are important for structuring marriage alliances, the building and settlement of villages, and warfare. I have also differentiated the Lese houses from those of these other societies by emphasizing that the house and extended kinship organization as villages and clans do not model

Before completing his house (right) a Lese man's Efe wife builds them a make-shift Efe hut. The Lese man has also built a *pasa* (center). *Photograph by R. R. Grinker.*

one another. Yet, the Mangbetu-Meje houses illustrate a pervasive social organizational concern in this region of Africa with managing coexisting principles of equality and inequality. The Lese oppose these two principles not within the house but between the house and the clan.

INEQUALITY AND THE HOUSE

As a Lese proverb puts it, in the clan "leopards give birth to leopards" while in the house "we know each other not by our spots but by our noses." In other words, clan members are identical, but house members know one another by living cheek by jowl, by knowing one another's differences. The village is the level of approved similarity and equality, whereas the house is the level of approved difference and inequality. At the level of the "house," in contrast to that of the "clan," the Lese find inequalities in status and access to resources to be the normal state of affairs. The house is characterized by dependence, and by the relations of inequality engendered in dependency. These relations characterize the links between the Lese and the Efe and are made at the level of the house—the meeting place of birth, marriage, death, social inequality, and ethnicity.

Marriage and Lese-Efe partnerships are two sets of unequal relationships that are integrated at the house. These two unions are, in fact, the basic constituents of the Lese house. In the preceding chapter, I noted that the terminology used to describe and define the marriage of a man and woman, and the formation of a Lese-Efe partnership, are the same. Adult men are expected to maintain both of these unions in their new houses, and to serve as the protectors of the house members. Indeed, an adult man is himself like a house because he encompasses and protects the members. A central metaphor is "the house is a body." One informant said: "[The] house [*ai*] is our shelter. We depend [*ogbi*] on the bones [*iku*] of our house. If you do not have a house, people will think you are not a man, that you have no family [*famili*]. My house is like the pangolin [whose scaly skin is called its *ai,* or house]." Houses, in short, are vital to the integration of difference. Within the house, the Lese and the Efe, men and women, are simultaneously differentiated and unified. To quote Dumont in a different ethnographic context (1970:191): "In the hierarchical scheme a group's acknowledged differentness whereby it is contrasted with other groups becomes the very principle whereby it is integrated into society." Difference is itself constitutive of integration.

The emphasis on equality *between* houses, and inequality *within* houses, is illustrated by the restriction on the movement of cultivated foods between Lese houses and the distribution of cultivated foods to wives and Efe. Giving cultivated foods symbolizes the dependence and subordination of the receiver to the giver. Many Lese say that to give cassava or peanuts or potatoes to another Lese is tantamount to calling the receiver an Efe. Only the Efe, it is said, should *ogbi*—that is, lean on, rest upon, depend on—another Lese, as the Lese say the Efe depend upon them for cultivated foods. Since every Lese man and woman expects that he or she will be the equal of the other men and women in their village, it is not socially acceptable, in terms of equality, for the members of one house to be deficient and to request or need goods that they should have already. For this reason, the Lese rarely trade or share cultivated foods with the Lese of other houses. In fact, some of my informants defined the house explicitly as the unit within which production, consumption, and the sharing of cultivated foods occur. No one but a house member should produce or eat the foods that come from that house. Likewise, only house members can eat within the house. One informant said, "My house is where I eat, and no one else eats there. Even if I ask someone to eat there he won't, because he will think I am trying to poison him, or raise myself over him [brag, *iba-ni*]. The house is where a baby drinks his mother's milk and grows."

CONCEPTIONS OF THE LESE-EFE ECONOMY

If the house mediates Lese relations of inequality, then we must seek its symbolic representation not only at the level of ideas and concepts but also in specific domains of social life, including the economy. Despite the range of Lese-Efe relations, the Lese and the Efe describe those relations as of the most impersonal and contractual nature. For example, both groups define their separate group identities as a matter of a strict division of labor between farming and hunting—an economic arrangement that is mutually beneficial: the farmers give cultivated foods and iron in return for the forager's meat and honey. The division of labor, along with the trade of goods that the Lese and the Efe say results from that division, is a central ethnic marker distinguishing the two groups, even though the farmers frequently hunt and gather, and most foragers know how to cultivate gardens (but rarely do so). The Lese accept the kinds of interactions discussed above, from child rearing to ritual to warfare, as more or less an associated, if not very important, part of the economy; the interactions are residual to the distribution of material goods, mere by-products of a meat-for-produce transaction. Members of both groups give the same definition: that they give things and get things; they act collectively, and the acts are embedded in economic relations. Together the Lese and the Efe give the impression that their relationship is founded on the giving and receiving of such items between groups.

For both groups, meat is by far the most highly valued good circulated. Some of my Lese informants say that the only reason that they live with the Efe at all is to obtain meat—and they even say that they are afraid to alienate the Efe because this might threaten the supply of meat. But the truth is that the Lese obtain most of their meat by themselves or from other Lese. Moreover, although the Efe provide much of the labor needed to cultivate the Lese gardens, my informants rarely mention the procurement of Efe labor as a defining characteristic of the partnership. Despite the Lese's silence on this aspect of the relationship, labor, as we shall see, is a vital part of the Lese-Efe relationship. The distribution of Efe meat to Lese partners symbolizes the participation of the Efe in the production and distribution of Lese cultivated foods. Labor aside, the Lese do not cite any of the other aspects of Lese-Efe interactions as central components of their partnerships. Efe also help raise Lese children, are the main participants in Lese rituals, and, among numerous other things, serve as guards and protectors, but the Lese whom I interviewed treated these aspects as secondary to the giving of meat for cultivated foods. It appears that the intimate relations that constitute *everyday* practice between Lese and Efe are dissociated from the *ideology* of practice. This seems to me an anomaly quite at variance with what is commonly said about the "gift economy" (Bourdieu 1977:172), that the "good faith" economy is costly because societies spend so much time and effort developing concepts of kinship, marriage, reciprocity, and so on, to disguise self-interested and economic acts. The Lese and the Efe do just the opposite. They frame interpersonal interactions with one another in an idiom of economy. "Forager" and "farmer" thus become encompassing ethnic categories.

However, despite the fact that the two groups generally speak of their relationships in a way that sounds very much like trade and material exchange, the actual words they use to describe the circulation of goods say something very different: the vocabulary used tells us that the Lese and the Efe are not involved in a trade at all, but rather in a "division" of shared goods to those who hold rights in them. The vocabulary used and the ideology articulated are indeed contradictory.

THE "DISTRIBUTION" OR "DIVISION" OF FOODS

The Lese use three general concepts to describe the transfer of material goods between people: division (*oki*), purchase (*oka*), and exchange (*iregi*). The verb *oki,* meaning, "to share," "to divide," "to give," refers primarily to transfers of goods for which reciprocity is generalized rather than direct or balanced. My informants translated the term *oki* into Swahili as *-gawa* (to divide), rather than as the more common Swahili term for the circulation of goods, *-leta* (to give, in KiNgwana; to bring in, in KiSwahili). This is because those things circulated are transferred between people who already have rights in them. For example, when a man offers his baby a piece of cassava to eat, he considers this a "division" of his foods, since all young children have a claim on the goods their parents produce. *Oki* denotes apportioning, distribution, and the possession of parts of a common good.

From here on, I shall thus translate *oki* as "distribution." Division might suffice, but it can imply an even or equal splitting up of goods which does not exist between the Lese and the Efe. Nor does "generalized reciprocity" capture the fact that access to goods is often unequal. The house merges the efforts of both Lese and Efe participation in the economy, but the individual does not necessarily get back what he/she puts in. Like a government that decides budget allocations, distribution is not always equal. Given that both the Lese and the Efe contribute to the foods of the house, redistribution might also be used, but redistribution implies that there is a single center from which all goods flow. Distribution has the advantage of implying a moral right, since distribution refers to the apportionment of goods held in common, as well as the potential for unequal apportionment.

The Lese and the Efe also consider the transfer of goods between trading partners to represent *oki,* or distribution, rather than purchase or exchange. Thus the Lese use the term *oka,* "to purchase," to express the transfer of goods between nonrelated Lese or between Lese and Efe who are *not* trading partners. When a Lese house gives cassava to a nonpartner, the Lese family views this transfer as a purchase of labor or some other form of reciprocity. Finally, for exchange (the term by which anthropologists have conventionally represented the relationship between the foragers and the farmers of central Africa), the Lese use the word *iregi,* which literally means "to turn around, to make into a circle." The Lese use this term only when speaking of the balanced exchange of identical or comparable items (swapping), such as when someone changes money from larger to smaller denominations or trades one knife for another. In short, the Lese-Efe relationship is founded not on exchange or purchase but rather on the distribution of common and shared goods.

The house is the single domain within which there are shared rights of access and consumption of cultivated foods. It is, in fact, the productive unit of the economy. Each Lese husband and wife cultivates a single garden together, usually with the help of their Efe partners. In polygynous houses, the two (or more) wives ideally plant separate gardens, but during very rainy seasons, when it is difficult to burn felled trees, they may work together in one garden belonging to their husband. When the wives are able to cultivate separate gardens, there is little food sharing between them. They will feed their children almost exclusively with the food produced in their own garden. If they cultivate a common garden, each wife will claim a portion of the garden as her own—*as if* there were separate gardens—and feed herself and her children with the food grown in that portion. But all the while, the Efe are present, in the Lese farmer's mind if not physically at hand, as participants in the garden. Even when Efe do not participate in the clearing and harvesting of the gardens, they maintain rights to the crops grown there. And so it is safe to say that no Lese farmer plants a garden without the expectation that some of his produce will be distributed to the Efe. Lese men and women, and the Efe, depend upon the gardens for their subsistence.

Part Two: Economy

LABOR

It is curious that so few Lese informants cite labor as a central aspect of their relations with the Efe. Despite their statements that labor is incidental, Efe labor is, for many Lese, highly desirable; the more Efe workers, the more likely it is that a garden will be large enough to provide for one's house, and for the Efe family linked to the house through its Efe member. Poorer Lese, with small gardens, may be unable to offer enough to keep active partnerships with their Efe, and so their Efe seek informal, often multiple, economic relationships with other Lese men. And just as wealthier men can afford to support a polygynous household, so too can they support more than one Efe partner and thereby ensure or expand their garden size. Although few men ever have more than one wife or Efe for very long, wealthier men sometimes try to maintain these multiple relationships.

Many of the researchers working in the Ituri have addressed the question of how much the Lese "rely" upon Efe labor for their survival. This question is of special importance because the Lese villages are so sparsely populated, and there are few children to help clear, cut, and weed. Bailey and Peacock have made the most definitive statement about labor in the Ituri. They note that, despite the desirability of Efe labor, the Lese are able to plant productive gardens without Efe labor:

> *There is much circumstantial evidence to strongly suggest that the Walese are far from dependent upon Efe labor for subsistence.* There are two convincing lines of evidence. The first is that there are many people living within the tribal lands of the Walese, in the same habitat using the same techniques to cultivate the same crops, who have virtually no dealings with Efe whatsoever. These people, from various tribes that include the Babudu, the Miaga, and the Banande, subsist independently of the Efe, and, by their own admission and that of the Walese, have a higher standard of subsistence than most Walese. Indeed, the Walese are generally recognized by the people of other tribes as being, among other things, impecunious due in large part to the

> draining relationship they maintain with the Efe. The second line of evidence is that there are numerous Walese within the study who have only infrequent contact with Efe. It is true that these are generally the poorer Walese; they maintain smaller gardens and sell very few, sometimes no, cash crops. They are less likely to want to spare the food to hire Efe or to trade for meat. Nevertheless, they can and do gain an adequate subsistence largely independently of Efe labor. These observations strongly suggest to us that the Walese *do not require* Efe labor. They may call upon Efe in an attempt to augment their living standard above bare subsistence—by enlisting Efe to increase the size of their gardens and to assist in harvesting and preparing cash crops—but they are not dependent for their livelihood upon Efe labor. (1989: emphasis mine).

The authors suggest rather explicitly that the Efe are a drain on Lese food production yet also state that those without Efe are generally poorer.

An obvious problem with the Bailey and Peacock analysis is that the discussion of subsistence is framed in terms of *need* or *survival,* concepts that, in the absence of social definitions of *need* are empty. Without investigations of needs as they are socially defined by the Lese and the Efe, and without detailed quantitative studies of Lese agriculture and labor, any assessment of necessity for survival on the part of the Lese has to be speculative. What we can state with confidence is that without Efe labor the Lese may cultivate smaller gardens. Since needs are everywhere culturally defined, and since people everywhere can find innumerable and innovative ways to make a living, I would suggest that such questions of dependence are not fruitful. A focus on ultimate needs might presume Lese-Efe relations to be an adaptation to preexisting conditions of reliance, rather than an outcome of creative efforts. In addition, whereas people certainly need food, many other activities, such as ritual service and witchcraft protection, are not limited to food production, yet they can be socially defined as labor.

Indeed, it may be fruitful to view Efe labor as vital not to the quantity of food production but to the Lese *model* of society and economy, a model founded upon the house. The actual structure of a Lese house only becomes a "house," in social terms, if it contains Efe and women. What do Efe and women do for the house? They *produce.* We can say that, with the exception of hired laborers, a person is a member of a house if he or she produces for it. Thus, when an Efe man works in the garden of his Lese partner, the actual act of labor signals that the latter is a social adult, that he has a house. I would also suggest that Efe labor is necessary for the symbolic and gendered incorporation of Efe as female. Farming is a female domain, as evidenced not only by the place of farming in the Lese conceptual scheme of the economy but also by the fact that in polygynous marriages each woman maintains her own garden.

With regard to how much the Efe labor actually contributes to the success of the Lese gardens, the question of reliance upon Lese labor is itself misleading. Bailey and Peacock state that the use of Efe labor in the Lese gardens appears to put the Efe in a position to simultaneously enlarge Lese gardens and drain Lese foods. But this is the case only if we assume that those foods belong to the Lese; if I am correct in my arguments, these are house foods, not Lese foods. If one conceives of cultivated foods as Lese property, then the Efe are in a position to help or hurt the Lese; the Lese can be seen to make a choice as to whether or not to use Efe labor, given that they must pay Efe laborers who are not partners and distribute foods to their Efe partners. However, it is entirely plausible to conceive of the situation differently: the Lese can be seen to make a choice as to whether or not to allow Efe to practice agriculture on Lese land. The Efe, as I have shown, are a part of the domain within which cultivated foods are distributed. The Efe have a right to foods grown in the gardens of the house to which they belong. From the perspective of the Efe, and as expressed in the language used to characterize the circulation of cultivated foods between the Lese and their Efe partners as division or distribution, the foods belong to the Efe as well. Despite the fact that the Efe are ethnically defined as hunter-gatherers, it may be appropriate, for some analytical purposes, to consider the Efe to be farmers. Obviously the Efe know how to farm since they carry out all of the agricultural tasks necessary for successful cultivation. The Efe choose not to build their own gardens because they conceive of themselves as hunter-gatherers, and no evidence from any researcher working in the Ituri suggests that the Efe are coerced into a hunting-and-gathering subsistence. Instead of growing food in their own gardens, they use the gardens of the Lese. In this way, the Efe reap several benefits: they maintain their sense of ethnic identity, and because they need not always live near the gardens—as the gardens are protected by the Lese who own the land—they may continue living, hunting, and gathering in the forest. Working in a Lese garden assures Efe men and women that they will be able to acquire some agricultural foods, even in the unfortunate event of a food shortage. The Lese gardens are in essence cooperative house gardens from which the Efe can expect to receive a share of the harvest.

AGRICULTURE AND THE ROLE OF THE EFE

Lese agriculture is described in detail elsewhere (Wilkie 1987), but it is necessary here to mention some aspects of agriculture that relate to the integration of the Lese and the Efe in a joint productive activity at the level of the house. The Lese practice long-term current cultivation of yams, manioc, maize, beans, rice, plantains, and peanuts. According to G. P. Murdock, the Lese fitted within the Sudanic complex, a complex that included "growing ambary, cow peas, earth peas, gourds, okra, roselle, sesame, water melons, and in the south oil palm, in addition to sorghum and millet" (1959:227), but there is little indication that the Lese of Malembi cultivated any of these crops, other than sesame. Following relocation, the Lese began to produce some rice, peanuts, and coffee as cash crops, and most men grow some coffee today in the hope that they can sell it for cash. But the Lese seldom grow more than a few different kinds of crops. Gardens are extremely small and produce barely enough to feed a single house (Bailey and Peacock 1989). Greater attention is thus paid to manioc and plantains, which can be planted and harvested at any time during the year, require little labor, and can be abandoned after a year or two without the feeling that a great investment has been lost.[4] Few Lese cultivate the palm oil trees (*Elaeis guineesis*), despite the fact that they are the major source of oil used for cooking meat and preparing the staple of cassava leaves (*odu-pi*). These trees take up to seven years to mature, and most Lese, by experience and habit, do not expect to remain in one village for more than a few years. The Efe, however, travel to the forest areas to look for wild palm nuts, and these may be processed and distributed in the kitchen of the Lese partners. According to oral history, the Lese before resettlement obtained the majority of their palm oil from Budu traders and also acquired oil from *siya* trees found growing wild. The Lese have little contact with the Budu today, and so they are continually searching for oil, either at the new Dingbo market or from their economic partners, the Efe. Domesticated animals are rare; the Lese keep no cattle, and only a few have goats (Bailey and Peacock [1989] note that only a handful of 200 houses sampled owned even a single goat); however, most people own at least one chicken.

4. In a 1916 report on plantain cultivation in the northeast Belgian Congo, Commandant Delhaise wrote of banana cultivation among the Rega who live to the north of the Lese: "They [the Rega] are content to stir the earth a little around the spot where the plant is to be planted. Most often, once planting is finished, no further attention is paid

The Efe often take an active role in the production of crops. Together, the Lese men and their Efe partners will clear gardens at a distance of between a few hundred meters and one kilometer from the village. They may clear up to two hectares, leaving one hectare fallow and seeding the other, but the average is about half a hectare of secondary forest each year. The same garden can be used for two years, after which time it is usually abandoned.

Lese plan their gardens in accordance with the rainfall cycle. Clearing is normally done in December and January, at the end of the rainy season, so that unwanted vegetation can dry and be burned in February during the dry season.[5] During this time of the year, the Efe frequently make hunting trips from forest camps, but they can return to the villages periodically to help the Lese cut back the forest since most of these camps are within a day's walk from the Lese villages and rarely more than an eight-hour walk from the villages of the Lese-Dese. During other times of the year, the Efe camps are constructed closer to the road, sometimes within fifty meters, but rarely further than nine hundred meters, of a Lese village (Fisher 1986). Even in December and January, the best hunting season, the Efe rarely use more than about twenty kilometers of a given trail, beginning near a village, or village garden, leading through old garden growth to the camps from which the Efe begin honey collecting and hunting expeditions.

In most cases, Lese and Efe men clear the gardens and Lese women and Efe men and women plant the crops. This is done in March and April, although bananas and cassava are sometimes planted as early as November or December; the harvest begins in late June and continues

to the field. Sometimes one or two weedings are given if weeds develop too much" (Lacomblez 1916:127–128; also quoted in Miracle 1967:46).

5. The Lese classify their gardens into several types. The general term for garden, *opu,* describes an area in which food is currently being cultivated outside the village area; thus, banana and coffee plants cultivated within the village plaza do not constitute an *opu.* One is either in the village (*ubo-ke*), or in the garden (*opu-ke*), and there is no overlapping; in the event that someone lives in their garden they are said to be without a village. A garden area that has been hoed but in which no trees have been felled is called an *ube* (from the verb *ube,* to cut) a term that implies that cutting is required. The *ubenatanga* (from the verb *ube,* to cut, and the verb *itanga,* to uproot or weed) is a burned garden that requires weeding. Four terms describe gardens not currently under cultivation: (1) *Ngoi,* or *opu-ngoi,* is secondary forest that has grown over a previously cultivated garden; (2) *opu-kogbe* is an area that has been hoed but left untended or uncut for one to two years; (3) *gbakba* is a general term that refers to any piece of land that at some point in the past was cultivated by one's fellow clan members; and (4) *chacha* refers in general to any old and abandoned garden that is open to use by anyone looking for a piece of land on which to cultivate food. The word *chacha* signifies that the prior holders of usufructuary rights

through December. The work of Lese men in the garden diminishes after clearing, and after peanut planting, but Lese women and Efe men and women, especially, continue to work in the gardens throughout the summer and autumn weeding, harvesting, planting rice (before the beginning of the heavy rains in August), and searching for potatoes or cassava for each day's meal (Wilkie 1987:116). At this time, an Efe woman's subsistence activities are, in large part, oriented toward the garden of her husband's Lese partner (if she is married) or her father's Lese partner (if she is unmarried), where she weeds and plants, and from which she receives cultivated foods. Efe men, meanwhile, if they are not hunting, spend considerable time caring for children, and preparing and cooking the food that their wives or sisters help to cultivate in the Lese gardens.

Once the foods are harvested, the distribution of foods between the Lese and the Efe begins. Despite the intricacy of Lese and Efe relations, food distribution is not marked by ritual or ceremonial activity. Transactions are usually made in Lese villages, but they may take place anywhere, at almost any time. Following the term *oki,* this is strictly a "division" or distribution of food, but in fact the transfers imply some recognition of reciprocal obligation. The distribution of foods consistently sustains debt and obligation between the parties, and there is a certain understanding of commitments, though vague and indeterminate, to continue distributing foods. These future distributions are not fixed according to time or to the quantity or quality of goods (see Sahlins 1972:194). This generalized and indeterminate reciprocity is made easier by the fact that the Lese and the Efe are transferring different kinds of goods—the Lese giving their garden produce and the Efe their meat and honey. By and large, the items given do not have any fixed or definite equivalence, but there are a few exceptions: honey, for example, should be reciprocated with cloth. There are no fixed amounts of honey or cloth, but the Efe expect that when they give pots of honey to their Lese partners, they will be given cloth. In general, the most important part of any transaction between Lese and Efe partners is an evaluation of the transfer as a social interaction, rather than an evaluation of the quantities of goods transferred. My Lese informants stressed the point that what was crucial to the structure and continuity of their relations was not so much the quantity of goods given as it was the act itself

over that land are not known. These classifications become very important in the allocation of usufructuary rights to land.

of dividing up specific kinds of goods as an expression of loyalty and relationship. The same feeling was not so true of my Efe informants: they appeared to demand frequent and substantial amounts of cultivated foods, and they were quite aware of how much they gave and received.

LAND RIGHTS

At this point it is necessary to make some comments about land rights, especially the rights of the Efe. Efe have rights to the foods grown by the Lese house to which they belong, but access is not without restrictions. The Efe hold that partnership obligations entail reciprocal access to land. According to my Efe informants, while no Efe or Lese owns a particular plot of land itself, an entire Lese or Efe clan may own access to land. There are two main types of land: *gbakba* (previously cultivated land), and *opu* (active gardens). Just as the members of a certain Efe clan will feel free to travel into an area in which their fathers and grandfathers lived, so too will they feel free to travel into the gbakba areas they have previously occupied, or which their Lese partners currently occupy. This right of access, they assert, is consistent with a Lese man's right of access to land that was cultivated previously by his agnates. Gbakba lands are usually overgrown and considered to have become "forest." The Efe will frequently go into their Lese partners' gbakba without asking for permission, in order to uproot old cassava or potatoes planted previously by the holders of the gbakba. But for the Lese, no man has the right to enter another man's gbakba or alter it in any way, without permission of the holders of access to it (the previous cultivator or his nearest agnate). The Lese take issue when food is removed by the Efe from the Lese gbakba because they believe that they must either distribute food themselves, or, at the very least, give permission for the Efe to forage for food there. On a number of occasions, Lese men and women reprimanded the Efe who violated the rules, but they did not publicize the disputes or present them to be adjudicated by the local or *collectivité* chiefs.

The Lese are more strict about how they view rights of access to active gardens (*opu*). If given permission, the Efe can enter the active gardens of their Lese partners. Indeed, the Efe frequently *reside* in the gardens of their Lese partners and are responsible for weeding portions of those gardens. Even so, when the Efe take food from those gardens without actually being given the food by the owners of the garden, the

Lese may consider it to be an act of theft (*iba-ni*). Still, the Lese do not wish to publicize the theft by their partners or seek adjudication, since such legal action, they suggest, would cause the Lese and the Efe to split from one another and would "destroy" (*ima-ni*) the relationship between the two groups. The most serious disputes occur when the Efe take food without permission from the gardens of the Lese with whom they are not associated or from gardens in which they have not worked as laborers. According to my observations, these constitute the most common kind of dispute in Lese-Efe society and are often adjudicated at tribunals.[6]

DISTRIBUTION AS A SYMBOL OF LOYALTY

It is not easy to quantify exactly how much food is transferred between the Lese and the Efe, or, given the division of labor, whether one group actually depends upon the other for its subsistence. According to Bailey and Peacock (1989), the Efe get more than 60 percent of their caloric intake from cultivated foods given to them by the Lese. And the food is usually acquired when Efe actively participate in garden labor. This figure tells us just how important Efe labor is to the partnership, and to the overall economy, despite informants' reluctance to identify labor as a primary definitional characteristic of Lese-Efe relations. I do not have substantial data on how much food the Lese acquire from the Efe, but my impression is that the Lese receive very little of their subsistence from them. When the Lese do receive meat from the Efe, the amount given is always small. When I pointed out to my Lese informants that the Efe seldom give them much meat, they did not answer directly but simply said that the Efe provide them with other material benefits such as honey. Some figures I collected support my observations that the Lese receive little meat or foods from the Efe. In 1987, 29 out of the 39

6. The Lese maintain customary rights to enter into the forest territory of their Efe partners. Lese men hunt and set traps, and women gather foods, only in areas that are inhabited by the Efe group with which they are associated. They travel on trails maintained by their Efe partners, and when they travel on longer trips, they spend nights in Efe huts, or in caves, situated along those trails. The Lese feel free to use the trails within a few hours' walk of their village to gather food and set traps. However, longer trips into deeper areas of the forest require some communication with the Efe. Before each of the long excursions into the forest that I have observed, the Lese informed their Efe that they would be traveling on the Efe trails. My Lese informants say that when they talk to the Efe about future trips into the forest, they do so in order to warn the Efe not to disturb the Lese snares; my Efe informants say that when the Lese talk to them about such trips, the Lese are asking the Efe for *ruusa,* a Swahili (KiNgwana) word meaning "permission."

houses (74 %) in the vicinity of the village in which I lived received some honey from an Efe partner, or from another Efe who may have struck up informal ties to a Lese house. Of the remainder, 4 houses received honey from other Lese, and 6 received none at all. In the month of July of 1987 (during the honey season, when most honey is circulated), only 9 out of 38 houses (24 %) received any meat, and 14 out of 38 houses (37 %) received some other kind of forest food from the Efe: kola nut (5 houses), opi fruit (3 houses), mushrooms (1 house), edible caterpillars (1 house), wild yams (2 houses), and palm oil nuts (1 house). Mark Jenike's superb data on meat acquisition (1988b), collected from a series of observations of Lese men made over a period of fifty-four days (between January 16 and March 2, 1986), show that these men received meat from the Efe in only 25 percent of the observations; in 37 percent of the observations, they received meat from another Lese; in 24 percent of the observations, they received meat from their own hunting efforts; finally, in 14 percent of the observations, they received meat from an unknown source. It is possible that Jenike might have reached a slightly higher figure had he sampled houses rather than men, but his figures, based on extensive fieldwork and observation, are consistent with my quite limited survey.

Neither the transfer of meat nor the transfer of honey explains why the Lese and the Efe interact with one another, or why they define their relationship in terms of the distribution of foods. Like the distribution of meat, the amounts of honey distributed are almost always small. But the transaction itself, in which a Lese couple gives an Efe a metal pot with which to collect the honey, and then gives a cloth to the Efe man upon the return of the pot full of honey, is a strong symbol of loyalty between Efe and Lese; of all items given by the Efe to the Lese, honey is the most consistently given. Yet honey takes second place to meat in the conception of the relationship. The giving of meat and honey for cultivated foods and iron implements is symbolic of the alliance between the two groups, but it is not necessarily the essence of actual Efe-Lese economic transactions.

The Efe also, from time to time, give mushrooms, wild yams and tubers, *opi* fruit, and kola nut. These are all considered by the Lese to be *teti* (luxuries), as honey itself is—foods that complement a more ordinary diet of garden produce. Honey is perhaps the most common of these luxuries, but it is available for at most two months per year and provides little nutrition. Obviously, honey is highly prized—many people say it is their favorite food and that they crave it. It is the only

En route to collect honey, an Efe woman decorates her face with bark powder, her ears with the calyx of a flower, her neck with a vine. *Photograph by R. R. Grinker.*

forest good that Lese men, women, and children do not, and will not, gather by themselves.

The Efe are the sole gatherers of honey, but they have no monopoly on the production of meat. The notion propounded by previous observers, notably Joset (1949), Turnbull (1965b), and Duffy (1984), that the Lese villagers do not enter the deep forest and are poor hunters, does not hold for the Lese of Malembi. The Lese are indeed afraid of the forest, but they often venture into the forest to hunt and trap, especially when they are able to cooperate with the Efe. In July of 1987, for example, when the Efe were living farther away from the Lese villages in order to collect honey, I ascertained that about two-thirds of the men at Malembi maintained animal traps in the forest. Five men trapped the animals in cooperation with their Efe partners, and four men who did not set any traps in 1987 said that they had done so in cooperation with the Efe the previous summer. So far as I know, no data have been published on the volume of the meat transferred from the Efe to the Lese. My observations of the few meat transfers during 1985 and 1986 lead me to believe that, even when the Efe give meat to the Lese, they give very small amounts. For instance, two of the Lese-Efe transactions that resulted in Efe acquisitions of kola nut and yams in July 1987 involved, in the first case, an Efe trading the skeleton of a small duiker (to be used in a soup), and, in the second case, one shoulder of a duiker.

A MORAL OBLIGATION TO DISTRIBUTE WITH THE EFE

The symbolic meaning of the Lese-Efe distribution of goods also carried, for the Lese, a definite sense of obligation. Even though they do not always receive material goods in return for the cultivated foods they divide with the Efe, the Lese on the whole feel morally obliged to maintain the division. In 1987, in two Lese villages at Malembi, villagers gave cultivated foods to their Efe partners or partners' families almost every day for more than a month. According to the Efe who received these goods, the quantities given in each instance were large enough to support an Efe man, woman, and child for one or two days. Whether the sense of obligation is wholly altruistic is questionable: some Lese informants indicated that they find it difficult to refuse giving foods to their Efe partners because they view the relationship as fragile and are afraid to alienate the Efe:

> One day he gives meat, and I give him food to feed his entire family. Later, I will finish all the meat in just one meal. Then when his food is finished, he will come to ask for more food—before he gets another animal—and you must give it to him. You have to give it to him because he is your Efe. He brought you meat, and maybe he will do it again. You are unable to refuse them. And you are afraid to make him angry, because then he will give the meat he does catch to someone else. Maybe he will no longer be your Efe.

Maruokbe, an elderly Lese woman who was quoted earlier in chapter 3, also stated that the Lese must give the Efe something when they come to the house. An important part of her statement is that she must empathize with the Efe partner in order to establish a quantity of cultivated food to be given.

MARUOKBE: When an Efe comes with meat, he comes with his wife. You must give them something; the Efe and his wife receive separate payments. They go directly to the wife with the meat, and show it to the wife. The wife will say, "Your Efe killed this." You give tobacco right away, and he will smoke it there. He will get happy and start to tell you the long story of just how he killed the animal. Later the *muto* [Lese] woman calls her husband to go to the house to discuss it. What kind of animal is it? You will look at it. The husband will ask his wife, "When will they return to the forest?" I will ask them. She asks them. They say they will return on some day, and that they will sleep at your village. Later, you ask your wife to go to the garden with them to give them food. She will show bananas, will cut them herself, and the Efe man waits back at the village. If the camp is near the garden, maybe the Efe man will go there on his way to the camp. If he wants to return he will want his wife to collect the pot and tobacco, and salt.

GRINKER: As you are telling this story, how much meat are you thinking of?

M: One leg of a duiker. Later, the Efe will beg again for an arrow. You give him one or two, or you tell him that there are none. He will say give me more tobacco, and I will have to go buy some from someone else to give to him. You refuse. He leaves. He goes to find his wife, and she asks for more than you have given her. Maybe I will show her a place to dig some food. Maybe I will refuse, but I will probably give it. If I do not give it to her, she will think: "I will come back and steal it."

Maruokbe, like other Lese, actually has in mind a certain customary amount of meat that she would like her house to receive. She thinks about needs, but not about supply and demand.

G: What do you prefer to receive from Efe?

M: Meat surpasses everything else.

G: If someone brings you one leg, how do you calculate what you give in return?

M: I think of the size of the Efe's family. Kebe has so many children, he will get more from me; Edimo has no children. You say to yourself, "Do I like this Efe? Does he give me meat? Is the piece of meat large or small? After you say these things, you give what you want. But he will also say what he wants. I give three heads of bananas [approximately 24 to 36 bananas] for one leg of *iti* [duiker], or maybe I give him one big root of cassava.

G: Do they ever give you a whole animal?

M: If they give you a whole animal, they bring it in a large basket [*kou*], and you fill it up with [cultivated foods] to the point where the meat had filled it up. You fill it with peanuts or *opi* fruit. Efe like peanuts more than *opi* fruit because peanuts are hard to find. *Opi* is not hard to get. It falls by itself.

THE FLOW OF GOODS BETWEEN HOUSES

One result of the isolation of Lese houses and villages from one another is that even in times of hunger the Lese find little assistance in their own or in neighboring villages.[7] This is in striking contrast to the norms of Efe food circulation. Different Efe groups transfer a variety of goods to one another, including cultivated foods obtained from their Lese partners. Between Lese villages the transfer of goods is limited to occasional reciprocity for the services of multivillage work groups at harvesting time, and the communal consumption of palm wine. Between houses, the circulation of cultivated goods is discouraged. A Lese man or woman will rarely share cultivated foods with any Lese who is not a member of his or her house, and any Lese man or woman, including elders, who asks for food or receives it, is thought to be like a child, or like an Efe. The Lese explicitly make the comparison between the dependence of elders and the dependence of children.

There is a Lese proverb: *Akbedu-akbedu muragbua ita,* meaning literally "It is not possible to mix the intestines of two *akbedu* [a species of monkey]"; that is, as my informants explained it, *Do not mix together things that are already divided.* My informants said that the proverb refers primarily to the house, and it is meant to discourage fellow villagers from sharing food with one another. Every village contains one or more houses, and these houses should ideally remain separated in their production, consumption, and distribution of cultivated foods. Each house is responsible for producing and consuming its own food, and the transfer of food from one to another is undesirable.

The evening meal demarcates the house boundaries. Although most people eat something at midday after returning from the garden, it is common for people to eat only one meal a day, an evening meal consisting of cassava and/or potatoes, and pounded and cooked cassava leaves (*odu-pi*). Every house eats separately, and within each house men eat apart from women and children. Women and children may eat before the men eat, but often they wait until the men are finished and then eat whatever is left. When boys begin puberty, they begin to eat

7. In cases of extreme hunger, parents may send their children to villages far from their own (up to 120 kilometers away). They may stay there for up to six months at a time (where they are fed entirely by the host family). Single men may travel 19 to 100 km to work at plantations where they receive free housing from the owners and are paid in palm oil, salted and dried fish, or money. In addition, they may obtain some agricultural foods from relatives living near the plantations. In most of these cases, the Lese obtain cultivated foods only far away from their own villages, and not from adjacent villages.

with their fathers in the pasa. The main exception to the confinement of food to houses that I observed was when a mother gave some of her house's produce to her married sons, and when, on one occasion, in an incompletely constructed village, married men shared cooking and eating areas with their fathers for lack of sheltered space. In this second case, however, the father ate food cultivated in his own garden, the son ate food cultivated in his, and their respective produce was kept in separate containers that their wives presented at mealtime specifically to their husbands; while eating, each man took one or two potatoes or cassava from the other's bowl. On several occasions, I observed a man to eat, with his father and with his son, pounded cassava leaves prepared by his and his father's wives.

THE FLOW OF GOODS BETWEEN VILLAGES

The Lese with whom I lived also maintained a normative standard against the circulation of foods between villages and between phratries. This has historical roots. I noted earlier that the Lese villages have always been highly independent residential and productive units. Before relocation, they were situated as far as fifteen kilometers from one another, and the area they occupied was in almost complete isolation from other ethnic groups, with the exception of the Efe. Clans clustered together into phratries, and the Efe clans, with whom the Lese traded, clustered along with them. After relocation, when villages were situated much closer together, the Lese continued to maintain the old values of insularity and self-sufficiency, and sought to continue their relations with the Efe rather than with other Lese, or non-Lese. For example, Lese men and women seldom admit knowledge of the Efe trading partnerships of other Lese houses or villages. The partnerships are said to be the personal affairs of each house, and although everyone knows everyone else's Efe networks, they feign ignorance for the sake of the idealized economic independence of houses.

Only on certain specific occasions is it permissible for the Lese to obtain some cultivated foods from other houses or villages. One occasion is the harvesting of peanuts, when members of the same phratry help one another, in what amounts to work parties; the current owner of the garden reciprocates directly for the help he or she was given by giving the helpers small bags of peanuts. Food may also be shared in the event that someone passes by another's village for talk or gossip and finds the members of that village in the process of eating. In such cases, the villagers will ordinarily offer food to the guest. However, I have never witnessed a villager prepare food especially for a guest; not only would this be an insult to the guest, it would be dangerous. People fear that meals prepared for them may contain poison or witchcraft substance. Some communal meals are eaten at occasional rituals or dances, at religious meetings held by missionaries in distant towns, and at peace-making ceremonies. I shall present one such eating ceremony in some detail in the next chapter, a ceremony in which two men who had not seen or spoken to one another for more than two decades tried to end their hostilities by eating a communal meal. Commensalism is a gesture of friendship and trust, for a man would never eat the food of another man if he felt that the other had murderous intentions. This has significant effects within the village. Since people fear most those who live in their own villages, they do not wish to eat their fellow villagers' cultivated foods.

The primary form of communal consumption between houses of the same village, and between villages of the same phratry, takes place under the palm tree when drinking wine. Some trees will give enough wine to last several weeks, and the owner of the tree has the social obligation of sharing it first with fellow clan or village members, and after that with fellow phratry members or, rarely, with members of an adjacent phratry. Wine drinking is strictly a male activity, and it commonly starts early in the morning, sometimes before the sun rises. Men gather together, and while they drink, they talk about the quality of the wine and tell stories of other palm wine trees, and they tease the women who beg to be given a drink. There are strong strictures against drinking palm wine alone, and people only infrequently do so (various myths express the moral that palm wine must be shared within the village). Even the group drinking is done in moderation, since most wine is sold for cash. Ordinarily the owner of the palm wine tree and the *fundi* (a Swahili term meaning an "expert" or "wise" person, who in this case is the person, not necessarily the owner, responsible for draining the wine and putting it into cups) decide to give certain men or villages a single day out of the week when they may drink the wine as their guests. These men are usually elders of neighboring clans within the same phratry as the owner of the palm wine tree. Women of the same village can also come to drink, although they are given the wine only if the men have finished theirs, or if they have paid for it. The Efe are excluded from the early morning palm wine parties, and are rarely given palm wine to drink at any time (the Lese frequently accuse the Efe of stealing the Lese palm wine). Besides palm wine, there are other forms of alcohol made with a still, including *kaikbo,* a liquor made from cassava, corn, or rice, and *njerekuma,* liquor made from plantains. These can be bought with Zairian currency, and consumption is, of course, limited to those who can afford to pay.

CIRCULATION OF NONEDIBLE GOODS

The strict standards governing the circulation of foods between houses, villages, and phratries do not apply to the circulation of nonedible goods such as money, tools, shoes, and bicycles. Items of this sort are frequently circulated between members of different villages, as well as between houses. It is significant that, whereas requests for money from the members of one's phratry are easily denied because money can be hidden, and the amount owned is very often kept secret, requests for more easily seen nonedible goods and for the loan of something from someone who, himself, has borrowed it, are often difficult to refuse. At Andingbana village, for instance, a man lent a hammer to another man; within a few days, in a sequence of intervillage loans, the hammer had traveled fifty kilometers and changed hands five times. In such cases, owners often have a difficult time retrieving their borrowed goods, and, in the event of a public dispute, are requested by the local chiefs to accuse the last one known to be in possession of the item, rather than the first borrower who set the item on its course. Placing blame on the person who does not return the item rather than on the individual to whom the item was originally lent helps preserve peaceful relations among villagers, since the original borrower is often a fellow village member, and the final one a stranger or distant acquaintance.

One reason that requests to use, to give, or to sell *noncultivated* or *nonedible* goods are difficult to deny is that things like radios, bicycles, and shoes are public knowledge, and moreover, it is unacceptable for one person or house to have a greater number of goods than other houses in the same village. One Lese man who worked at a plantation earned enough money to buy a bicycle but instead of bringing it home to his village he stored it at another village some distance down the road. He told me that if he brought the bicycle home his "brothers would ruin it"—by which he meant that he would be obliged to share the bicycle with his fellow clan members, and that the bicycle would wear out quickly from overuse. One sharing legend tells of a widowed man who asked a fellow villager for the "use of his wife's vagina," and, when the villager refused him, he and his family split apart from the village, and renamed it "Andikufengope" (that is, "the people who refuse to give vaginas"); the village retains that name today.

Lese legends of village breakups, like that of Andikufengope, abound; most of them have to do with the refusal of one or more members to share noncultivated goods (usually meat) with a member of another village, but the refusal to share within a village has perils, mostly because of the jealousy with which villagers view perceived differences in productivity. In part, the jealousy is related to beliefs in supernatural malevolence: villagers express their jealousy through their fear of being accused of bewitching the more wealthy. It is not at all uncommon for poor villagers to be taken to tribunals on charges that they used witchcraft or sorcery to cause the misfortune or death of others. Lese men and women also complain of a lack of affection and loyalty among village members, and sometimes they threaten to leave their settlements, saying if relations between coresidents were truly loving, they would all be equal.

It is not considered to be improper for one village or phratry to exceed another, nor are the different villages that constitute the phratry expected to remain always at the same level of productivity. They are not partners, but neither are they openly competitive with one another. Fellow phratry members certainly conflict with, are jealous of, and wish ill upon one another, but they do not see one another as inherently harmful or hostile. Although economic successes in other villages are viewed with ambivalence, no Lese plans or hopes to benefit from them.

Relationships within the village are thus full of much of the tension and conflict that might otherwise exist between different villages or between two different populations. F. G. Bailey has noted the extent to which gift giving among equals generates stressful and conflict-laden social relationships:

> A gross difference in power and in status usually has the effect of putting people so far apart, that they cannot compete (although they may, of course, seek to use one another). Hence the paradox and, I suppose, the tragedy: people remain equal because each one believes that every other one is trying to better him, and in his efforts to protect himself, he makes sure that no-one else ever gets beyond the level of approved mediocrity (1971:19–20).

Bailey's statement applies to the Lese, where villagers seek their economic relationships at the level of their own house, and within the Lese-Efe partnership. It is as if the Lese were saying: I should not give to you because you should be inherently equal to me. The circulation of goods has profound social consequences because it is linked to ideas about egalitarianism, hierarchy, and competition. The Lese are competing with one another not so much for actual resources as for equality.

SHARING MEAT

Meat, like cultivated foods, is not something to be transferred between villages, nor is it something to be given by the Lese to the Efe. However, in contrast to cultivated foods, meat *should* be shared between Lese houses. One possible reason why this is so is that acquiring meat is frequently a cooperative effort, unlike the growing of cultivated foods. Lese men do sometimes hunt or trap alone, but often several men from the same clan leave the village together and help one another to hunt or set snares. It is thus profitable to distinguish between sharing and distribution. Both entail a moral obligation to transfer foods, but while the latter term refers to allocation on the basis of rights to a common good, the former connotes the spirit of the gift. Meat symbolizes kinship, brotherhood, and the spirit of giving between equals. Cultivated foods, however, have a potency due to the common participation of unequal house members in garden labor. Meat invokes the clan and common descent, cultivated foods speak of gender and ethnicity.

When a Lese man captures an animal on his own, he keeps the best parts, usually one or two hind legs, and gives the rest to other members of his clan. He may give the entrails to a dog if a dog was involved in the hunt. A single house will almost never acquire a piece of meat without sharing some of it with members of other houses, even with those who did not help in the hunt. One informant, Nestor, idealized the meat sharing between members of the same clan: "No one kills an animal for himself. You killed your brother's animal, and your brother killed yours. Ubotedi killed meat for Ngote, and Ngote killed meat for Ondekomvu, and Ondekomvu killed meat for Ubotedi."

So important is the sharing of meat that failure to do so can indicate a lack of mutual kinship and affection. Clan schisms are commonly attributed to the failure of the clan members to share meat, or if not meat, then other noncultivated goods such as wild fruits or mushrooms. Moreover, the Lese are well acquainted with the legends of what happened in the past to break up villages that were once united. The following legends, the first four collected from different clans within the same phratry in my study, the fifth from a clan of a more distant phratry outside the study area, all have the theme of fragmentation caused by not sharing.

1. We [the Lese-Dese] are all from Sudan. From there we left because of wars of men, who came to burn everyone's beards. We arrived at Mount Menda. We left Menda over a fruit. We had one tree with many branches, and the nduku fruit would fall off and everyone would divide them. Then only one remained. One woman had a house at the bottom of a hill, and she was sitting in the house because she had a new baby. The nduku fruit fell, and rolled into her house. People returned from the gardens and saw that the fruit was gone. Where did it go? they asked. The husband of this woman said, "It fell and went inside my house, and my wife ate it." From there we all split up. (Andingire clan informant)

2. Andikose and Andifuru were one. The old men went to the forest every day and killed many animals. The young men went to the forest every day but came back with *furu* mushrooms only, the kind called furu. The young became angry that their fathers did not give them enough meat, and so they left in sadness. The old men had beards, and so took the [clan] name Andikose (*kose* = beard), and the young men took the [clan] name Andifuru. Now we are separate villages, but once we lived under one pasa. (Andikose clan informant).

3. Andikose [clan] was with Andisopi [phratry] . We split over a genet. We had separate places for our houses, on the sides of the pasa. We set a trap, and one man killed the genet. He told his child, "Go give this piece of the genet to your father's brother [the man's elder brother]." The child took a long route, and passed a fallen tree. He sat on it, and ate all the meat himself. When the child returned, he said that he had given the animal. The older brother prepared banana alcohol and brought it to his younger brother to drink. He saw the genet skin and said, "Why didn't you give me any?" The man told his brother that he had sent meat to him. They asked the child, and he said he had given the meat. They found the Akawakawa tree on which the child had eaten the meat, and they saw the pot and the bones. The brother said, "This is very bad—will we leave each other like this?" One Andikose [man] left to go to the BaBudu people, the other began to live with Andisopi villages. Now we all call ourselves Andisopi. (Andikose informant)

4. Long ago all the Andisopi were together. One day, they set traps. They killed animals. There was a woman, Okato. The Andisopi went to look at the traps, and near the village a tree stump stubbed the toe of one boy. "Oh! My foot hurts! Why did this happen? I am hurt because of a trap, and the women don't even give us the meat they cook!" Okato heard this problem. She said, "Why are they stating our names? We will not cook their food." Okato took some meat, and cooked it in a huge pot. After two days of cooking, the meat was ready. She cooked a lot of bananas, and when everyone was in the pasa, she came to the pasa and put the meat on the ground. They all split up after this to go on their own. The men were saddened by

this, and so Andisopi split up to live in separate villages. (Andisopi informant, Andimoma clan)

5. Andikefe and Anditara [clans] of the Andipaki [phratry] split up at Akbera. There was an Andikefe woman who married a man from Anditara. She [already] had a small child. When she arrived there she found [married] a man with bananas called njeru. "I found these in an old garden." He was putting *njeru* (ripe, sweet bananas) into four clay pots. He put water in the pot, and they ate the njeru after two days. The water was sweet. They ate three pots and one remained. Her brother's wife was in the village [indicating that a sister exchange had taken place, hence the Andikefe woman's brother's wife is a member of the Anditara clan]. She [the Andikefe woman] went to her garden but left her child behind. When she came home she found that the last pot of njeru had been eaten. She asked, "Where are my njeru?" The husband said, "My sister gave them to our child." The woman became angry and asked how they could have eaten the njeru without permission. She said, "If it is this way, you should kill my child." After this, the whole Andipai [phratry] left to go to Menda. (Andipaki informant)

Not only in legend but in everyday life, the failure to share, especially meat and other noncultivated foods, causes unified groups of Lese to split into two or more villages. The difficulties of sharing are highlighted in the fourth legend, in which a woman serves food improperly; instead of serving some meat to each man sitting underneath the pasa, she places the entire pot of meat at their feet. The men refuse to eat the meat, leave the pasa for their respective houses, and then establish separate villages. Reflecting on the story, one informant stated that men will not eat meat that has not been rationed for them: one man might eat more than his share;[8] another informant, referring to the same legend, stated that men will not eat meat such as this because it is "cooked with sadness"—that is, the characters of the story are afraid that the woman put poison into the meat. These legends, symbolic representations of the genesis of intervillage conflict, tell clearly of competitiveness, anger, selfishness, and the suspicion of evil intent; even more striking is the fragility of the relationships between groups that once lived together—fragile because Lese social relationships are intrinsically antagonistic and opposing. These are tales of woe, of clans splitting up and individual Lese houses remaining alone. The greatest dispersion takes place among those who are similar to one another, the greatest integration among those who are different.

8. Generosity is restricted to the extent that a giver of food or meat must specify the quantity to be taken. When offering food to someone it is inappropriate to extend a bowl or plateful of food and leave the decision of what quantity to take to the receiver.

A Lese man (left) who has trapped a duiker gives some meat to a fellow clan member's Efe partner (center). *Photograph by R. R. Grinker.*

GOOD AND BAD EFE

The conflicts inherent in the circulation of goods between persons result in constraints on distribution and sharing. Cultivated foods are given to those who are supposed to occupy a subordinate position in a hierarchy, whereas meat is given to those who are equals or kin members. Obviously, when the Efe give meat to the Lese the transfer does not imply equality between the Lese and the Efe. But neither does it imply inequality. From the Lese point of view the transfer does imply a recognition on the part of the Efe of a common bond between the Lese and the Efe, one that is often framed in kinship terminology. Thus, it is the flow of agricultural goods rather than the flow of meat that helps to construct hierarchical relations. The Lese emphasis on meat sharing within Lese villages explains why the Lese define "good Efe" or "bad Efe" (*Efe irembe,* or *Efe inda,* respectively) in terms of meat sharing. The Efe, the Lese's classificatory kin, are good Efe if they give meat, bad Efe if they do not share meat. In the same way, Lese village members are good or bad depending upon whether they distribute their meat with their fellow Lese villagers. Meat sharing is, very clearly, *an act of friendship, loyalty, and kinship rather than an act of dependence on a source of nutrition.* The Lese want to receive meat not because they are unable to get it themselves, but because they desire expressions of loyalty and affection. The Efe are obliged to give meat to the Lese not because the Lese will not hunt or trap, or because meat functions as a tribute to a higher status group. In giving meat, the Efe are doing only what is expected of any kin or village member. If we were to examine the Lese concern for sharing meat between Lese and Efe in isolation from the social meanings that Lese attribute to sharing meat among themselves, we might overemphasize the significance of meat in defining the Lese-Efe relationship. The sharing of meat is a symbol of brotherhood; the sharing of cultivated foods is a symbol of inequality.

MEAT IS TO CULTIVATED FOODS AS MALE IS TO FEMALE

The difference between meat and cultivated foods parallels the differences between male and female roles in Lese-Efe society. In chapter 3, I described how meat is symbolically classified as female, in the sense that it is red and wet and is integrated into Lese symbolic representations of women and reproduction. The *acquisition* of meat, however, like the acquisition of women, is a male activity. Cultivated foods are symbolically classified as male (in the sense that they are white, hard, and dry), yet the acquisition of cultivated foods is a female activity. Women cultivate the gardens and play no role in hunting or trapping, other than occasionally to travel with their husbands to the forest where they prepare food while their husbands go off to set or check on their traps. Lese men view women as of lower social value than men, and they also view farming as having a lower value than hunting. It follows that meat acquired and distributed by men (often as the result of a cooperative effort among agnates) is channeled into the clan, which is idealized as a solidary organization of men. Women's goods represent *private* interests, the interests of the house; while men's goods represent *public* interests, the interests of the clan or village.

In childhood, boys learn from their fathers and/or father's brothers about hunting and trapping as a collective venture, and they are told the legends that attribute clan disruption to selfishness and the refusal to share meat. When hunting or whittling arrows, agnates are thus brought together in a common activity. Groups of boys frequently go off to the edge of the villages to hunt mice, rats, and other small animals. Hunting expresses an opposition between men and women, and it mediates oppositions between men. Girls, however, are taught to help the mothers in house activities and to keep cultivated foods within the houses.

Although men will work in their gardens, farming becomes the domain of women and Efe. One who "cuts down" the forest (clears a garden) is male, one who works in a garden is female. Lese men thus identify themselves as farmers to the extent that they have harnessed the forest, cut it back, and encroached upon it with their houses and villages. In fact, when a man wishes to clear an area of forest, or a gbakba, he first builds a small pasa, or begins building a house within the garden itself. While women, children, or Efe work on the garden, he will (ideally) refrain from cultivation and remain under the pasa fashioning tools or building an animal trap.

The gendered separation of farming and hunting is expressed as well in the uneasy relationship between hunting-trapping and sexual activity. Every clan has its own special rules, but all without exception have strong restrictions against men engaging in sexual intercourse while they are hunting or trapping. Generally, this means no intercourse from the day before setting the traps until the day the traps are examined (from three days to one week later). The sexual restriction extends to any contact with sexual acts: at Dingbo, a violent dispute erupted when it was discovered that a couple had had sexual intercourse on the sleeping mat of a man from a neighboring village; the man who owned the mat had set his snares but had yet to investigate them, and though he himself had observed the prohibition against intercourse, his sleeping mat and therefore his own trapping skill were spoiled.

Furthermore, although there is some variation in the prohibitions, according to whether one uses metal trapping wire or the indigenous kinga cord that grows wild in the forest, the prohibitions generally equate failure at trapping with things slippery (the vagina). A snare that is slippery will not hold the animal. One informant from the Andingbana clan gave the following description: "People used to set more kinga traps before we had metal. If you had a trap you wouldn't eat catfish, or squash, or anything slippery, because then the animals would slip out of the trap. My father told me also not to put my hand under a bed, or on top of a drying rack, and not to eat with dirty hands while the traps are set." A man from the Andimoma clan said, "One week before setting the trap, you will stop having sex, and three animals must be killed before you can have sex again. If you don't have sex, you can make [innumerable] traps from the same tree, and it will not ruin the tree." A man from the Andibeke clan said, "When you have set traps, you cannot eat elephant skin, or *gbara-ta* [a kind of leaf]. If a woman is sad she will rub banana peel on your kinga. You cannot eat anything slippery. I was also told that, with regard to the Lese practice of setting up spear falls for the killing of large animals, the restrictions were even more severe, including prohibitions on sexual intercourse for several weeks. I do not know whether these prohibitions were actually followed.

The sexual contradiction in Lese men's conceptions of hunting should be fairly obvious by now: Lese men idealize hunting as a masculine activity and yet they feminize the hunters. I have already commented on a distinction between the good itself and its acquisition. Meat, for instance, is a female substance but its acquisition is male. Given the denigration of the Efe as female, the association between meat and women helps explain why the color of Efe bodies is paired with the color of meat. But how can the Efe be denigrated as female when they are identified with such a male activity? The resolution is that hunting simultaneously represents low and high status. Efe men are denigrated because they hunt and do not build houses or clear gardens of their own. Similarly, Lese men who hunt too much are denigrated as Efe. But a Lese man who is able to capture meat is idealized as a successful farmer who, by virture of his success, has the time to hunt, and, moreover, can do so in a more technologically advanced way—with traps rather than with the simple bows and arrows of the Efe. A Lese man who hunts makes a statement to the world that he has a house, that he has women and Efe who are taking care of his garden, that he has command over his social world.

CONCLUSION: THE CIRCULATION OF INTERACTIONS

Lese intragroup relations and Lese-Efe relations have to be analyzed together because each depends on the other for its particular forms and functions. Each set of relations presupposes the other. We have also seen that the house model of the economy is composed of many metaphors that have to do with maleness and femaleness, equality and inequality, and the symbolic incorporation of the Efe into Lese life. The house model encompasses not only the production, consumption, and circulation of foods but also the relationship between the two ethnic groups.

One of the curious aspects of the Lese-Efe relationship is the number of different kinds of interactions that take place between affiliated Lese and Efe, in contrast to the more limited number of interactions between Lese of different villages. This "social exchange," for lack of a better term, is in part a function of the ethnic integration of the Lese and the Efe that takes place in the house. The Lese of different villages within the same phratry have only a few activities they can carry out together. They may drink palm wine together, participate in rituals with one another, and on rare occasions organize work parties for harvests. They may meet at tribunals to discuss local affairs, meet at the market to gossip, and may sometimes sell secret medical potions to one another. These are ideally strictly Lese activities, in which Lese interact with other Lese. The Efe do not participate in these activities. They do not attend tribunals together unless an Efe man or woman is accused of a crime or must serve as a witness. The Efe do not drink palm wine together and seldom attend the market or participate in work parties.

But if the Efe are forbidden from those kinds of activities with the Lese, they and their Lese partners have a wide range of other mutual activities permissible to them as fellow house members but forbidden to Lese of different villages. Some of these activities, such as administering medicines and raising Efe children in a Lese house, are of a very intimate nature, and the Efe are also allowed more freedom in personal exchanges. They can argue with the Lese (usually without fear of violence), and they can work together about the house. Between the Efe and the Lese there is also, as we have seen, a regular division of meat and cultivated foods, quite different from the restrictions on such transfers, either by gift or purchase, between Lese of different villages. It is customary for Efe to go with their Lese partners on hunting, fishing, and trapping trips; they provide music for Lese dances; they protect their Lese from witchcraft; Efe girls prepare and cook food for their father's partners. They also cooperate with the Lese to name one another's babies; and when an Efe dies, the Lese provide burial cloths. It is also noteworthy that, whereas the intervillage transactions that do occur between the Lese usually are of a pecuniary nature, such as brideprices and cash payments for noncultivated goods, and may be carried out once and never again, the material transactions between the Lese and their Efe partners usually involve the distribution of goods and the performance of services and are carried out in the context of an ongoing partnership.

The freedom in the range of interactions between the Lese and the Efe may be related to the fact that inequality between the two groups is institutionalized in the house. To the extent that inequality is a key concept in comprehending the range of interactions within the house, the interactions can be seen as distributions in a Maussian sense. Anthropological orthodoxy accepts that gift giving often establishes social and political links between persons in relations of domination; it is also not uncommon, aside from certain relations of domination, such as those of tax and tribute, for the givers to be superior to the receivers. From this, we would expect that, where there are constraints against forms of inequality, there would be constraints on exchange and gift giving specific to those forms. Indeed, cultivated foods, though not highly valued by the Lese as a cash crop or exchange item, are strongly valued in symbolic terms. The transfer of cultivated foods from one party to another generates relations of inequality between persons, and so there are many restrictions on the movement of these goods between Lese. We would also expect that, from the point of view of both the Lese and the Efe, where hierarchy is already accepted by the parties as a legitimate form of social and political relationship, there will be fewer constraints on the circulation of goods. The circulation of goods will not threaten relations of equality between givers, because the givers are not expected to be equals. By the same token, there may be fewer constraints on the variety of interactions that occur between unequals. The Efe have the freedom to walk in and out of their partner's villages and gardens, to help care for children, and to help in various kinds of village work, because their inferior status is almost never openly questioned. Both dissenting voices among the Lese about Efe inferiority and overt expressions of resistance against hierarchy among the Efe remain as "hidden transcripts," to use J. C. Scott's phrase (1990), and rarely enter into the dialogues about interethnic relations. The Lese-Efe relationship can be seen in the analytical framework of gift giving to constitute a semiautonomous field of social action (Moore 1978) in which the Lese carry out interactions with Efe that, within their own social group, are unacceptable or jeopardize idealized relations of equality.

In the next chapter, we will see just how dangerous competition and inequality can be. We will see that in witchcraft, as well as in economics, the Efe are valued because they transcend the social boundaries that separate and protect the Lese from one another.

CHAPTER V

Witchcraft and the Opposition of Houses

"My heart has died. Where will I find another muto? I am shaking."

An Efe man at the funeral of his Lese partner, December 1986

Enmity between kinsmen and neighbors is a common ethnographic phenomenon, especially in eastern and central Africa (see Evans-Pritchard 1976 [1937]; Middleton and Winter 1963; Douglas 1970); witchcraft accusations and other accusations of supernatural harm-doing occur most often in situations of intimate personal contact. In Malembi, as among the Amba, witches kill only people who live in the same villages with them. Since Lese villages consist of an average of nineteen adults (child witches do not kill), people have reason to fear witchcraft from only a few of the people with whom they come into daily contact. Despite the efforts of each village to isolate itself from all others, all of the members of the nine Lese villages in Malembi, some 140 adults who inhabit a four-kilometer stretch of road, come into frequent contact with one another; they see one another on the road, they meet at the market, they dance together, they may be lovers, and they are usually related affinally. Yet despite such frequent contact, the members of neighboring villages are not harmful to one another in terms of witchcraft.

Earlier, we looked at the organization and meanings of the Lese house and began to examine the house as a model for social and economic practices, such as the Lese-Efe partnership and the growing and circulating of foods. In this chapter we look not only at the house but at the village (clan). We will see that two forms of harm-doing—sorcery (*aru*) and witchcraft (*kunda*)—are related to two different levels of social organization: the village and the house. Sorcery is carried out between villages, and when an act of sorcery occurs, the entire village of the victim comes together to thwart the malevolence. Witchcraft obtains only between houses. The witch is the sibling, the menace next door, the constant threat to any person who lives with his or her relatives. As Winter (n.d.) puts it, the house next door is "the enemy within." The Efe, the outsiders, far from being feared by the Lese for supernatural malevolence, are idealized by them as witch hunters and protectors of the living. Whereas in sorcery the village unites against the sorcerer, in witchcraft Lese and Efe partners unite against the Lese of other houses.

The importance of the distinction between witchcraft (*kunda*) and sorcery (*aru*)—yet another opposition neatly drawn by many Lese—and the reason why I detail the distinction, lies in two areas: the parallel opposition between the house and the clan, and the integration of the Efe into Lese houses. First, by separating houses from one another, witchcraft reinforces the house as a central social unit in Lese society, one that is characterized by relations of inequality among its members. By separating the villages from one another, sorcery unites clan members in relations of equality. Thus, the simultaneous appearance of two theories of malevolence is a powerful and pervasive cultural expression of two coexisting models of social organization. Second, the emergence of witchcraft fears and accusations accompanies the affirmation of the Efe as loyal friends, hunters, and house members. Harm-doing necessitates the closing of clan and house boundaries and a ritualized reacceptance of the Efe into Lese social organization.

I should point out at the start that I have little evidence on how Lese ideas about malevolence have changed over the years. The cases of sorcery and witchcraft that I shall discuss cover only a short time and are perhaps only a handful of the total that may have occurred in that time. Though they highlight a broad range of important issues and reveal some general principles of the organization of supernatural malevolence, they are in no way a complete account of Lese sorcery and witchcraft. A more complete account would situate witchcraft within its historical context, but for lack of data, oral or written, I have been unable to do so. I have considered that the witchcraft beliefs I describe below may be a response to exogenous forces, to economic marginalization and state predation, but given the data available to me, any such argument would be speculative. Nor shall I discuss the various potions, herbs, and other materials that the Lese employ in sorcery or in what might be categorized as "good magic" (preventative medicines, love potions, rites that contribute to health and fertility or that ward off natural catastrophes). That, certainly, is a different subject altogether.

INTERVILLAGE HARM-DOING: MARRIAGE-RELATED SORCERY

Witchcraft, "the enemy within" (Winter 1963), is the latent threat to clan unity. Yet sorcery, the threat to conjugal and intervillage unity, is seen to emanate from outside of the village. Few cases of sorcery involve village coresidents, and the majority of cases of sorcery involve men from distant villages or phratries practicing sorcery against their lovers or against their lovers' husbands. Many of these cases also involve female sorcerers acting against their lovers or their lovers' wives. Marriages are threatened by the fact that wives frequently travel between their affinal and natal villages and engage in adulterous liaisons. Sometimes these liaisons are merely imagined by suspicious spouses, but men and women usually do have lovers in other villages—in fact, men and women expect their spouses to have lovers—and it is generally believed that it is the male sexual partner who becomes the sorcerer. The sorcerer's intention is to disrupt the lover's marriage, thus liberating the lover so that she (or he) can marry the sorcerer. The sorcerer may also wish only to punish a lover who refused him, and so he inflicts illness upon her. Although I was never able to interview sorcerers (few will ever admit to their practices), informants told me that sorcerers hope that the harm they do to the spouses of their lovers will make the adultery public knowledge, shame the spouses, and force them to dissolve the marriage. That is not the usual result, however. The most common outcome of acts and accusations of sorcery is that spouses and their clans seek to protect the afflicted wives or husbands (sometimes by prohibiting them from travel) from the members of other villages. In conflict-ridden village settings, the problem of locating the sorcerer contributes at least for a time to ties of affection between husband and wife, and more generally between wives and their affines. Sorcery is thus a variation on the opposition between the ideal of group unity and the kind of village fragmentation that results from interpersonal conflicts.

Among both the Lese and the Efe, when a husband and wife experience great difficulties in their marriage—disputes over theft, adultery, jealousy between co-wives, neglect, or beating—one of the spouses may become ill and go into convulsions (*itare-ni*). In the handful of cases I have witnessed, and in all those reported to me, an Efe or Lese man or woman administered drops of medicine to the eyes of the victim. The victim was then expected to state the name of his or her lover, and indeed muttered something; the muttered word was interpreted to be the name of the suspected lover, who was then said to have caused the convulsions. I recorded six detailed reports of convulsions that occurred during the years 1980–87 within the nine villages in my study area. Three of these occurred in the Andingbana village, a village I shall discuss in more detail below; four of the six victims were wives, and in all but one case the convulsions had to do with adultery (one Lese man fell victim to sorcery because he had failed to repay a debt). None of these persons had ever had convulsions before, and so far as I know, they have not had them since. None had any history of epilepsy, and they were apparently conscious during the convulsions.[1]

My Lese informants believed that all these convulsions were induced by sorcery. They did not make a conscious connection between the illness and unhappy marriage, though I knew that, except for the man who had not paid a debt, the others were experiencing extreme trauma in their marriages when the convulsions began. In each of the five cases of marriage-related sorcery, including the two I present below, the initial conflict that led to discord was ignored after convulsions began. Instead, people focused on the conflict between the victim and the sorcerer. In other words, the community attempted to manage the real problem of marital conflict by shifting attention to a new problem.

NESTOR AND ANETI

Sometime in 1982, Nestor married Aneti, and a year later he married a second wife, Aruoka. The marriage to Aneti had been arranged many years earlier by Nestor's classificatory father, Ondekokbi, who had made marriage payments to a woman with whom he had lived, and who was Aneti's classificatory mother. Aneti's mother left Ondekokbi, however, as the result of disputes with her co-wife, and Aneti's clan promised to give Ondekokbi another wife as compensation. Instead, Aneti was given to Nestor as compensation, and Nestor thus paid no bridewealth. The nonpayment of bridewealth seemed to Aneti a humili-

1. I did, however, record several other cases of what seemed to my untrained eye to be epileptic seizures. Neither the Lese nor the Efe appear to attribute epilepsy (*ode riku riku*) specifically to sorcery. Various informants offered a wide range of etiologies for epilepsy, including poor nutrition, excessive use of marijuana, and idiosyncratic behaviors inherited and held in common by the members of particular clans.

ation, and her feelings of worthlessness were exacerbated when Nestor took Aruoka as his second wife and paid a large bridewealth for her. The payment was large enough to become the subject of conversation in several villages, though it was no doubt exaggerated through all the gossip. Aneti realized that the second marriage was based on mutual affection, and she took the bridewealth for Aruoka as an insult. When she complained to Nestor, he beat her, whereupon she accused him of neglecting her and threatened to leave him. One month after Aruoka moved into Nestor's house with Aneti, Aneti became feverish and went into convulsions, throwing her body on the ground and shaking uncontrollably. According to Nestor, during her convulsions, Aneti stated the name of a man who lived several miles away in Dingbo. Most members of Nestor's phratry came to visit Aneti, and they privately accused Aruoka of having caused the illness. Publicly, however, people said that the sorcery had been the work of a man from a distant village who long ago had wanted to marry Aneti; she had refused him, and so he harmed her with sorcery. Nestor stayed with Aneti, cared for her during her illness, and did not sleep with his new wife for several days. Aneti was treated with medicines applied to her eyes.

FILIPE AND ABIYE

In 1981, Filipe and his wife, Abiye, began to argue often. Rumors circulated that Abiye had committed adultery with Efe men, a most heinous act in the eyes of the Lese. One day, during an argument, Filipe publicly accused Abiye of the crime. She, in turn, accused him of being worthless as a farmer or as a lover, and at the same time picked up a burning branch and stabbed him in the eye. Filipe's half brothers told me that they took spears and pointed them at Abiye and that all the village members believed that "Filipe's eye had died." At first Abiye ran away into the forest, but later she came back to find Filipe and to sit beside him. Throngs came from their villages to walk past Filipe's pasa and look at his eye. Filipe sat in a chair, while Abiye sat on the ground beside him. According to my informants, the passersby screamed obscenities at Abiye and threatened to destroy her eye in revenge. Some weeks later, Abiye became feverish and began to convulse. Witnesses say she threw her body against the walls of her house in an attempt to collapse it and then tried to run deep into the forest. During her convulsions she stated the name of a Budu man living in Dingbo, a man who she claimed had propositioned her, but whom she had refused. Filipe called in his Efe partner to look for medicines in the forest and applied them to Abiye's eyes. When he applied the medicines, she again stated the accused lover's name. Filipe's classificatory and half brothers went to Dingbo, found the man, and asked him to give some of his own medicines as an antidote. Because the medicine was not of Lese but of Budu origin, they argued, the best antidote ought to be Budu as well. Though he did not admit to the accusation, he did offer some medicines. The brothers administered them to her eyes and healed her.

With the exception of the case in which a man refused to pay a debt to his brother, all the convulsions followed the same pattern: first, a series of arguments between spouses, leading to severe conflict between them; second, the onset of convulsions; third, the statement of the name of the sorcerer during convulsions; fourth, the accusation that the sorcerer's actions were motivated by sexual rivalry; fifth, the sympathetic response of the community to the victim; and sixth, the replacement of the original argument between husband and wife with a new one between sorcerer and spouse.

In the case of Nestor and Aneti, the illness began just at the time when the marriage was in jeopardy. Many Lese and Efe men and women acknowledge that their polygynous marriages seldom last more than a year or two. Aneti's illness brought her and her husband closer together, allied against outside third parties, her co-wife, and her apparent suitor in Dingbo. For Nestor, the main issue to be confronted became the protection of his wife, rather than the argument between them over his second wife. In the case of Filipe and Abiye, Abiye's convulsions began a few days after she was first physically threatened by men armed with bows and arrows and spears. Besides those threats, Abiye was verbally abused by Filipe's half sister, for example, who publicly called her a *dole idlofe* (a person who fornicates indiscriminately) and said that it was well known that she had had sex with Efe men; the sister also warned Abiye that she would soon be murdered, or at least would lose one of her eyes as punishment. Other insults concerning physical deformity were leveled against Abiye's vagina, and she was accused of fornicating with her lovers without being given gifts in return (an insulting charge that implies men view her as worthless). She was told that she was a poor worker and was reminded that she was infertile. As a result of the convulsions, sympathies turned around: Abiye's coresidents became concerned with how to protect their clan member's unfortunate wife, rather than with how to express anger at the damage she had done to her husband. When the convulsions brought out the name of a third party upon whom all blame could be placed, Abiye was on the way to reintegration into the local community. Had it not been for the illness, Abiye would very likely have been imprisoned by local authorities for attacking her husband or forced to leave the village.

INTRAVILLAGE FEARS OF HARM-DOING: WITCHCRAFT

Fear of witchcraft unfolds after the death of a village member. The family of a deceased person, or of a person who is near death, advertises neither the death nor the illness. If the death was expected, the family may conceal the victim's body, hide the death for several hours, and consider precisely how best to release the information about the circumstances of the death. Death is seen as an embarrassment, as well as a real threat, to the village in which it occurs. A village that suffers many deaths is said to be worthless and problem ridden, for if it were a healthy and morally good community, its members would be reproducing instead of diminishing. More importantly, death means there is a witch living inside the village of the deceased. The surviving members of the village will accuse one another of witchcraft, bringing on even more shame. The members of the victim's village and, depending upon the popularity of the deceased, the members of neighboring villages of the same phratry of the deceased, will gather together (men under a pasa, women in a *mafika,* or kitchen) to discuss the misfortune.

For fellow villagers and clan members, death is a real trauma. They will come together to mourn, but most people will try to avoid contact with a deceased or dying person. Even those in the victim's immediate family are cautious about administering medicines, food, or water, and may even withdraw almost entirely from the ill person unless the person is ambulatory or can sit up. I twice witnessed families shunning a dying family member, not even giving them water though they seemed to me to be dehydrated. The fear is not only that severely ill people are thought to be bewitched and capable of contaminating others; it is also the fear that, if someone touches the body of the sick person and administers medicines, and the sick person dies soon after, the charge of witchcraft could fall on the survivor.

It follows, then, that mourners, too, must take care to protect themselves from witchcraft. At several of the small meetings of older men and women that take place during funerals, I listened as mourners talked about their fears. They said that witches are cannibals, who will try to take the corpse from the grave to eat it. Within a few hours after the "final breath" (*kiu*) of one who has died, and the onset of rigor mortis (*ekbe*), family mourners begin to chew *akbe-pi* (literally, "orphan leaves"). These leaves are supposed to protect the survivors from witches. It is understood that if someone is dying, or has died, witches must be present in the village. Women take extra precautions in preparing food to be eaten after the burial; no food must be cooked during or immediately after the funeral because food cooked under such unfortunate circumstances would be cooked "with sadness" (*igi*)—that is, open to suspicion. Funerals are a time of witchcraft accusations, and it is thought that either angry, sad, or revengeful mourners may want to poison the food, or, even worse, witches may still be lurking about in order to poison the food with their witchcraft substance. My informants told me that, in the past, it was sadness that led mourners to become headhunters. Though everyone knew that witches' murderous activities are limited to the villages in which they live, compensation for death was frequently sought outside the village. The survivors would become so full of grief (*igi*) that they wished to "diminish another *gili* [social group, see p. 122] as we were diminished [*iranja*] by the death in our clan."

Precautions against witchcraft also govern the interment. The grave diggers are carefully chosen by elders from among the young men of a village *different* from that of the deceased but of the same phratry; men of the same village may be contaminated, or they may be witches who will want to eat the corpse. It is always best to get as diggers men who are known to have dug graves that were "successful"—success being determined by there having been no deaths in the particular village for several years following the burial. Women and Efe, if they are present, go to the edge of the village to cut banana leaves to cover the floors of their houses and pasa, it being proper for mourners to show the signs of diminishment by sitting and sleeping only on banana leaves, rather than on furniture, for at least a week after the burial. Metal cups and kitchen utensils are stored away so that the mourners must drink out of leaves, and eat with their hands. Using leaves for sleeping, sitting, and cooking is a symbol of poverty, and death is understood to diminish the survivors, making them *iranja,* that is, "stupid," "poor," and "without," "dirty like an orphan." All luxury goods (radios, toothbrushes, combs, ballpoint pens, brassieres, and shoes), are also, of course, put away; mourners put on their worst clothes, occasionally rub dirt on their bodies, and begin to fast. Men and women who meet at funerals ask of one another the everyday question, "Have you defeated the day?" Instead of the usual reply, "Yes, and you?" mourners reply, "Only with iranja have I defeated the day." Some more educated Lese substitute a French translation for iranja, and reply, "Now that [the deceased] is gone, we are *sans valeur* [without value]."

Within a few hours after death, the eldest same-sex sibling, or preferably, a same-sex Efe man or woman associated with the clan of the deceased, washes the corpse. Except for the anus, every part of the body is washed with soap and cold water. Men then carry the corpse into the darkest and coolest room in the village, where it is left uncovered, or covered only by a thin cloth so that heat will not hasten the decomposition. Generally, the oldest women of the deceased's lineage, or the deceased's Efe partners and relatives, sit near the corpse and keep flies and other insects from touching it. The body is positioned straight, with the hands at the sides.

Washing a body is looked upon as a dangerous task. All body products, even gas, are considered to be potentially pathogenic, and fluids from a corpse are especially potent because they may contain witchcraft substance. That is why the Lese want nonvillage members to dig the graves and prefer their Efe to touch the corpse. Several people told me that the Efe are already polluted (*uche-ani,* with dirt), and so the corpse cannot harm them. Others told me that they prefer the Efe to touch the corpse because the Efe are not susceptible to the witches who dwell in the Lese village and may have caused the death.

WITCHCRAFT AS INVOLUNTARY HARM-DOING

The appropriateness of the terms "witchcraft" and "sorcery" deserves some comment. Evans-Pritchard's classic distinction (1976 [1937]) between sorcery and witchcraft is now well known to be inappropriate for some societies (see Marwick 1965; Macfarlane 1970; Thomas 1971), including, some would argue, the Azande. Even where the partition between the two forms of malevolence is an emic one, there remains ambiguity and uncertainty in specific cases of perceived harm-doing. Among the Lese, the elders clearly distinguish between witchcraft and sorcery, as I have described these two concepts; younger people often refer to all malevolence as witchcraft. The latter usage of the term "witchcraft" may be due to a general belief that one who has power in one domain, say sorcery, will also have power in other domains and will be able to use that power in any way he or she wishes.

For example, when someone dies, the cause of death is almost always attributed to witchcraft, but when someone becomes ill the cause is less easily defined. Some people will say that witches are "at work," but by this they simply mean that very powerful forces are at work, and they may even include sorcerers in the category "witches." When witchcraft and sorcery are spoken of in the abstract there is far more uniformity than when they are appropriated to refer to actual ongoing instances of misfortune. One has to be careful about using these terms as if they were unambiguous or understood clearly and in the same way by all people.

My purpose from here on is to explore in more detail the opposition between witchcraft and sorcery in general and between involuntary and voluntary malevolence in particular. I believe that the distinction between witchcraft and sorcery can be useful for analytic purposes. I also believe that the distinction holds quite unambiguously with regard to the Lese definition of witchcraft and sorcery as mechanisms of harm-doing. Although people may not reach a consensus about the cause of an illness, they will not dispute the fact that witches harm only within the village, whereas sorcerers harm within or without—usually without. I begin with a general outline of witchcraft as involuntary malevolence and then go on to compare it with the Lese model of sorcery. The data on which this outline is based were gathered largely from older Lese men and women.

According to Evans-Pritchard (1976 [1937]), the Azande hold that witchcraft is a biological and hereditary phenomenon. It is biological in the sense that witchcraft is contained within the human body and can be discovered through postmortem examination of internal organs. Azande witchcraft is hereditary in that children inherit witchcraft substance from their same-sex relatives. The Lese, who live in the same region as the Azande, do not believe that witchcraft is inherited; rather, malevolent witches transmit their powers by forcing or tricking children into consuming a witchcraft substance called *kunda.* Only if a child eats kunda will he or she become a witch. A witch may either spit the substance into a child's mouth, or surreptitiously place it in a child's food. The child will then unknowingly consume the kunda, which will grow larger as the child grows. The larger the substance, the more powerful the witchcraft will be. My informants told me that this is the reason why witches are, as children, only disobedient and mischievous, whereas old witches are dangerous murderers (cf. Evans-Pritchard

1976:7–8).[2] Although elder widows are thought to be especially dangerous as witches, I found little indication that one sex is in general more feared for witchcraft than the other.

Witches are always witches, and they act malevolently because they are witches. Although they may commit specific murders because they are jealous of the wealth or good fortune of certain members of their village, they will murder members of their own village regardless of whether or not they are provoked by intravillage inequalities. In this sense, witchcraft is an involuntary practice. Some witches kill more than others, however, and though witches cannot help being witches, they are believed to be able to limit the number of people they must kill in order to satisfy their appetite for human flesh. Sorcerers, however, can act at will. They are people who decide to act malevolently and use bad medicines. Referring largely to Evans-Pritchard's data on Azande witchcraft, Keith Thomas describes the distinction concisely:

> Witchcraft is an innate quality, an involuntary personal trait, deriving from a physiological peculiarity which can be discovered by autopsy. The witch exercises his malevolent power by occult means, and needs no words, rite, spell, or potion. His is a purely psychic act. Sorcery, on the other hand, is the deliberate employment of maleficent magic; it involves the use of a spell or technical aid and it can be performed by anyone who knows the correct formula. (1971:463)

A Lese informant stated the distinction:

> Not all people have kunda.[3] If it is inside of you, you will know it, and you will eat people because this is what witches do. . . . You can be a sorcerer (*hai-aru*) if you want to be. You must find the people with bad medicines, and tell them what you want to do. You will hurt women who refused you their vaginas, maybe you will hurt the husbands of those women, or maybe you will give your brother a disease. A woman wants to hurt her co-wife with bad medicine.

2. Witch doctors (*noko todu*) are an exception. They are witches who have in the past been given witchcraft substance by other witch doctors but have harnessed their powers to help victims of witchcraft. I point out here that the witch doctors act on their own behalf; their "good witchcraft" is considered to bear no relation to the other members of the witch doctor's clan. Although the clans of these doctors are said to be free of witches, they and their fellow clan members are susceptible to harm if witchcraft is introduced into the village by a new resident.

3. The word *kunda* is used in a variety of ways. It is frequently used to mean witchcraft, or witch substance, and sometimes to mean witch or witches. Someone is said to be *kunda-ani*, to be with witches. *Hai-kunda* is a more common term used to mean "possessor of witches."

The important aspect about harm-doing revealed in this explanation is that while witchcraft activities are not *necessarily* motivated by conflict or malevolent intention, sorcery is always employed for specific purposes between people in conflict. Sorcerers are necessarily selective.

MECHANISMS OF HARM-DOING

Lese witches kill by using witch's medicines and eating their victims. Sorcerers only make people sick by using medicines, called *aru,* which means any substance that produces profound bodily effects, good or bad—a wide range that includes everything from herbs that may be used by infertile women to harm their fertile co-wives, to penicillin and chloraquine. These substances can be placed in a person's food or flicked on the path over which an intended victim will pass.

Since sorcerers do not ordinarily cause their victims to die, witchcraft is obviously the more dreaded; those who are singled out by witches nearly always die. Witches' medicines are stronger and can cause large-scale catastrophes. A Lese witch can do nearly everything the sorcerer does, only with greater force. One Lese man reported: "Witches have medicine [*aru*] too. Only witches can know what kind of medicine it is. They kill at night or in the day. They can destroy a garden, and can call baboons to eat it, and can call wind and rain to destroy it." Witches will not, for example, destroy a garden by hand, but will instead manipulate the environment so that the crops fail. Both witches and sorcerers may act covertly, but witches are more dangerous because they kill at night, and because they can be seen only by other witches, or by the Efe. Sorcerers are simply human beings with bad intentions, and they will commit their crimes during the day and may not even attempt to hide their intentions. The mechanism by which sorcerer's medicine works upon the victims is supernatural, but the action of the sorcerer, unlike actions of witches, has an empirical status in the natural world. People actually attempt to harm others with medicines that can be bought and sold. Witchcraft, however, is something entirely supernatural, and the actions of a witch are never straightforward or completely understandable by human beings.

One of the most significant differences between sorcery and witchcraft is that sorcerers can harm anyone they have reason to harm, although their victims are usually members of villages other than their own. Witches, however, can harm only members of their own villages; hence the suspicion and fear attached to a death in the village. It is believed that one or more witches can murder a victim, as he or she sleeps, in the supernatural world, before the person dies in the natural world. All witches take leave of their own human bodies at night so that they can kill the members of other houses, or so that they can walk, in spirit, from village to village in search of freshly killed villagers, leaving their human bodies asleep in their houses. If they intend to kill someone in their own village, they remove the victim from his or her house, and distribute body parts to the witches who have traveled from other villages. They eat, vomit, and piece the body back together, so that they can eat it again after burial. The victim will die within a few days or one week after such an attack. Sometimes witches kill their victims by shooting them with "witches arrows" and then eating them later. Witches, then, are both human and supernatural—ordinary human beings by day and witches at night. All witches know they are witches, and they know when the "witches inside of them" leave their bodies. Human beings and their witchcraft are thus both integrated and independent: witches are human victims who have become witches not out of their own doing but because they were at some time poisoned with witchcraft substance; at the same time, after becoming witches, they are in some sense lost to the ordinary human world and only by destroying them can the witchcraft be ended.

It will be seen that, because witches attack members of their own village, whereas sorcerers usually work their spells on members of different villages, the solidarity of different social units is differently altered. Witchcraft comes from the houses and threatens the unity of the clan, and in this sense witchcraft represents the consolidation and opposition of houses. Sorcery, which comes from outside and threatens harmonious relations between different villages, represents the consolidation and opposition of clans. One expression of this distinction is the common fear that sorcerers prefer above all to poison palm wine, one of the few foods shared among members of different clans.

There are several other important distinctions. First, because witches are invisible and will surely murder members of their own village, witchcraft is not controllable. Witch hunters may look for witches, and certain techniques may be used to frighten witches from committing murder, but witches can almost never be discovered, identified, and imprisoned or executed. Sorcerers, in contrast, are controllable in the sense that their actions are comprehensible, and they can be identified, apprehended, and imprisoned. Furthermore, sorcerers may act only once, and never again, but witches will kill until they and their human bodies die. Second, while witch's motivations are never clear, witches must satisfy their desire for human meat. Therefore, they may kill anyone in their village, if only for the food. Sorcerers, however, are motivated principally by sexual and reproductive interests. They want to disrupt the marriages of their lovers or punish those who have refused to have sexual intercourse with them. Third, the most dangerous witches are old people, whereas the most dangerous sorcerers are young, sexually active men and women. When conflict motivates witches, it is usually conflict over access to food and material wealth, whereas sorcerers are motivated not by inequalities in goods but by unequal access to sex and children. For example, I recorded two cases, told to me by the victims, in which particularly fertile clans had been subject to a number of acts of sorcery.

DIFFERENCES BETWEEN LESE WITCHCRAFT AND SORCERY

Witches	Sorcerers
most harmful agents are elders	most harmful agents are the young
supernatural activity	human activity
cannibalize	employ medicines
cause death	cause illness
act at night	act during the day
limited pool of victims	unlimited pool of victims
act inside village	act outside village
uncontrolled	controlled
not necessarily select in choosing victims	select in choosing victims
appearance transmutable	appearance not mutable
motivated by hunger for human meat	motivated by sex and reproduction
involuntary	voluntary
contagious	not contagious
usually cause incurable illness and death	usually cause curable illness
malevolent actions are cooperative	malevolent actions are individual
not necessarily hostile	hostile

Many of the differences between witchcraft and sorcery are subsumed by a general opposition between inhumanity and humanity. Witches represent inversions of the natural order of things. Like the witches of many other eastern and central African societies (Middleton and Winter 1963), Lese witches eat human flesh, walk naked, travel at night, have a desire to fornicate with persons of an inappropriate age (for example, their classificatory grandparents or classificatory children), can change themselves into leopards, eat salt when they are thirsty, and regurgitate or vomit the meat they have eaten.

Another significant aspect of witchcraft is the way in which the distribution of meat among witches parallels and is differentiated from the distribution of meat in the human world. Witches and nonwitches alike follow the same normative standards of "dividing" (*oki*) food, the division of meat being a symbol of unity and brotherhood. But there are two important differences; first, witches eat and distribute human meat, whereas nonwitches eat and distribute animal meat; second, whereas nonwitches distribute meat only within villages, witches distribute their human meat between villages. Every time a witch murders in a particular village, the witches of other villages wait nearby to claim the parts of the body they want to consume. The murderer is obliged to distribute the parts to the other witches: "Among witches, the butcher is the one in the family of the corpse. He gives permission for others to butcher it. Everybody calls out the part of the body they want to eat. Someone wants a hand, someone else a foot, someone else a shoulder" (interview with a *noko todu* [witch doctor], 1987). The distribution of meat between witches thus represents an inversion of meat distribution between nonwitches. The sharing of meat, and relations of meat debt, between the witches of different villages expresses their binding relationships to one another, and a witch's failure to repay a meat-sharing debt can result in his or her destruction at the hands of other witches.

A witch may want to kill someone because of craving for human meat or jealousy of kin, but a witch may also be obliged to kill a relative because of a meat debt to a witch of another village. A witch called upon by another witch to repay a debt must murder a member of his or her family. This echoes Winter's account of Amba witchcraft, "The Enemy Within":

> The witches in various villages are bound together in a system of reciprocity. Thus if the witches in a particular village kill a person they invite the witches from another village to share the ensuing feast. At a later date, the witches of the second village must reciprocate by inviting their previous hosts to a feast at which they will serve the corpse of a victim from their own village. (1963:292)

Intervillage distributions of human meat carried out by witches result in potentially hostile debt relations between the witches of different villages. At two Lese funerals that I attended, mourners suggested that the deaths were the result of debts of limbs owed by members of their village to members of other villages.

MEAT AVOIDANCES[4]

Another important aspect of witchcraft beliefs has to do with meat avoidances, which every Lese observes in one way or another. A villager who eats meat prohibited by meat taboos inherited from the clan tempts witches to kill. Since many of these meat taboos are inherited from the same-sex parent, all the men in a village who are descended from a common male ancestor will tend to have the same taboos or avoidances; their wives, on the other hand, having different mothers, will each have another set of avoidances. Other types of avoidances are not inherited but are observed only as the result of specific circumstances. For example, men and women avoid eating certain meats when they are expecting a child and avoid other meats from the time a child is born until it begins to walk; some clans have specific taboos against the consumption of certain meats by children, adolescents, or women, and some taboos are applicable only when members of the village are actively engaged in hunting or trapping activities. Thus it can happen that, at any given point, nearly all the members of a village will avoid eating, even touching, different kinds of meat.

The consequences of eating a prohibited meat depend on the nature of the prohibition. If the prohibition is not inherited (that is, it is not a clan prohibition) or if it has to do with specific circumstances (for example, pregnant women have particular prohibitions), eating a prohibited meat can result in the severe illness or death of the person or of that person's children. But eating a meat that is an inherited taboo is rarely fatal and may not even cause illness. Indeed, the fear among Lese men and women on this score is far less than the fear of being caught doing so by a village coresident. Several men reported that they would gladly eat their inherited prohibited meats outside the village, but that within the village, someone might find them out and use the crime as an excuse for murdering a fellow clan member. What this seems to mean is that someone may murder a relative with witchcraft and then say that the death was caused by eating a prohibited meat. Remember that meat should be distributed between houses. If a man eats a prohibited meat,

4. My analysis is preliminary. I refer the reader to Robert Aunger (1992).

he eats it alone, and in so doing he flouts the normative standard and commits a crime against his "brothers." The crime of selfishness is provocation enough for, at the very least, arousing anger and hostility, and, at the worst, stimulating witches to kill.

HIDING PREGNANCY

Witchcraft and fears of malevolence are also involved in the tendency of Lese women to try to hide their pregnancies for as long as possible. In the spring of 1987, a young woman named Janeti became ill. Her resting pulse rate was well over 120, and she was short of breath. After several days, when it seemed that she was having uterine contractions, she admitted with considerable hesitancy that she had been pregnant for more than six months. Her mother-in-law denied that she was pregnant, and other members of the village expressed surprise at the news. Janeti's husband did not express surprise, however, and indeed told me that he had known about the pregnancy but had hidden it from his mother. I learned, upon further investigation, that Janeti had miscarried the year before, and that her husband's agnates had encouraged him to leave her and find a new wife, one who would be able to carry a child to term. Miscarriages and stillbirths are often attributed to witchcraft, and, on occasion, to sorcery practiced by the deceased baby's mother or by other women in the village who may be jealous of the pregnancy. In this case, Janeti's mother-in-law, recently widowed and now supported by her son, forbade her to become pregnant again, lest she murder another child by whatever means she had murdered the first. Janeti assured me that she had told no one about her pregnancy, for fear that her affines would be angry with her and that she would miscarry again. Probably Janeti believed she had successfully hidden the pregnancy from many people, but she was unlikely to have fooled everyone, for by the beginning of her third trimester she was quite large, and the intimacy of village life precludes keeping many secrets. Why, then, did Janeti try to hide her pregnancy, and why did her village coresidents deny knowledge of it?

The length of time that Janeti was able to hide her pregnancy is unusual. But the fact that she tried to keep her pregnancy a secret is not. Two other informants, including Janeti's husband, asked me why I was surprised that the pregnancy was hidden. Didn't I know, they asked, that pregnancies often terminate prematurely in the first few months? And didn't I know that fetuses in their first trimester are more easily affected by witchcraft and sorcery? Finally, did I not realize that many Lese and Efe women are infertile, and that there is extreme jealousy between kin over reproduction? In fact, most Lese women and their husbands inevitably try to hide pregnancies for as long as possible. In Janeti's case, her earlier conflict with her mother-in-law exacerbated the problem.

Indeed, Janeti's mother-in-law, as an unmarried widow, posed a severe threat to her. The mother-in-law depended on her son for food, and she was able to remain at her affinal village only because she had been fortunate enough to have a son who survived to adulthood and could build her a house in which to live. Janeti's mother-in-law was seen by many of her coresidents as a possible witch, and she was classified privately as *basari—basari* being an unmarried middle-aged woman, usually childless. Lese women who are childless cannot remain with their affines once they are widowed; they must seek residence in their natal village or in the village of their mother's brother. *Basari,* although, by definition not witches, are occasionally accused privately of a specific kind of witchcraft that does not cause death, "vagina witchcraft" (*kunda kufe-ba*); that is, they and others like them singly or cooperatively employ supernatural powers to attract young men to their vaginas (*kufe*). The victim becomes obsessed with his elder's vagina and is thus prevented from becoming attracted to women of his own age, and from reproducing. One young informant described the dangers of basari:

> The basari have medicine [*aru*] and they will shoot you [*oti*] with it. They want to have sex with young men, they will shoot you, and they will ruin your life. You will want to have sex only with her, and you will not want any other woman. You will want only her, and she will never let you go until you die.

Another informant's definition of the basari parallels the first:

> The basari are like witches (*hai-kunda*) of the vagina. They will want a man to have sex with her, even if he is an old man, it will not matter. The first drop of his sperm will go directly to her witchcraft substance. The man will not like any other woman. So you should not sleep with older women. It will ruin the marriage path of a man because he will like only her.

Basari are thought to be hostile to younger women, and it is likely that for this reason, as well as the mother-in-law's warnings against pregnancy, Janeti intended to hide her pregnancy for as long as possible.

THE MOTHER'S BROTHER AND SISTER'S CHILD AS PROTECTORS

After her pregnancy became public knowledge, Janeti strongly considered moving to another village until the baby was born. Shifting residence is, in fact, one of the most common ways that the Lese of Malembi address their fears of witchcraft or sorcery. When someone dies, my informants say, it is natural to want to move; when someone becomes ill, it is natural for the victim to leave his or her agnates. Misfortune, including witchcraft, is frequently blamed on residence, and many Lese respond to misfortune by traveling to distant villages or plantations, or at least to another village well removed from home. Perhaps the most common place to move is to one's mother's brother's (*andi*) village, as the following cases illustrate:

1. In 1985, Jean-Claude of the Andali phratry moved into the Andimoma village to live there permanently. He had become ill at his own village and was now, in his early thirties, nearly completely blind. He attributed his illness to the malevolent intent of the members of the village in which he had been living (his own patri-clan's village). In order to escape witchcraft and sorcery, he decided he would move to the village of his deceased mother's brother. The Andimoma clan, as the representative of his deceased mother's brother, offered him security and protection against malevolence.

2. Karusa is a thirteen-year-old girl from the Andipaki phratry. Her mother, Albertina, is from the Andimoma clan, but Albertina lives with her husband sometimes at his own clan and sometimes at the Protestant mission with which he is affiliated. For most of her childhood Karusa lived apart from her mother with her mother's brother Padi. The father travels extensively, and attends classes at distant missions for training as a Protestant preacher, but both he and her mother are quite ill and cannot support a family with their small garden. Both her mother and father suffer from leprosy, and her mother is nearly blind. Although her mother and father today live only three-quarters of a kilometer from Andimoma, Karusa spends little time with them, and she most often sleeps in the village of her mother's brother. Karusa stays with her mother's brother at the Andimoma village so that she does not become ill herself.

In many instances, people will seek refuge with their sisters' children (*ungbaro*):

3. During the summer of 1986, ImaMani and her infant, Mani, lived at the Andimoma village for three months, while she waited for her husband to return from his work at a plantation in the distant town of Wamba. ImaMani's husband had sent ImaMani to Andimoma to live with her classificatory sister's child (*ungbaro*) so that his wife would be safe until his work

was completed. Although ImaMani's own patri-clan is Andingbana (a fifteen-minute walk from the Andimoma village), she remained at her ungbaro's village, Andimoma, for maximum safety.

4. Baudouin and Oboni, both of the Andibeke phratry, lived at Andimoma for three months. Oboni was ill with swollen lymph nodes, and, like Jean-Claude, sought refuge with her ungbaro (sister's children). Baudouin, who had just reached the age at which he could enter school, lived at Andimoma because his own clan Andibeke was located beyond a reasonable walking distance from the primary school.

The ungbaro is the favorite category of person. The mother's brother, it is said, "cannot refuse" and "cannot harm" the ungbaro. By this it is meant that people will give their various ungbaro what they ask for and will never deny them hospitality. The mother's brother, individually, and as a group, is viewed as affectionate, generous, and nondisciplinary. The mother's brother gives freely to the ungbaro and helps to raise, feed, and nurture the child. An ungbaro knows that he or she can travel to the mother's brother (and vice versa), and be received warmly and given food. People say, "If you arrive at the village of your andi they will kill a chicken for you" (a huge sacrifice given the small number of chickens owned by the Lese). Many of my Lese informants also said that whereas agnates intend to murder one another, andi would murder their ungbaro only by accident. The andi is loving and acts with only good intentions.

The andi-ungbaro relationship is based on a mutual interest that binds the individuals from each of these groups together. Thus although the relationship always involves the classificatory extension of the ungbaro relationship to the entire group to which the ungbaro or andi belongs, it is not entirely accurate to assume that it is conceived in this way. The Lese who spoke with me about these relations characterized them as ties between individuals, rather than as ties between groups. The term may even be applied freely between people whose andi-ungbaro kinship cannot be reckoned, or whose social relations are formed on the basis of affinal ties, but for whom the *quality* of their relationship is one of personal affection, and sentiment, borne out in action as well as in belief.

The differences between agnatic ties and ties between the andi and ungbaro are consistent with the differences between the roles of one's father's and mother's clans in a person's social life. The patri-clan represents the interests of the clan; the mother's brother (an extension of the mother, from whom clan identity is *not* derived) represents personal interests. It is not surprising, then, that the term *ungbaro* should be used so frequently to refer to groups of intimates who are related even very distantly through uterine kinship; thus, a friend is "like an ungbaro" (cf. Fortes 1949 on the mother's brother's relationship [*soog*] among the Tallensi). In addition, although agnates bewitch or ensorcell one another, andi and ungbaro do not. This is not unusual, since the greatest hostilities seethe within the residence groups. Because marriage is exogamous, and the ungbaro relationship is established by exogamous marriage, ungbaro and andi do not live together. In fact, with the exception of extended visits, and the rare village relocation in which a person chooses to change his clan identity, the two kin relations usually live quite far apart and so offer to one another safe haven.

DEATH AND VILLAGE FRAGMENTATION AT ANDINGBANA VILLAGE

The safe haven of the villages of the mother's brother or the sister's child is usually only temporary. Fears of witchcraft may result in the splitting of villages into subvillages or even into separate villages. Andingbana village is a case in point.

In December 1986, two young women and one middle-aged man from Andingbana village died from eating wild poisonous yams; in January 1987, in the same village, a woman suffered a stillbirth, and in June, an elderly woman and a young woman died there, too; in July, the eldest Andingbana man died. In November 1986, the village of Andingbana had had a population of about thirty-three adults, which meant that, in addition to the unfortunate stillbirth, 18 percent of the adult population had died within less than eight months.

Witchcraft was the most common explanation for these misfortunes, and even before 1986, fears of witchcraft had already caused the village to become increasingly fragmented. In 1984, Andingbana had had no subvillages, but starting in 1985, after consulting with the local witch doctor, the noko todu, four out of the seven houses in Andingbana village moved their residences from a few hundred meters to one-half kilometer away from their previous residences in order to establish subvillages and distance themselves from the relatives they suspected of witchcraft. Formerly, the seven houses in the village had been close together, all well within view of the others. The men of these houses shared a common pasa. But the son of a man named Kebi died in 1985, and Kebi told me later that the noko todu had identified Angofe, a half brother of Kebi, as the witch who had murdered his son. Within a few months, Kebi moved his residence, building a new house and pasa. The wife of Kebi's half brother Nestor then became ill. Nestor reported to me that the noko todu had named Filipe (another half brother of Kebi and Nestor) as the witch who had caused her illness; if Nestor did not move away from Filipe, his wife would be sure to die. Nestor's wife recovered, but within two months Nestor moved his residence half a kilometer away from Filipe. Later, another Andingbana man moved his residence to his garden, saying that he had reason to believe Filipe would murder him because of a long series of disputes about the validity of the former's membership in the Andingbana clan and about the ownership of a certain goat. Finally, in December 1986, after Angofe and his two wives died from eating wild poisonous yams, Filipe, who lived next door to Angofe, fearing that he would be accused of causing that and any other misfortune in Andingbana village, and also fearing that he himself would be murdered by the witch or witches who had murdered Angofe, decided to move out of the village and establish a subvillage one-quarter of a kilometer away. During 1986 and 1987, two other houses dissolved completely as the result of four deaths in those houses. As it stands today, Andingbana village consists of two houses in the main plaza where the united village had been in 1984, and four other houses set well apart and constituting four distinct subvillages. One whole family unit, that of Angofe and his wives, no longer exists; Angofe's two young children are currently being raised by one of the accused witches, Filipe. All the abandoned houses have been destroyed so that witches' spirits can no longer use them as feasting rooms. It remains to be seen whether or not the fragmentation of the Andingbana village will eventually lead to the fusion of two or more houses into a new village with a new clan name.

AZIMA AND BELI OF ANDIMOMA VILLAGE

A little more than one kilometer away from the main Andingbana village plaza lies the Andimoma village. Here, accusations of harm-doing, and the placing of blame between two classificatory brothers, led in 1966 to the fragmentation of the Andimoma clan into two villages separated by more than thirty kilometers of forest. Twenty years later, the brothers reunited, but this time only into subvillages.

According to oral histories collected at Andimoma village, members of the Andimoma clan, and other clans of the Andisopi phratry, were murdered by members of the clans of the Andoa phratry around the turn of the century. Apparently, Andimoma also killed some members of Andoa in retaliation, but I was not able to elicit many specifics about the violent relationship between the two groups. In about 1962, Azima of the Andimoma clan convinced a fellow clan member named Beli that they might seek peace with Andoa through a marriage alliance. Although Azima was childless, Beli had a daughter of marriageable age. Beli's daughter would be given in marriage to a man from the Andoa phratry. The plan was carried out, and Beli's daughter moved to Andoa to live with a new husband and his affines. Unfortunately, her husband died a few years later of a disease that was said to have afflicted his genitals. Since Beli's daughter had no children, she was obliged to leave Andoa and return home to Andimoma. Within a year after her return to Andimoma she, too, died. Beli accused Azima of killing his daughter, saying that it was Azima who had arranged the marriage, and that had she not gone to that marriage village she would not have died. Beli cited as motivation for the murder Azima's own misfortune, when two of his children died before reaching adulthood. At that time, Azima had, in fact, accused Beli of bewitching his children, so it was not surprising that Beli should argue that Azima killed his daughter out of revenge.

Before their final split, Beli and Azima had already begun living apart. After his children died, Azima moved away from Beli to establish a separate village at his pre-1940s residence. After Beli's daughter died, in 1966, both men vowed never to see each other again. And I was told that they did not see each other until the Andimoma clan decided in 1986 to allow Azima to move to the roadside. Azima, one of the oldest Lese-Dese men, had become ill and was afraid that he was approaching death. He and his wife decided to leave his sapu village, which he thought might have caused his goiter, blindness, and sore joints, and move to Andimoma so that he could be within four days' walk of the missionary hospital. Azima hoped he could find a cure among the missionaries. It was also made clear to me by the members of the Andimoma village, the village in which I lived, that Azima expected me to drive him to the hospital. He spent three months living at the Mandima mission hospital in Mombasa, after which I drove him 120 kilometers (a full day's drive) to Andimoma. Azima and his wife moved into a house in a subvillage at Andimoma (the subvillage in which I lived), about one hundred meters from the subvillage where Beli lived. A narrow path connects the subvillages, but the villages are hidden from each other's view. Azima and Beli saw one another from time to time when

Beli passed through Azima's village on the way to the road, but Beli usually took a roundabout path to the road to avoid the village. When Beli and Azima did see each other, they did not sit together, and I never saw them shake hands.

Azima had been profoundly influenced by his experiences at the mission hospital. In April 1987, he told me that he thought he was about to die, and he feared he would not go to heaven unless he settled the old problem with Beli. He decided that he wanted to celebrate his return to Andimoma. He would eat a communal meal with Beli in order to mark the end of their hostilities. He said to me, "How can I die without confessing?" He invited all the older men from every Andisopi phratry, as well as a Lese minister who had been associated with the Mandima mission. The discussion that took place between Azima and Beli, parts of which I give here, illuminates some aspects of witchcraft:

AZIMA: I am a bad man, but I do not have bad medicine or witchcraft substance. These two things only I do not have. Your [Beli's] problem found me. Why? When my children died I stayed here and cried, and I didn't go to the *sapu*. My children died, I cried, but I did not say anything about you [Beli]. All of your children died too [Beli and his wife Ondekila's five girls and one boy died at a young age, four of them in early childhood]. I am a child of sadness. I know about the forest, that it is bad, and that we should stay away from it. God [*mungu*] gives us all illness. Do you think I did not hear what was going on? You told Nekubai [*chef de collectivité* until the late 1960s] that I killed [your daughter]. You talked about me, and your mouth was bad.

BELI: When you came last year to live here I sent you food so that we could eat together, but you took my food and left for the hospital. And you were saying, "I will never go to Andisopi again."

AZIMA: That is right, I said that.

BELI: And people said you were dying. And then you started to walk. And you walked to Lui's, and you walked to

Avio's, and you walked to Andingbana, and then you went to Mandima. So I asked, why is he walking everywhere but not coming to my place? He is giving me a problem!

ASINA (ELDER FROM ANDINGBANA): Today you will say it all! (followed by applause).

AZIMA: Quiet! . . . It was my mouth and not my heart that was bad. If things were bad, I would not have eaten that food. But I ate it! I ate it! I ate all of it! . . . If I had prepared bad medicine, I wouldn't be here doing this. When I was talking about these things, God saw me, and watched me, just like Mufanofigile [the anthropologist] writes things down. God knows I didn't lie. I arrived here and I ate! I ate that food all the way to the hospital.

After some discussion in which both men recalled the deaths of other children, the two ate a meal of cassava and rice and meat all served in the same large bowl. When they had eaten, they gave some of the meat and food to the other men participating in the meeting. After the food was finished, Azima and Beli stood up, faced each other, and spit on each other's foreheads, both of them screaming out, "Your body will be strong! [*igbara*]." Witchcraft substance, and the bad medicine of sorcerers, is transmitted often in food. By eating cultivated foods communally, something that even the most amicable of brothers rarely do, the participants communicate to each other that they do not suspect the others of harm-doing. Thus, Azima's emphasis on the fact that he consumed all of the food that Beli had given him.

THE NOKO TODU

Beli and Azima spoke of their fears of witchcraft, but they did not speak of the actions they might have taken to avoid accusations or to protect themselves and their children from supernatural malevolence. Taking action is difficult because witches are so deceptive that the Lese are usually unable to identify them. Furthermore, specific accusations of witchcraft are rarely made, and I know of no cases in which someone has actually admitted to being a witch. As with the Amba (Winter

1963), Lese witches can be identified by hiring a diviner,[5] or by administering a poison to the members of the clan of the deceased. As I shall discuss below, Lese witches can be identified by the Efe.

The Lese diviners, or witch doctors [noko todu], are able to identify the witches responsible for certain misfortunes, but they cannot identify all witches, and they have little power with which to counteract witchcraft or defeat the witch itself (Winter 1963:287).[6] If the noko todu identifies a witch that is currently bewitching someone, he or she can advise a client to move away from the residence of the witch or may try to find the witch at night. By threatening to reveal the witch's identity to the public, the noko todu may perhaps frighten the witch into halting the activities. Witches, and witch doctors also, are said to have powerful medicines that can heal afflicted persons and also keep certain witches from inflicting further harm. For example, it is possible for witch doctors to convince witches to put a person's body back together even after it has been partly eaten. If the noko todu identifies a witch who has already murdered someone, then he or she can only inform the client of the witch's identity. Apparently, in the past, the Lese chiefs tried and convicted persons charged by the noko of witchcraft killings, but today, neither the local nor *collectivité* chiefs have anything to do with adjudicating cases of witchcraft. The administration, however, has in the recent past, investigated cases of overt sorcery.

In many ways, the noko todu resembles an oracle, but the ability to see into the future is very limited. Although Lese and Budu noko todu can identify witches and forecast whether someone will die of witchcraft, they can see no further than their clients' immediate futures and can answer few questions more specific than whether their clients will live or die. They do not ordinarily try to address the smaller issues of everyday life, such as minor illnesses, financial problems, and concerns about love. Their main duty is simply to identify the witch or witches within a client's clan. As one noko todu explained it:

5. I do not know how often people consult the noko todu. Many go to these diviners to receive medical care, rather than to discover witches' identity. In these cases, afflicted persons may spend one or two weeks living at the diviner's village. My impression is that most people consult the diviners at some point in their lives.

6. The term "witch doctor" is as appropriate here as the term "diviner." The noko todu is said to be both a doctor (*nganga*) and a witch (*hai-kunda*); Lese listen to the noko todu primarily because he or she is a witch, putting powers to good use. *Noko* refers to the actual instruments used in divining; the noko todu throws sticks called noko and reads the position of the sticks in order to read the future. Another noko is a ball that hangs from a stick and which spins faster if a client is bewitched, slower if he or she is unharmed.

> I have a noko, and it tells me whether my person [client] will die or not. I take two sticks and rub them together and ask the question. The noko told me about Kebi's witch. I take a ball and hang it on a string, and ask it if the situation is bad. If it turns fast, I know that people will be falling on the ground, and rolling in the dirt, crying for someone who has died. If it is steady, the people are standing still. No one will die. If it turns, I will start to state the names of the people who live in the same village as my [client]. The ball will turn fastest when I say the name of the witch.

In short, the noko todu limits the investigation to the members of the village in which the victim lives and does not necessarily look for hostile relations in general as a clue for identifying a witch. His or her power lies in the ability to see witches and to communicate with the noko oracle. The noko todu is most effective at stimulating Lese villagers to move away from the residence of the witch and establish new residences elsewhere. When the noko todu tells a client the name of the witch that has caused misfortune or killed someone, the client frequently leaves the village to establish a new house but will not speak publicly of the witch. This reticence makes it difficult to pin down any facts, and I heard of only a few cases of a witch being said to have bewitched someone at one particular time and place.

At this point a general conclusion can be drawn concerning the strategies the Lese employ to manage crises that are believed to be caused by supernatural forces. As we have seen, the strategies for dealing with both witchcraft and sorcery minimize *intravillage* hostility. In sorcery, when the apparent source of conflict between spouses is judged to be a village outsider, that person is named and becomes the focus of a specific discourse and ritual. In witchcraft, the perpetrator is judged to be a village insider, and is unnamed, or, more precisely, unmentionable.

For very practical reasons, most people do not consult the diviners often. In the first place, because the dangerous witches are the witches of one's own village, people only consult diviners who belong to clans and phratries other than their own, and that can mean traveling some distance and perhaps having to leave gardens and houses unattended. Moreover, the diviners are extremely expensive. One man from Andingbana village incurred a debt of three thousand zaires (at that time, approximately 100 days' wages at a coffee plantation, about $25 U.S., or half the average annual income of a Lese-Dese house), a debt he will probably never be able to pay. The expense prohibits people from consulting diviners on trivial matters, and they do it only in cases of extreme fear of witchcraft murder or when they are quite certain that their illness, or that of their spouses or children, is life threatening. I do not know why diviners do not lower their fees. Beyond the trouble and expense, there is also the very important deterrent of wanting to avoid an explicit act of hostility against the members of one's village. Trips to the village of the witch doctor inevitably become public knowledge and stimulate much gossip in all the villages. Traveling to a witch doctor is like saying to one's fellow villagers, "There are witches among you, and I will find out who they are." Such an act makes the suspicious villager the object of anger and fear: agnates and/or coresidents are outraged and worried about the possibility of being unjustly accused. Yet as one man from the Andingbana village said, "Just by going to the village of the noko todu, I can frighten the witches. Maybe they will run. They know I will learn who they are."

Oral history tells us that the Lese and the Efe of Malembi have in the past used a poison called *sambasa* as a way of identifying witches. Winter (n.d.) says that the Amba, too, used a poison for identification. By most accounts I heard, sambasa was declared illegal by the colonial administration and is seldom used today; it was not used during my stay, but the Lese talked about it at every one of the thirteen funerals I attended. I was told that, in the past, members of the village of the deceased would drink the sambasa, and those who vomited (or died) would be accused of witchcraft, and banished from the village. Before the poison was outlawed, those who vomited were sometimes tried by the appointed chiefs and, if convicted, were beaten and sent to prison. According to my informants from Andingbana village, at the funeral of Ngote, the most prolific man in the history of the Andingbana village, their Efe partners angrily administered sambasa to every Andingbana villager. There were no deaths or vomiting. In the 1950s, at least three people died from drinking sambasa at a funeral for a man of the Andipaki phratry. One man from the Andipaki phratry who attended that funeral told me that although he was not a witch, he was afraid that the sambasa would kill him; he saved himself, he insisted, by consuming human feces taken from an outhouse. Indeed, my informants stressed that the failure of suspects to vomit or die when given sambasa does not prove innocence; it only means that the witches are able to elude its powers. As Winter (n.d.) notes, the administration of poison may reduce some tension following death, but it never eliminates the fear of witchcraft from the village.

At the same time, however, there does not appear to be a general view that all deaths are the result of witchcraft. These points were highlighted by an elderly man at the funeral of another elder: "It might be witchcraft. He had a lung disease in February, and he did not die. Why should he die now? He had pain at the bottom of his stomach, he did not defecate, and he kept vomiting. I think he died of a 'man's disease' [hernia], but people should still talk about witches, because there are always witches somewhere. It is dangerous to say there are no witches —they will start to eat everyone." Witches may, of course, eat a corpse regardless of whether or not the death resulted from witchcraft. Thus, even in the event that witchcraft is not considered to be the proximate determinant of death, care needs to be taken to protect the corpse from being eaten by witches. By stressing witchcraft as a cause of death, the mourners hope to frighten away any witches, thereby protecting not only the corpse but themselves.

THE EFE AS NONHARMFUL KIN

Although the Lese incorporate the Efe into their houses, the Efe are not included within the group of potential murderers. This is perhaps because the Efe, despite being house members, are not clan members. The Lese also believe that the Efe know how to hunt witches, and because they look upon the Efe as powerful protectors, they sometimes encourage them to be vocal accusers at Lese funerals. At the funeral of Ondekokbi of Andingbana village, several mourners suggested that the death occurred because the Efe had not been present in the Andingbana village for some time: "The witches saw that Kazumiri and Mimu [the deceased's two Efe partners] were not here, and so they [the witches] came to kill Ondekokbi." Indeed, it was the Efe who, in the past, administered sambasa and thereby tried to protect the village from witches. During my stay, Efe men connected with Andingbana village twice brought blood-stained arrows to their Lese partners as proof that they had killed a Lese witch in the forest. Efe not only have a reputation as witch killers; they also have the ability to kill the witches of any village, not just those of the village in which their Lese houses are located.

When a Lese man has to travel somewhere at night or has to travel long distances, he will often ask his Efe partner to accompany him. At Lese funerals, Efe men and women are asked to sleep at the village of the deceased in case of a disturbance by witches, and they also act as the chief mourners, whose loud anger and protestations can frighten off

A Lese boy (left) and his future Efe partner, standing in his father's unfinished house. *Photograph by R. R. Grinker.*

the witches and declare to all that the deceased was a victim of village enmity.

My impression is that the Efe are, on the whole, much less violent at Lese funerals than they are at their own, but they appear to be just as vocal, angry, and resentful of the loss specifically of their *muto* (Lese partner) or member of their muto's family (a loss that they sometimes believe is more severe for them than for the deceased muto's extended family and coresidents). Efe men and women seemed to me to mourn louder and longer than Lese did, and they give longer and more frequent speeches, thereby contributing most to the "noise" of funerals, which, according to the mourners I interviewed, stimulates grief. Funerals are also one of the few occasions, in addition to dances and festive adolescent initiation rituals, when Efe men and Lese men interact with one another for a prolonged period. At funerals, Efe and Lese men may mourn together in the house containing the corpse, and Efe men, women, and children will most often sleep at the village until the body is buried. Nonetheless, at all the funerals I attended, the Efe men and women sat with Lese women near the corpse and spent the rest of their time sitting together in an area far away from the Lese men. But several times a day at these funerals, Efe men confronted Lese men to ask for food or tobacco or marijuana, and they began long monologues about their relation to the deceased, and about how their relations with the deceased were, unlike the Lese's relations with one another, caring and affectionate. In every case, the Efe speakers blamed the villagers for the death, stated that the Efe partners were entitled to inherit or destroy all the dead man's possessions, and declared that upon this death their amicable relations with the village's survivors had ended.

All this is exactly what the Lese want from the Efe: they are supposed to express their commitment to their Lese partners. Filipe's narrative on Efe loyalty is an example of such an idealized expectation of the Efe. Filipe accompanied his own Efe partner, Albert, to the funeral of an Efe man, one of Albert's affines. Filipe spoke:

> Albert gives me meat, and so I cry for your Efe. When I die, Albert will come to the place of my death, and he will clean my body well, and wrap it up, and then say "Mafu! The men that killed my muto will die." Albert, you will kill them at the water path. And then you will die. You will go to heaven, and your problems with the Efe will end. You will pay for my problems, and we will see each other in heaven.

At another funeral, this one for a stillborn boy, one of the few persons to express explicitly any outrage at the misfortune was a young Efe woman who cried out to the mother of the deceased child: "You killed this little boy because he has a penis. You like children with vaginas. The child of my muto gave birth to a boy. Why did you destroy our new boy?" By behaving in a hostile manner toward the survivors, the Efe in effect treat the corpse as a victim of enmity between villagers.

Robert LeVine (1982) has similarly interpreted some Gusii witchcraft accusations as the mourner's identification with the deceased. The Gusii mourners may make wild accusations of witchcraft that are intended not to accuse any particular person of the murder, but rather "to give voice to what they construe as the dead person's reaction to his or her own death, that is, to blame it on enemies or on hitherto unknown conspirators." Similarly, Lese and Efe mourners may reconstruct parts of the victim's life, often retelling every statement made by the victim in his or her final days. The Efe mourners appear, in effect, to deny the fact of death itself, and in replaying, indeed reexperiencing, their conversations with the dead person, they recall the person from death and give her or him voice. Before the burial of Ondekokbi of Andingbana, the Efe mourners sitting beside the body were talking excitedly. The funeral was well attended by Efe and Lese alike, to honor the deceased and discuss the reasons why he died. Ondekokbi was especially well liked by the Efe because he had raised several Efe children in his house, and because he had two Efe partners and was able to support their families with cultivated foods and clothing. In the conversation reproduced below, one of Ondekokbi's Efe partners, Kazumiri, eventually begins a dialogue with his own brother's wife, Marko-di, in which they together give explicit voice to the corpse, speaking about the corpse's wishes with first person singular pronouns and verb forms. They effectively *become* the corpse. In the conversation, we also hear the voice of Albert (an Efe man whose partner lives in the village of the deceased), Mimu (Ondekokbi's other Efe partner), Azima (a Lese elder who took charge of directing the funeral), and Ude-ni (Ondekokbi's brother's son). The conversation took place on the second day after death, before the burial, with the Efe participants seated on the floor beside the corpse. The Lese participants stood around the corpse.

KAZUMIRI: Go, let's go to the house, to see the quiver he left, and see the arrows he left. Really! Come, let's take them out of the house "so the face of the quiver does not get dizzy" [so the quiver does not get lost (*idle a ue a itau-ni*)]. My heart has been taken out of me, I no longer have a muto, and I cannot stay here. The women here will tell me mouth [say angry things]. I speak the truth. I am speaking the voice of Ondekokbi.

ALBERT: When I left the village for the forest, Ondekokbi said, "Don't go, let us, the two of us, defeat the day together under the pasa."

KAZUMIRI: Your two boys have returned.

ALBERT: He [Ondekokbi] told me, "I and your mother's sister want to sleep and vomit." So I said, "What is happening to you my muto [Ondekokbi]?"

MIMU: In our absence, they killed him.

AZIMA: His wife told me this: Ondekokbi was fixing his peanut storehouse across the river, and he was tying up the house. He stopped working, went into the pasa, something ripped inside of him. He vomited right away.

MIMU: The corpse is starting to swell.

UDE-NI: A hernia kills a man.

ALBERT: What will we do? We must watch him.

At this point, when the mourners bring attention to the swelling of the corpse, they are implying that the death was caused by witchcraft. Mourners at the funerals I attended expressed the belief that when a cadaver swells quickly, it is because of witchcraft substance present in the body; a cadaver that has not been affected by witchcraft will not swell.

AZIMA: This problem is mixed with witches. There are two things: witches and illness.

ALBERT: True.

KAZUMIRI: Yes.

AZIMA: If it is illness, it is hard to die.

UDE-NI: Even with a big illness, witches did not come into it, and he did not die in February when he was ill . . .

As the conversation proceeds, Kazumiri begins to mix pronouns. He looks confused. He and Marko-di recreate a dialogue that occurred before the death, in which Ondekokbi asked his Efe partners to go to the forest to find honey for him. While they were in the forest, the witches took advantage of the absence of the Efe and murdered Ondekokbi. Kazumiri's speech is nearly incomprehensible, not only to me, but to the listeners as well. He cries, slaps his hand to the ground, and does not speak directly to either the other mourners or to the corpse. When Kazumiri states "I told you to go to the forest," he and Marko-di begin to speak as if they have become the corpse.

KAZUMIRI: . . . My muto, my muto, your wife told you bad things, and he got sad because she told him bad things. I [the deceased] told you to go to the forest. I told you [Efe] to find me meat.

MARKO-DI: And so I went to the forest.

KAZUMIRI: I told you to go to the forest for honey.

MARKO-DI: And then I died.

KAZUMIRI: Bury him, bury him.

MARKO-DI: Do not take my corpse out of the house, leave my corpse here.

KAZUMIRI: Now other [Lese] will kill me, I am not strong without you.

MARKO-DI: So now there is no one to whom we can give Ondekokbi's seeds. Who will feed our children?

KAZUMIRI: My heart has died. Where will I find another muto? I am shaking.

In the context of such a discourse, the deceased become victims, the survivors become enemies. Only the Efe are beyond suspicion. Moreover, the mourner's words are consistent with the Lese idealizations of the Efe. That is, the Lese and the Efe are incomplete without one another.

CHAPTER VI

Conclusion

A Union of Opposites

"It is not the resemblances, but the differences, which resemble each other."

Claude Lévi-Strauss, Totemism

A number of anthropological studies illustrate the ways in which the meanings and structures of the house can constitute cosmology, religion, psychology, society, and politics (Fernandez 1976 in central Africa; Feeley-Harnik 1980 in Madagascar; J. Comaroff 1984 in South Africa; and in West Africa, Fortes 1949; and Blier 1987). Other studies confirm that political and ethnic relations can be established in the context of the house (in Ghana, Schildkrout 1975, 1978; and in Sudan, Evans-Pritchard 1940—see my discussion below). These data suggest that the social organization of some African societies, with or without attached foragers, might very well be recast in terms of the house. Yet my account of the Lese of Malembi differs from these studies in at least one crucial area: its separation of the house and clan as distinct cultural models. In this sense, my study contrasts with the numerous studies in Africa that have shown that elements of the house—for example, spatial orientation, the division of rooms, and house-building materials—serve as models for clans and lineages. R. A. LeVine and S. LeVine (1990:6), for example, note that, for the Gusii of Kenya, the word *egesaku,* meaning "the smaller doorway into the traditional house, from its cattle pen," refers to the lineage and to more inclusive political units including the nation-state. And of the Nuer, Evans-Pritchard writes: "*Thok dwiel,* lineage, means this: it is the entrance to the hut, the mother's hut. The tiny twigs we see in the *gol,* household, grow into the great branches of the lineages" (1940:247). In these cases, the house is meaningful primarily in the service of descent groups. The Lese house is not just another figuration of clan relations, for, ideally, the house and clan are separate social organizations that refer to very different kinds of social processes. Whereas clans are agnatic organizations in which the members should remain at the same level of economic productivity, and in which all competition should be muted, houses are organizations (based on marriage and interethnic interaction) in which the members are placed in hierarchical relationship to one another.[1] The house is especially significant because it is both an institution and a model for relations of inequality, including, of course, relations between ethnic groups. As an institution that organizes both marriage and the Lese-Efe relationship, the house brings together people who are separated in most other social contexts. As a model, the house provides the meanings and metaphors through which house members symbolically represent their relations with one another. These gender and ethnic relations are characterized by inequality and dependence. Just as the mud or organs of the house depend upon the trees or skeleton of the house, so do wives and Efe depend upon Lese men for their social identity in a Lese village.

The house is central to an analysis of Lese social organization in part because it resonates with their ideas about social organization. In particular, the isolation of the house from other social units, especially the clan, resonates with Lese ideas about their ethnic identity. Throughout chapter 2, I pointed out the ways in which the Lese seek simultaneously to isolate themselves from and integrate themselves with non-Lese and non-Efe Zairean groups and outside urban or agricultural systems. I argued that the Lese rationalized their externally imposed political and economic isolation as internally imposed; that is, at some point, many Lese began to conceive of their increasing isolation as a product of their own agency rather than as a product of both the oppression of the state and indigenous cultural values. One contributing factor to this conception is a Lese cultural disposition toward the separation of settlements into distinct houses. We cannot be certain about causality—that is, whether the structures and functions of the Lese house were determined primarily by their more recent political and economic isolation or by

1. Although the individuals in any given Lese clan often adhere to an idealized equality, we should not exclude the consideration that clans themselves may be juxtaposed hierarchically. However, my data do not indicate a systematic hierarchical ordering of clans, despite the fact that clans are not expected to remain equal to one another. In other ethnographic contexts, of course, clans become incorporated into hierarchies. Among the Nuer and many other East Africa and central African groups, there are aristocratic and commoner lineages and clans; in northern India, clans are important elements in the construction of social stratification (Parry 1979).

enduring cultural dispositions—but it would appear that isolation and the cultural patterning of local social organization have accompanied each other through history. Oral histories suggest that the political organization of the Eastern Uplands societies of central Africa have long been both unstable and house centered (Vansina 1990a, 1990b).

INCORPORATION AND MARGINALITY

The boundaries of the Lese clan are fixed and fairly impenetrable. Immigrants may live in houses within a village, and their offspring may even become clan members (usually by altering genealogical memory in favor of clan membership), yet outsiders find it difficult to live in the Lese villages. But it is possible for someone to become a member of a house without becoming a member of the clan. Indeed, the house is the site for the incorporation (and marginalization) of outsiders. The contrast between marginality and incorporation is highlighted by the integration of the Efe into Lese houses. By marginality I refer to the outsider who has crossed a social boundary but does not obtain full membership in the new group (Kopytoff and Miers 1977:18). By incorporation, I follow R. Cohen and J. Middleton's usage (1970), whereby group boundaries are crossed to form a new unit, such as a nation. Along these lines, I consider the Lese house to be a form of social organization made possible by the incorporation of the Efe (outsiders) into the Lese house.

The Efe and the wives are the two groups that cross the boundaries, and in doing so they pose the problem of their symbolic and social incorporation. Incorporation takes place *symbolically* through denigration and the establishment of a discourse on biological and cultural differences (thus reinforcing the outsider's marginality) and *socially* through the incorporation of outsiders as subordinates in the Lese house. One depends upon the other, for marginality is a kind of incorporation. The contrast between the Efe's dual insider and outsider status is also related to the organization of both witchcraft beliefs and economics. Recall that, for the Lese, witchcraft emanates from inside the village and threatens village unity. Since witchcraft can only be carried out between members of the same village and is usually carried out between the members of different houses, witchcraft *is* the opposition of houses. The production, distribution, and consumption of foods are patterned similarly: foods should be produced, distributed, and consumed within the house.

I find parallels between the Lese-Efe relationships and the joking relationships between in-laws as described by Radcliffe-Brown (1952 [1940]), not so much because the Lese and the Efe engage in playful antagonism or teasing, but because both sets of relationships involve attachment and separation, or what he referred to as "social conjunction" and "social disjunction" (1952:91). In chapter 3, I showed that the Lese draw an equivalence between the incorporation of Efe and wives. The formation of an Efe partnership, like the formation of a marriage, necessitates a "readjustment" of the social structure, since a house must be created and occupied by the new outsiders. Wives actually reside in the house, but the Efe, although symbolically included as members, are spatially excluded. Like in-laws, the Lese and Efe men avoid social contact.

THE HOUSE: DOMESTIC AND PUBLIC

As briefly noted in chapter 3, I treat inequality narrowly as ideological inequality. That is, I focus on how the Lese pattern social and cultural differences among human beings so that they are unequal to one another and are vertically arranged. I follow J. Rousseau's definition of ideological inequality as "conceptual sets which establish the superiority of some categories over others" (1990:163). Forms of political and economic inequality (for example, control over decision-making processes and the means of production) often accompany ideological inequality, but these more objective bases are to be found in detailed studies of politics and the relations of production. I am concerned primarily with the images and ideals of difference as they appear in a particular Lese discourse about the Efe.

It is in light of inequality that the house holds promise for a critical anthropology of Africa, a field that has relied so heavily on analyses of clans, descent groups, and other units that are, sometimes by definition, egalitarian social organizations, and often have little to do with gender or ethnic relations. The tendency to explore clan relations, for example, as if they could explain a social totality has undoubtedly affected the data we choose to gather and the interpretations and conclusions that ensue from them. Neither Winter nor Turnbull, for example, ever approached the signs and practices of inequality because they did not explore the contexts in which they exist. Clans tell us something very important about the ideologies framed by men about men, but they often tell us mainly about sameness and equality, egalitarianism and solidarity. It is in the context of egalitarianism, of course, that the clan, descent, and lineage become so important to the Lese. The organization of descent lines into clans is especially important in times of conflict in which the clan ideology of organization is invoked. Clans unite in opposition to other clans and can mobilize for collective action in the case of dispute or illness. This is the principle behind segmentary opposition: there are groupings, some of which may be short-term, which must be solidary and egalitarian for the purposes at hand. But while the clan is essential to Lese social life, it is simply one level, one location, at which to analyze social organization. One location is not more important than the other, but an accurate anthropological picture depicts society as the product of the relationship between these two coexisting models.

The salience of the house also tells us something more general about egalitarianism and the so-called "agnatic principle" in patrilineal societies (Evans-Pritchard 1940, 1951). Evans-Pritchard explained Nuer social organization by positing a structural principle that achieved a degree of social equilibrium and integrated all persons into agnatic social units: "tribes," "clans," "lineages," and "lineage segments." I noted, however, that Evans-Pritchard translates the Nuer terms for these social units as "house," "hearth," or "entrance to the hut." Kathleen Gough has located other inconsistencies with the agnatic principles. In her reanalysis of Evans-Pritchard's data, she found that just as the whole of Nuer society could not accurately be termed egalitarian, so, too, not all Nuer were equally "agnatic." Aristocrats conformed fairly consistently to the agnatic pattern, but commoners varied considerably in how they reckoned descent and formed marriages and households. The variation was due, in part, to the fact that the Nuer had been expanding at least since the mid-nineteenth century and had absorbed numerous captured or immigrant Dinka into their households (Kelly 1985); by establishing a number of customary legal fictions, many Nuer could interpret the new social situations to fit the patrilineal principles, but "the less successful layers had to abandon strict patrilineal principles and adhere to the former [more successful layers of the population] through cognatic and affinal ties in order to reintegrate themselves into society" (Gough 1971:117). Despite his repeated descriptions of the integration of Dinka into Nuer households in his *Kinship and Marriage among the Nuer,* Evans-Pritchard, Gough argues, found an unstable and internally differentiated society in transition but sought to explain it with a timeless, homogeneous, and egalitarian structural principle that obscured the unequal distribution of status and property, and the social composition of households (see also Hutchinson 1992). Gough's reanalysis suggests to me that a focus on the house might have revealed the social and historical complexities masked by Evans-Pritchard's specific focus on patrilineages.

The relationship between the house and clan brings us back to the conventional analytical distinction between domestic and public domains, a distinction that led to a methodological choice by most anthropologists to study one domain or the other, or to describe the domestic domain somewhat superficially and to employ more sophisticated analyses for the public domain. Those with an interest in politics studied bureaucracies, descent, and corporate groups, while those with an interest in domestic issues (a small minority in social anthropology) studied the household and relations between men and women. Indeed, the numerous studies of households and their economic functions in sub-Saharan Africa (see Guyer 1981) tend to isolate the household from "exogenous" social, political, and economic processes (Heald 1991:131). The infrequency with which the two domains have been systematically linked in anthropological analysis is in large part due to the tendency to bring such an analytic dichotomty with us to the field—a dichotomy that has been a part of Western social thought at least since the late nineteenth century (Coward 1983)—but it may also be due to the tendency for anthropologists to accept informants' renderings of their world at face value. The separation between the domestic and the public sometimes reflects local models of society as represented by our informants quite as much as it represents our own concerns or ideologies. But we must compare those models with ethnographic observation and experience, for ethnographic analysis cannot simply mirror local models, and the empirical and the ideological rarely agree.

Fortes himself made numerous caveats about this analytical distinction, remarking that the domestic and public domains are usually linked empirically. "The actualities of kinship relations and kinship behaviors are compounded of elements derived from both domains. . . . Every person is an agent, actual or potential, in all domains" (1969:251). Yet, as Yanagisako says of the Fortesian dichotomy, "There is, in fact, a tendency for the terms to be employed to refer to whole social relations (rather than to their contexts and implications) and to entire social institutions (rather than to facets of social institutions)" (1979:187). In addition, where the split is expressed by informants, it has to be contextualized as an indigenous or local model. In some societies, as in South

Asia, the domestic/public split will refer to the sexual purity and impurity of women, while in some, as in the United States, the same ideological split will refer to the opposition of love and money (Rapp 1979:510). In still others, such as among the Lese, where the private is to the public as wives and the Efe are to Lese men, "domestic" relies upon an ideology of ethnicity as well as gender.

ETHNICITY AND HIERARCHICAL OPPOSITION

One of the particularly significant aspects of ethnicity is that it can be analyzed in terms of underlying structural oppositions. John Comaroff (1987) describes ethnicity as first and foremost a process of symbolic classification. We have seen that the Lese classification or marking of Lese-Efe relations opposes whole social groups to one another, but it also opposes the particular elements that comprise the whole. Lese-Efe relations thus turn on several oppositions that have to do with social statuses (male and female, forager and farmer, house and village/clan member) and social structural principles (marginality and incorporation, equality and inequality, masculinity and femininity).

These oppositions are expressed here in the language of anthropology, but the realities they represent are not simply the result of a perspective that assumes, for analytical and methodological purposes, that Lese and Efe society is composed of a well-patterned series of oppositions. It is true that societies everywhere place some emphasis on what D. Maybury-Lewis (1989:1) refers to as "polarities of logic or experience." Structural analyses have revealed that totalities frequently comprise a "union of opposites" (Maybury-Lewis 1989:5). These oppositions are illuminating because the Lese and the Efe, like many other people in the world, do concern themselves with antinomies in their everyday lives. But such dualistic thinking (on the part of both anthropologists and the people they study) cannot be embraced uncritically. As I have noted, to accept the sharp separations posited by informants, such as the private and public, female and male, is to embrace and enshrine the local ideologies it is our task to deconstruct.

Structural oppositions are also framed so abstractly that they can seem to stand on their own, divorced from everyday life and the hierarchies of value associated with them. One critic of Lévi-Straussian structuralism, Louis Dumont, has consistently found fault with what he considers to be an anthropological aversion to the study of hierarchy, especially the reluctance to explore the logic of hierarchy underlying egalitarian ideology in the West. More recently, Dumont has extended his campaign for hierarchy in a criticism of the use of binary opposition in anthropological analysis. His theory of caste hierarchy turns on structural oppositions, namely, the pure and the impure, status and power (Dumont 1970). But Dumont wishes to criticize not the postulation of oppositions but the treatment of oppositions as equal to each other. Taking up the issue of right and left as polarities (Needham 1973), Dumont argues that, as with other structural oppositions, that of right and left tends to be viewed as a simple polarity or complementarity (1986:228). If right and left are considered in relation to each other as terms or poles, it is their structural equivalence that makes possible the opposition. The poles do not have equal status *in relation to the whole,* however, for right is, in general, socially and symbolically superior to left. The poles are not equally opposed because they are valued differently.

Such differences in value have a direct impact on how we view ethnicity, since ethnic groups can be unequally opposed rather than balanced. Following Dumont, B. Kapferer (1988) argues that many classic analyses of ethnicity are placed in an egalitarian framework. He suggests that F. Barth and Abner Cohen, among others, have drawn on Evans-Pritchard's concept of balanced segmentary opposition, a concept that is embedded in European ideas about egalitarianism in modern industrial societies. Kapferer criticizes the concept of segmentary opposition for masking an underlying inegalitarianism; he argues, for example, that although Australians appropriate a nationalist ideology of equal opposition, in doing so they create a false sense that various national or cultural identities are homogeneous, and at the same time they subordinate Asians and other immigrants of non-European descent in a hierarchy. If everyone is equivalent in the sense that they are, as individuals, homologous and thus opposable elements, and if this sort of egalitarianism is applied to whole societies or ethnic groups, then it is only a short step to racial stereotyping; for just as the categories "Vietnamese" or "Sri Lankan," for example, are naturally opposed to the category "Australian," so are all Vietnamese conceived to be like all other Vietnamese, Sri Lankans like all Sri Lankans, and so on. " 'Australian' and 'Vietnamese' are patently not equivalent units, although their phenomenal constitution is in accordance with egalitarian principles" (Kapferer 1988:197). Thus hierarchy and equality are not necessarily opposed to each other; they may actually encompass each other. In fact, Dumont argues that in the United States "race prejudice is, in a sense, a function (a perversion) of egalitarianism" (1970:264). He goes on to say: "Where equality is affirmed, it is within a group which is hierarchized in relation to others, as in the Greek cities or, in the modern world, in British democracy and imperialism, the latter being tinged with hierarchy" (1970:265). Hierarchical relations encompass equal opposition despite egalitarian efforts to suppress them.

These criticisms of structural opposition negate neither its value in anthropological analysis nor its salience as the basis of political ideologies, but rather they lead us to consider the hierarchical nature of the oppositions underlying Lese-Efe relations. Inequality is engendered in equality, marginality in incorporation. Structural oppositions can explain the cultural logic of hierarchical social forms and practices, for the sides of any given opposition may be differentially valued. The Lese and the Efe provide a compelling ethnographic example of how ethnicity is structured by underlying oppositions and mediated in social organization. For all their differences, the Lese and the Efe remain a union of opposites.

EQUALITY AND INEQUALITY

If equality and inequality can emerge simultaneously it becomes important to look at the relationship between them in a specific ethnographic context. In the Ituri, we find that the Lese idealize relations between Lese as equal and relations between the Lese and the Efe, and between Lese men and their wives, as unequal. In their efforts to maintain equality, the Lese discourage economic and political inequality at the level of the village, but encourage it at the level of the house.

The significance of equality in the Lese village is evidenced by the struggle to achieve it. The Lese *compete for equality,* but the form that it takes is the inverse of what Americans call "keeping up with the Joneses' ": economic success for the Lese of a single clan means having the same or less, but never more, than your neighbor. Witchcraft beliefs form an integral part of that struggle. Indeed, the Lese compete with one another by suspecting that their agnates are hoarding unshared meat, and this suspicion is expressed by informants both in their statements and in the myths they report about village fission.

Within the realm of witchcraft, the associations between competition and the relations between equality and inequality are brought into relief. Witches represent an inversion of humanity, but they also constitute an image of the conscious hostility and suspicion that obtains between village comembers; tales of witchcraft pit villagers against one another in cannibalistic feasting and trading, and thus constitute a very real and understandable form of intravillage competition. What the Lese exclude from social action they practice intrapsychically.

These fears of witchcraft are fears about loss of identity within the clan as well as the fragmentation of the clan into isolated houses. In a different context (Sri Lanka and Australia), Kapferer has related the fears of the submerged self and the shattered society to distinct kinds of ideological systems:

> A fear expressed in egalitarian ideology is that the individual will be consumed, obscured, and will lose its identity in more inclusive orders and that those who command such orders will negate the autonomy of subordinates. . . . In hierarchical ideology . . . the individual in society can be an object of fear and terror. This is clearest in the idea of the demonic, an outsider within, which asserts the determination of its individuality against encompassing and incorporating forces. (1988:15)

In Malembi, both these fears emerge because there are elements of both systems. As with the demons described by Kapferer, witchcraft is the expression of individuality against the community. The clan is idealized because it gives its members a social identity that extends beyond the clan, and because the members share all their wealth and are "of the same blood." Witchcraft is the primary threat to the integrity of the clan, and a clan that is fragmented will produce only poverty and will be destined for death, since fragmentation disrupts the birth potential or "uterus." But there is also reason to suspect that the Lese clan threatens individual identity for the sake of the community. Clan members are supposed to be alike. The ideal of the Lese clan is that a man and his brothers should always have the same quantity and quality of noncultivated goods, should grow the same crops (though in different gardens), and should never exceed one another in agricultural production. Witchcraft asserts the house and individual over and above these standards of equality within the community. Witchcraft is about losing oneself and finding oneself: "I am not just like my brother," a Lese man may say, for "he is a witch." When the Efe are integrated into the house and through their witchcraft-fighting powers protect the Lese from themselves, they suppress the disintegration of the clan but at the same time reaffirm the integrity of the house and therefore of the persons who constitute it. Witchcraft incorporates both inequality and equality as ordering principles of social life.

ETHNICITY AND INEQUALITY

Equality and inequality may coexist in distinct social contexts, but each has its own agony. Equality, however defined, usually fosters some degree of competition and contention, and inequality involves power relations that can lead to exploitation, coercion, and oppression. Yet relations of inequality in general, and significant differences in power and status in particular, may in certain cultural contexts be so great as to restrain overt competition and violence, especially on the part of the subordinates. Differences may be so great that the open expression of competition, or what Scott (1990) has termed the "hidden transcripts" of subordinates, is either illegitimate or unfeasible. In addition, the lower- and higher-status individuals and groups may not compete on the same terms, but instead struggle to appropriate distinct discourses of contestation. In other words, persons of different social, economic, and political status may compete with one another by emphasizing their differences, rather than by trying to emulate one another. In his dissertation on the socioecology of the Efe, Robert Bailey (1985) repeats Gluckman's well-known hypothesis (1958) that groups in competition will emphasize their "endoculture," thus reinforcing the dominant cleavages between them.[2] Bailey thus suggests that, for the Lese and the Efe, the hunter will not try to compete with the farmer at the marketplace by attempting to cultivate a garden, but he will put greater effort into his own hunting, the performance of which further underscores his difference.

Under these conditions, it is easy to imagine how competition and division might lead to cooperation if not symbiosis. We know well from the Latin American ethnography on *compadrazgo* relationships and godparenthood how friendship and trust are generated within hierarchical dyadic partnerships; patrons and clients establish and maintain relationships that are frequently far more intimate and loyal than the relationships they maintain with members of their own group. Loyalty is to some degree a consequence of hierarchy. And the hierarchy may never be questioned because the social boundaries are so clearly defined. In hierarchy, equality is never at stake; in idealized egalitarian

2. Gluckman may have made this hypothesis well known to anthropologists, but the idea has older roots—for example, Rousseau's advice to the Corsicans and Poles of the mid eighteenth century to accentuate their differences if they were to survive (Smith 1986:136).

relations, such as those the Lese wish to have with their fellow villagers, equality is always at stake, always negotiable, always at risk.

The complex nature of the Lese-Efe ties reminds us that although ethnic relations are everywhere characterized by inequality and conflict, they need not always involve violence. At a time when so many areas of the world seem destined to suffer the violent passions of ethnic conflict, the Lese and the Efe are an anomaly. Or are they? Lese-Efe relations suppress overt interethnic conflict and promote loyalties, but it is a peace that is perhaps achieved only in opposition to a world of disorder and violence. As I have argued, the Lese and Efe each achieve a level of ethnic solidarity by imagining themselves to be isolated from the waves of Arab, colonial, and national oppression to which they have been subjected. The Lese and the Efe have, of course, never been totally independent of their neighbors, or of colonialism or nationalism, despite their efforts to convince themselves otherwise. If, as I have suggested, the Lese and the Efe must be seen as parts of a larger Lese-Efe social system, then it follows that they must also be situated in more inclusive systems such as the region or nation. Given the political and economic collapse of Zaire and the current civil and military unrest, of which the Lese and Efe will inevitably be a part, the Lese and Efe will probably continue to value their isolation, real or imagined. We shall have to await the day when we can assess to what degree the isolation of the Lese and the Efe during the 1980s, and the organizational principles I have shown to underlie their relations with one another, are replicated and transformed over time.

References

Anderson, B. 1991 [1983]. *Imagined Communities: Reflections on the Origin and Spread of Nationalism.* Second ed. London: Versor.

Aunger, R. V. 1992. "An Ethnography of Variation: Food Avoidances among Horticulturalists and Foragers in the Ituri Forest, Zaire." Ph.D. diss. Department of Anthropology, University of California, Los Angeles.

Bahuchet, S. 1992. "Spatial Mobility and Access to Resources among the African Pygmies." In *Mobility and Territoriality: Social and Spatial Boundaries among Fishers, Pastoralists and Peripatetics,* ed. M. J. Casimir and A. Rao, pp. 205–258. New York and Oxford: Berg.

Bahuchet, S., and H. Guillaume. 1982. "Aka-Farmer Relations in the Northwest Congo Basin." In *Politics and History in Band Societies,* ed. Richard Lee and Eleanor Leacock, pp.189–212. Cambridge: Cambridge University Press.

Bailey, F. G. 1971. *Gifts and Poison: The Politics of Reputation.* New York: Schocken Books.

Bailey, R. C. 1985. "The Socioecology of Efe Pygmy Men in the Ituri Forest, Zaire." Ph.D. diss., Department of Anthropology, Harvard University.

Bailey R. C., G. Head, M. Jenike, B. Owen, R. Rechtman, and E. Zechenter. 1989. "Hunting and Gathering in Tropical Rain Forest: Is It Possible?" *American Anthropologist* 91 (1): 59–83.

Bailey, R. C., and N. R. Peacock. 1989. "Efe Pygmies of Northeast Zaire: Subsistence Strategies in the Ituri Forest." In *Coping with Uncertainty in the Food Supply,* ed. I de Garine and G. A. Harrison, pp. 88–117. Oxford: Clarendon Press.

Baltus, M. 1949. "Les Walese." *Bulletin des Juridictions Indigènes* 17:114–122.

Barnes, J. A. 1971. *Three Styles in the Study of Kinship.* Berkeley, Los Angeles, London: University of California Press.

Barth, F. 1969. *Ethnic Groups and Boundaries.* Boston: Little, Brown & Co.
———. 1974. "On Responsibility and Humanity: Calling a Colleague to Account." *Current Anthropology* 15 (1): 99–102.
Begler, E. B. 1978. "Sex, Status, and Authority in Egalitarian Society." *American Anthropologist* 80 (3): 571–588.
Ben-Ari, E. 1987. "Pygmies and Villagers, Ritual or Play? On the Place of Contrasting Modes of Metacommunication in Social Systems." *Symbolic Interaction* 10 (2): 167–185.
Bender, D. R. 1967. "A Refinement of the Concept of Household: Families, Coresidence, and Domestic Functions." *American Anthropologist* 69:493–504.
Bentley, G. C. 1981. *Ethnicity and Nationality: A Bibliographic Guide.* Seattle: University of Washington Press.
Berger, P. 1983. Review of Colin Turnbull's *The Human Cycle. New York Times Book Review,* April 10, p. 13.
Berreman, G. 1975. "Bazaar Behavior: Social Identity and Social Interaction in Urban India." In *Ethnic Identity,* ed. George De Vos and Lola Romanucci-Ross, pp. 71–105. Chicago: University of Chicago Press.
Bird-David, N. 1988. "Hunters and Gatherers and Other People—A Re-examination." In *Hunters and Gatherers,* vol. 1: *History, Evolution, and Social Change,* ed. T. Ingold, D. Riches, and J. Woodburn, pp. 17–30. New York: Berg.
———. 1992. "Beyond the 'Original Affluent Society': A Culturalist Reformulation." *Current Anthropology* 33 (1): 25–47.
Blier, S. P. 1987. *The Anatomy of Architecture: Ontology and Metaphor in Batammaliba Architectural Expression.* Cambridge: Cambridge University Press.
Bloch, M. 1991. "The Resurrection of the House." Ms., Departmental Seminar; Dept. of Anthropology, University of California, Berkeley, Spring, 1991.
Boahen, A. A. 1985. *General History of Africa,* vol. VII: *Africa under Colonial Domination, 1880–1935.* London: James Currey.
Boon, J. A. 1990. "Balinese Twins Times Two: Gender, Birth Order, and 'Househood' in Indonesia/Indo-Europe." In *Power and Difference: Gender in Island Southeast Asia,* ed. J. M. Atkinson and S. Errington. Stanford: Stanford University Press.
Bourdieu, P. 1971. *The Berber House of the World Reversed. Echanges et communications: Mélanges offerts à Claude Lévi-Strauss à l'occasion de son 60 anniversaire.* Paris: Mouton.
———. 1977. *Outline of a Theory of Practice.* Cambridge: Cambridge University Press.
Bradford, P. V., and H. Blume. 1992. *Ota Benga: The Pygmy in the Zoo.* New York: St. Martin's Press.
Bulmer, R. N. H. 1960. "Leadership and Social Structure among the Kyaka People of the Western Highlands District of New Guinea." Ph.D. thesis, Australian National University, Canberra.
Casati, G. 1891. *Ten Years in Equatoria and the Return with Emin Pasha.* London: Frederick Warne.

Cashdan, E. 1989. "Hunters and Gatherers: Economic Behavior in Bands." In *Economic Anthropology,* ed. S. Plattner. Stanford, Calif.: Stanford University Press.

Cavalli-Sforza, L. 1987. *African Pygmies.* Orlando: Academic Press.

Cohen, R. 1978. "Ethnicity: Problem and Focus in Anthropology." *Annual Review of Anthropology* 7:379–403.

Cohen, R., and J. Middleton. 1970. Introduction. In *From Tribe to Nation in Africa: Studies in Incorporation Processes,* ed. R. Cohen and J. Middleton. Scranton, Pa.: Chandler.

Cohn, B. S. 1987. *An Anthropologist among the Historians and Other Essays.* Oxford: Oxford University Press.

Comaroff, Jean. 1984. *Body of Power, Spirit of Resistance.* Chicago: University of Chicago Press.

Comaroff, Jean, and J. L. Comaroff. 1991. *Of Revelation and Revolution,* vol. I: *Christianity, Colonialism, and Consciousness in South Africa.* Chicago: University of Chicago Press.

Comaroff, J. L. 1984. "The Closed Society and Its Critics: Historical Transformations in African Ethnography." *American Ethnologist* 11(3): 571–584.

———. 1987. "Of Totemism and Ethnicity: Consciousness, Practice, and the Signs of Inequality." *Ethnos* 52:301–323.

Cooper, F., and A. L. Stoler. 1989. "Tensions of Empire: Colonial Control and Visions of Rule." *American Ethnologist* 16 (4): 609–621.

Coward, R. 1983. *Patriarchal Precedents.* London: Routledge & Kegan Paul.

Dentan, R. K. 1988. "Band-Level Eden: A Mystifying Chimera." *Cultural Anthropology* 4:276–284.

DeVore, I. 1989. "The Human Place in Nature." *NAMTA Journal* 15 (1): 35–46.

District du Kibali-Ituri (P.V. No. 222-246). Historical Papers. Zone de Mambasa Archives, Mambasa, Zaire.

Douglas, M. T. 1963. *The Lele of Kasai.* London: Oxford University Press.

Douglas, M. T., ed. 1970. *Witchcraft Confessions and Accusations.* London: Tavistock.

Duffy, K. 1984. *Children of the Rainforest.* New York: Dodd, Mead & Co.

Dumont, L. 1970. *Homo Hierarchicus.* Chicago: University of Chicago Press.

———. 1986. *Essays on Individualism.* Chicago: University of Chicago Press.

Ekeh, P. P. 1990. "Social Anthropology and Two Contrasting Uses of Tribalism in Africa." *Comparative Studies in Society and History* 32 (4): 660–700.

Ellison, P., R. Peacock, and C. Lager. 1986. "Salivary Progesterone and Luteal Function in Two Low Fertility Populations of Northeast Zaire." *Human Biology* 58:473–483.

Endicott, K. 1984. "The Economy of the Batek of Malaysia: Annual and Historical Perspectives." *Research in Economic Anthropology* 6:29–52.

Errington, S. 1987. "Incestuous Twins and the House Societies of Insular Southeast Asia." *Cultural Anthropology* 2 (4): 403–444.

Evans-Pritchard, E. E. 1933. "The Nuer: Tribe and Clan," Part One. Sudan Notes and Records.

Evans-Pritchard, E. E. 1940. *The Nuer.* Oxford: Clarendon Press.

———. 1951. *Kinship and Marriage among the Nuer*. Oxford: Clarendon Press.

———. 1971. *The Azande: History and Political Institutions*. Oxford: Clarendon Press.

———. 1976 (1937). *Witchcraft, Oracles, and Magic among the Azande*. Oxford: Clarendon Press.

Feeley-Harnik, G. 1980. "The Sakalava House (Madagascar)." *Anthropos* 75:559–585.

Fernandez, J. W. 1976. *Fang Architectonics. Working Papers in the Traditional Arts*. Philadelphia: Institute for the Study of Human Issues.

———. 1982. *Bwiti*. Princeton, N.J.: Princeton University Press.

Fisher, J. W., Jr. 1986. "Shadows in the Forest: Ethnoarchaeology of the Efe Pygmies." Ph.D. diss., Department of Anthropology, University of California, Berkeley.

Forbath, P. 1977. *The River Congo*. New York: E. P. Dutton.

Fortes, M. 1945. *The Dynamics of Clanship among the Tallensi*. Published for the International African Institute. London: Oxford University Press.

———. 1949. *The Web of Kinship among the Tallensi*. London: Oxford University Press.

———. 1969. *Kinship and the Social Order*. Chicago: Aldine Publishing Company.

———. 1978. "An Anthropologist's Apprenticeship." *Annual Review of Anthropology* 7:1–30.

Fried, M. 1968. "On the Concept of 'Tribe' and 'Tribal Society.' " In *Essays on the Problem of Tribe*, ed. J. Helm, pp. 3–22. *Proceedings of the 1967 Annual Spring Meeting of the American Ethnological Society*. Seattle: University of Washington Press.

Gardner, P. M. 1972. "The Paliyans." In *Hunters and Gatherers Today*, ed. M.G. Bicchieri, pp. 404–447. New York: Holt, Rinehart & Winston.

———. 1989. Comment, on T. N. Headland and L. Reid's "Hunter-Gatherers and Their Neighbors from Prehistory to the Present." *Current Anthropology* 30 (1): 55–56.

Geertz, Clifford. 1956. "Religion in Modjokuto: A Study of Ritual and Belief in a Complex Society." Ph.D. diss., Department of Social Relations, Harvard University.

———. 1960. *The Religion of Java*. New York: Free Press of Glencoe.

Geluwe, H. Van. 1957. "Mamvu-Mangutu et Balese-Mvuba." Annales du Musée Royal Congo Belge, Monographies Ethnographiques, vol 3.

Gluckman, M. 1958. *Analysis of a Social Situation in Modern Zululand*. Rhodes Livingston Paper 28. Manchester: Manchester University Press.

Godelier, M. 1977. *Perspectives in Marxist Anthropology*. Cambridge: Cambridge University Press.

Gough, K. 1971. Nuer Kinship: A Re-examination. In *The Translation of Culture*, ed. T. O. Beidelman, pp. 79–122. London: Tavistock.

Grinker, R. R. 1990. "Images of Denigration: The Structuring of Inequality between Foragers and Farmers in the Ituri Forest, Zaire." *American Ethnologist* 19 (1): 111–130.

———. 1992a. Comment, on N. Bird-David's "Beyond the 'Original Affluent Society': A Culturalist Reformulation." *Current Anthropology* 33 (1): 39.

———. 1992b. "History and Hierarchy in Hunter-Gatherer Studies." *American Ethnologist* 19 (1): 158–163.

Gudeman, S. 1986. *Economics as Culture: Models and Metaphors of Livelihood.* London: Routledge & Kegan Paul.

———. 1990. *Colombian Conversations: The Domestic Economy in Life and Text.* Cambridge: Cambridge University Press.

Gulliver, P. H. 1971. *Tradition and Transition in East Africa: Studies of the Tribal Element in the Modern Era.* Berkeley, Los Angeles, London: University of California Press.

Gupta, A., and J. Ferguson. 1992. "Beyond 'Culture': Space, Identity, and the Politics of Difference." *Cultural Anthropology* 7 (1): 6–23.

Guyer, J. I. 1981. "Household and Community in African Studies." *African Studies Review* 24 (2/3 June/September): 87–137.

Hammond-Tooke, W. D. 1985. "In Search of the Lineage: The Cape Nguni Case." *Man* (N.S.) 19: 77–93.

Harms, R. 1975. "The End of Red Rubber: A Reassessment." *Journal of African History* 26 (1): 73–88.

Harries, L. 1956. "Notes on the BaLese Language of the Ituri Forest." *Kongo-Overzee* 22 (2–3): 152–170.

Hart, J. A., and T. B. Hart. 1984. "The Mbuti of Zaire: Political Change and the Opening of the Ituri Forest." *Cultural Survival Quarterly* 8(3): 18–20.

Headland, T. N. 1987. "The Wild Yam Question: How Well Could Independent Hunter-Gatherers Live in a Tropical Rainforest Ecosystem?" *Human Ecology* 15:465–493.

———. 1988. "Why Foragers Do Not Become Farmers: The Competitive Exclusion Principles and the Persistence of the Professional Primitive." Paper presented at the twelfth International Congress of Anthropological and Ethnological Science (ICAES), Zagreb, Yugoslavia, July 24–31.

Headland, T. N., and L. Reid. 1989. "Hunter-Gatherers and Their Neighbors from Prehistory to the Present." *Current Anthropology* 30 (1): 27–43.

Heald, S. 1991. Tobacco, Time, and the Household Economy in Two Kenyan Societies: The Teso and the Kuria. *Comparative Studies in Society and History* 33 (1): 130–157.

Helm, J., ed. 1968. *Essays on the Problem of Tribe.* Proceedings of the 1967 annual spring meeting of the American Ethnological Society. Seattle: University of Washington Press.

Hutchinson, S. 1992. "The Cattle of Money and the Cattle of Girls among the Nuer, 1930–83." *American Ethnologist* 19 (2): 294–316.

I.D. 1213, *A Manual of the Belgian Congo,* London: Naval Intelligence Division.

Ichikawa, M. 1978. "The Residential Groups of the Mbuti Pygmies." *Senri Ethological Studies* 1:131–188.

———. 1981. "Ecological and Sociological Importance of Honey to the Mbuti Net-Hunters, Eastern Zaire." *African Study Monographs* 1:55–68.

Jackson, J. 1983. *The Fish People: Linguistic Exogamy and Tukanoan Identity in Northwest Amazonia.* Cambridge: Cambridge University Press.

Jenike, M. 1988a. "Seasonal Hunger among Tropical Africans: The Lese Case." M.A. thesis, Department of Anthropology, University of California, Los Angeles.

———. 1988b. "The Acquisition of Meat from Pygmies by Villagers with an Example from Two Ituri Forest Populations." Ms., University of California, Los Angeles.

Jewsiewicki, B. 1983. "Rural Society and the Belgian Colonial Economy." In *The History of Central Africa,* vol. 2, ed. David Birmingham and Phyllis Martin, pp. 95–125. London: Longman.

Johnson, M. 1931. *Congorilla: Adventures with Pygmies and Gorillas in Africa.* New York: Bewer, Warren & Putnam.

Johnston, H. H. 1903. "The Pygmies of the Great Congo Forest." Annual report of the Board of Regents of the Smithsonian Institution, for the year ending 1902, pp. 479–91.

Jones, G. I. 1963. *The Trading States of the Oil Rivers.* London: Oxford University Press.

Joset, P. E. 1949. "Notes ethnographique sur la sous-tribu des Walese Abfunkotou." *Bulletin de Juridictions Indigènes* 17:1–97.

Kapferer, B. 1988. *Legends of People, Myths of State: Violence, Intolerance, and Political Culture in Sri Lanka and Australia.* Washington, D.C.: Smithsonian Institution Press.

Keim, C. A. 1979. "Precolonial Mangbetu Rule: Political and Economic Factors in Nineteenth-Century Mangbetu History (Northeast Zaire)." Ph.D. diss., Department of History, Indiana University, Bloomington.

Kelly, R. C. 1985. *The Nuer Conquest: The Structure and Development of an Expansionist System.* Ann Arbor: University of Michigan Press.

Kopytoff, I., ed. 1987. *The African Frontier: The Reproduction of Traditional Societies.* Bloomington: Indiana University Press.

Kopytoff, I., and S. Miers, eds. 1977. *African Slavery: Historical and Anthropological Perspectives.* Madison: University of Wisconsin Press.

Kuper, A. 1982. "Lineage Theory: A Critical Retrospect." *Annual Review of Anthropology* 11:71–95.

Lacomblez, M. 1916. L'agriculture indigène dans la région du Haut-Ituri. *Bulletin Agricole du Congo Belge* 7, 1–2:1–164.

Leach, E. 1954. *Political Systems of Highland Burma.* London: Althone Press.

Lee, R. B., and E. Leacock. 1982. *Politics and History in Band Societies.* Cambridge: Cambridge University Press.

Lévi-Strauss, C. 1962. *Totemism.* Boston: Beacon Press.

———. 1976. *Structural Anthropology* Vol. II. New York: Basic Books.

———. 1979. *The Way of the Masks.* Seattle: University of Washington Press.

LeVine, R. A. 1982. "Gusii Funerals: Meanings of Life and Death in an African Community." *Ethos* 10: 1: 26–64.

LeVine, R. A., and S. LeVine. 1990. "House Design and the Self in an African Culture." Ms., Graduate School of Education, and the Department of Anthropology, Harvard University, Cambridge, Mass.

Lloyd, P. C. 1957. *The Itsekiri: The Benin Kingdom and the Edo-speaking Peoples of Southwestern Nigeria.* London: International African Institute.

Louis, W. R. 1966. "The Triumph of the Congo Reform Movement, 1905–1908." In *Boston University Papers on Africa,* ed. Jeffrey Butler. Boston: Boston University Press.

McCall, Grant. 1975. More Thoughts on the Ik and Anthropology. *Current Anthropology* 16 (3): 343–348.

MacCormack, C., and M. Strathern, eds. 1980. *Nature, Culture, and Gender.* Cambridge: Cambridge University Press.

McDonald, G. C., D. W. Bernier, L. E. Brenneman, E. M. Colligan, W. A. Culp, S. R. MacKnight, M. L. Missenburg. 1971. Area Handbook for the Democratic Republic of the Congo (Congo Kinshasa). Foreign Areas Studies Pamphlet DA PAM 550–67. Washington, D.C.: American University.

Macfarlane, A. 1970. *Witchcraft in Tudor and Stuart England.* London: Routledge & Kegan Paul.

Marriot, M. 1955. Little Communities in an Indigenous Civilization. In *Village India,* ed. Mckim Marriot, pp. 171–222. Memoirs, American Anthropological Association.

Marwick, M. G. 1965. *Sorcery in Its Social Setting: A Study of the Northern Rhodesian Cewa.* Manchester: Manchester University Press.

Mathieu, N. 1978. "Man-Culture and Woman-Nature?" *Women's Studies* 1:55–65.

Maybury-Lewis, D. 1989 "The Quest for Harmony." In *The Attraction of Opposites: Thought and Society in the Dualistic Mode,* ed. D Maybury-Lewis and U. Almagor. Ann Arbor: University of Michigan Press.

Meillassoux, C. 1975. *Meals, Maidens, and Money.* Cambridge: Cambridge University Press.

Merriam, A. 1959. "The Concept of Culture Clusters Applied to the Belgian Congo." *Southwestern Journal of Anthropology* 15:373–395.

Middleton, J., and E. H. Winter, eds. 1963. *Witchcraft and Sorcery in East Africa.* London: Routledge & Kegan Paul.

Miracle, M. 1967. *Agriculture in the Congo Basin.* Madison: University of Wisconsin Press.

Mitchell, J. C. 1956. *The Yao Village: A Study in the Social Structure of a Nyasaland Tribe.* Manchester: Manchester University Press.

Modjeska, N. 1982. "Production and Inequality: Perspectives from Central New Guinea." In *Inequality in New Guinea Highlands Societies,* ed. A. Strathern, pp. 50–108. Cambridge: Cambridge University Press.

Moore, H. 1988. *Feminism and Anthropology.* Minneapolis: University of Minnesota Press.

Moore, S. F. 1978. *Law as Process: An Anthropological Approach.* London: Routledge & Kegan Paul.

Morel, E. D. 1906. *Red Rubber.* New York: B. W. Huebsch.

Morgan, L. H. 1881. *House and House-Life of the American Aborigines.* Contributions to North American Ethnology. Washington: Government Printing Office.

Mosko, M. S. 1987. "The Symbols of the 'Forest': A Structural Analysis of

Mbuti Culture and Social Organization." *American Anthropologist* 89 (4): 896–913.

Murdock, G. P. 1959. *Africa: Its People and Their Culture History.* New York: McGraw Hill Book Co.

Needham, R. 1973. *Right and Left: Essays on Dual Symbolic Classification.* Chicago: University of Chicago Press.

Newbury, C. 1988. *The Cohesion of Oppression: Clientship and Ethnicity in Rwanda, 1860–1960.* New York: Columbia University Press.

Ortner, S. B. 1974. "Is Female to Male as Nature Is to Culture? In *Woman, Culture, and Society,* ed. M. Rosaldo and L. Lamphere, pp. 67–88. Stanford, Calif.: Stanford University Press.

Ortner, S. B., and H. Whitehead, eds. 1981. *Sexual Meanings: The Cultural Construction of Gender and Sexuality.* Cambridge: Cambridge University Press.

Pak, O. K. 1986. "Lowering the High, Raising the Low: The Gender, Alliance, and Property Relations in a Minangkbau Peasant Community of West Sumatra, Indonesia." Ph.D. diss., Department of Anthropology, University of Toronto.

Parry, J. 1979. *Caste and Kinship in Kangra.* London and Boston: Routledge & Kegan Paul.

Peterson, J. T. 1978a. "Hunter-Gatherer/Farmer Exchange." *American Anthropologist* 80 (2): 335–351.

———. 1978b. *The Ecology of Social Boundaries: Agta Foragers of the Philippines.* Illinois Studies in Anthropology, No. 11. Urbana: University of Illinois Press.

Putnam, P. T. 1948. The Pygmies of the Ituri Forest. In *A Reader in General Anthropology,* ed. C. S. Coon, pp. 322–342. New York: Henry Holt.

Radcliffe-Brown, A. R. 1952 [1940]. *Structure and Function in Primitive Society.* Chicago: Free Press.

Rapp, R. 1979. Review essay: "Anthropology." *Signs* 4 (3): 497–513.

Redfield, R., and M. Singer. 1954. "The Cultural Role of Cities." *Economic Development and Cultural Change.* 3:63–73.

Rousseau, J. 1990. *Central Borneo: Ethnic Identity and Social Life in a Stratified Society.* Oxford: Oxford University Press.

Sahlins, M. 1972. *Stone Age Economics.* Chicago: Aldine Publishing Co.

Sapir, J. D. 1977. "The Anatomy of Metaphor." In *The Social Uses of Metaphor,* ed. J. D. Sapir and J. C. Crocker, pp. 3–33. Philadelphia: University of Pennsylvania Press.

Saul, M. 1991. "The Bobo 'House' and the Uses of Categories of Descent." *Africa* 61 (1): 71–97.

Schebesta, P. 1933. *Among Congo Pygmies.* London: Hutchinson & Co.

———. 1936. *My Pygmy and Negro Hosts.* London: Hutchinson & Co.

———. 1952. "Les Pygmées du Congo Belge." Mémoire de l'institut Royal Colonial Belge, ser. 8, vol. 26, fasc. 2.

Schildkrout, E. 1975. "Economics and Kinship in Multi-Ethnic Dwellings." In *The Changing Social Structure in Ghana,* ed. J. Goody, pp. 167–179. London: Oxford University Press.

———. 1978. *People of the Zongo: The Transformation of Ethnic Identities in Ghana.* Cambridge: Cambridge University Press.

Schildkrout, E., and C. Keim. 1990. *African Reflections: Art from Northeastern Zaire.* Seattle and London: University of Washington Press, New York: American Museum of Natural History.

Schlegel, A., ed. 1977. *Sexual Stratification: A Cross-cultural View.* New York: Columbia University Press.

Schloss, M. R. 1988. *The Hatchet's Blood: Separation, Power, and Gender in Ehing Social Life.* Tucson: University of Arizona Press.

Schmidt, S., L. Guasti, C. H. Landé, and J. Scott, eds. 1977. *Friends, Followers, and Factions: A Reader in Political Clientism.* Berkeley, Los Angeles, London: University of California Press.

Schrire, C., ed. 1984. *Past and Present in Hunter-Gatherer Studies.* Orlando: Academic Press.

Schultz, M. n.d. "Forager-Farmer Relations: Some New Fieldwork on the Batua and the Baoto, Equateur, Zaire." Ms.

Schweinfurth, G. 1874. *The Heart of Africa,* Vol. II. New York: Harper & Brothers.

Scott, J. C. 1990. *Domination and the Arts of Resistance: Hidden Transcripts.* New Haven, Conn.: Yale University Press.

Seddon, D. 1976. "Aspects of Kinship and Family Structure among the Ulad Stut of Zaio Rural Commune, Nador Province, Morocco." In *Mediterranean Family Structures,* ed. J. G. Peristiany. Cambridge: Cambridge University Press.

Slade, R. M. 1959. *English-Speaking Missions in the Congo Independent State (1878–1908).* Brussels: Academie royale des sciences coloniales.

Smith, A. D. 1986. *The Ethnic Origin of Nations.* London: Basil Blackwell Publisher.

Solway, J. S., and R. B. Lee. 1990. "Foragers, Genuine or Spurious? Situating the Kalahari San in History." *Current Anthropology* 31 (2): 109–147.

Southall, A. 1970. "The Illusion of Tribe." In *The Passing of Tribal Man in Africa,* ed. P. C. W. Gutkind, pp. 28–50. Leiden: E. J. Brill.

Stanley, H. M. 1891. *In Darkest Africa, or, The Quest, Rescue, and Retreat of Emin, Governor of Equatoria.* New York: Charles Scribner's Sons.

Strathern, A., ed. 1982. *Inequality in New Guinea Highlands Societies.* Cambridge: Cambridge University Press.

Strathern, M. 1987. Introduction. In *Dealing with Inequality,* ed. M. Strathern, pp. 1–32. Cambridge: Cambridge University Press.

Sulloway, F. 1979. *Freud, Biologist of the Mind: Beyond the Psychoanalytic Legend.* New York: Basic Books.

Tambiah, S. J. 1986. *Sri Lanka: Ethnic Fratricide and the Dismantling of Democracy.* Chicago: University of Chicago Press.

Tanno, T. 1976. "The Mbuti Net-Hunters in the Ituri Forest, Eastern Zaire: Their Hunting Activities and Band Composition." *Kyoto University African Studies* 10: 101–135.

———. 1981. "Plant Utilization of the Mbuti Pygmies with Special Reference to Their Material Culture and Use of Wild Vegetable Foods." *Kyoto University African Study Monographs* 1:1–51.

Terashima, H. 1983. "Mota and Other Hunting Activities of the Mbuti Archers: A Socioecological Study of Subsistence Technology." *African Studies Monographs* 3:60–71.

———. 1984. "The Structure of the Band of Mbuti Archers." In *Afurika Bunka no Kenkyu,* ed. J. Itani and T. Yoneyama, pp. 3–41, Kyoto: Academica Shuppan-kai.

———. 1985. "Variation and Composition Principles of the Residence Group (Band) of the Mbuti Pygmies—Beyond a Typical/Atypical Dichotomy." *African Study Monographs,* Supplementary Issue, 4:103–120.

———. 1987. "Why Efe Girls Marry Farmers: Socio-ecological Backgrounds of Inter-ethnic Marriage in the Ituri Forest of Central Africa. *African Study Monographs* 6:65–84.

Thomas, K. 1971. *Religion and the Decline of Magic.* London: Weidenfeld & Nicolson.

Thompson, R. H. 1989. *Theories of Ethnicity: A Critical Appraisal.* New York: Greenwood Press.

Tonkin, E., M. McDonald, and M. Chapman, eds. 1989. *History and Ethnicity.* London: Routledge & Kegan Paul.

Turnbull, C.. 1961. *The Forest People.* New York: Simon & Schuster.

———. 1965a. "The Mbuti Pygmies: An Ethnographic Survey." *Anthropological Papers of the American Museum of Natural History* 50 (3): 139–282.

———. 1965b. *Wayward Servants: The Two Worlds of the African Pygmies.* New York: Natural History Press.

———. 1968. "The Importance of Flux in Two Hunting Societies." In *Man the Hunter,* ed. R. B. Lee and I. DeVore. Chicago: Aldine Publishing Co.

———. 1972. "Demography of Small Scale Societies." In *The Structure of Human Populations,* ed. G. A. Harrison and A.J. Boyce, pp. 283–312. Oxford: Clarendon Press.

———. 1983a. *The Mbuti Pygmies: Change and Adaptation.* New York: Holt, Rinehart & Winston.

———. 1983b. *The Human Cycle.* New York: Simon & Schuster.

Turner, V. 1967. *The Forest of Symbols.* Ithaca, N.Y.: Cornell University Press.

Turton, D. 1986. "A Problem of Domination at the Periphery." In *The Southern Marches of Imperial Ethiopia,* ed. D. Donham and W. James, pp. 148–171. Cambridge: Cambridge University Press.

Tyson, E. 1751 [1699]. *The Anatomy of a Pygmy Compared with That of a Monkey, an Ape, and a Man.* Second ed. London: T. Osborne in Gray's Inn.

Vail, L., ed. 1988. *The Creation of Tribalism in Southern Africa.* Berkeley, Los Angeles, London: University of California Press.

Vanderstraeten, L.-F. 1985. *De la force publique a l'Armée Nationale Congolaise: Histoire d'une mutinerie, juillet 1960.* Bruxelles: Academie Royale de Belgique.

Vansina, J. 1980. "Lignage, idéologie et histoire en Afrique Centrale." *Enquêtes et Documents d'Histoire Africaine* 4:133–155.

———. 1982. "Towards a History of Lost Corners in the World." *The Economic History Review,* second series, Vol. XXXV, no. 2: 165–178.

———. 1990a. *Paths in the Rainforest.* Madison: University of Wisconsin Press.

———. 1990b. "Reconstructing the Past." In *African Reflections: Art from Northeastern Zaire,* ed. E. Schildkrout and C. Keim, pp. 69–88. Seattle and London: University of Washington Press, New York: American Museum of Natural History.

Vellut, J.-L. 1983. "Mining in the Belgian Congo." In *The History of Central Africa,* vol. 2, ed. David Birmingham and Phyllis Martin, pp. 126–162. London: Longman.

Vierich, H. 1982. "Adaptive Flexibility in a Multi-ethnic Setting: The Basarwa of the Southern Kalahari." In *Politics and History in Band Societies.* ed. Richard B. Lee and Eleanor Leacock, pp. 213–222. Cambridge: Cambridge University Press.

Vorbichler, A. 1971. *Die Sprache der Mamvu.* Hamburg: Verlag J. J. Augustin.

Waehle, E. 1985. "Efe (Mbuti Pygmy) Relations to Lese-Dese Villagers in the Ituri Forest, Zaire: Historical Changes during the Last 150 Years." Paper presented at the International Symposium: African Hunter-Gatherers, Cologne, January.

Wilk, R. R. 1989. *The Household Economy.* Boulder, Colo.: Westview Press.

Wilkie, D. S. 1987. "The Impact of Swidden Agriculture and Subsistence Hunting on Diversity and Abundance of Exploited Fauna in the Ituri Forest of Northeastern Zaire." Ph.D. diss., Department of Forestry and Wildlife Management, University of Massachusetts, Amherst.

Williams, B. 1989. "A Class Act: Anthropology and the Race to Nation across Ethnic Terrain." *Annual Review of Anthropology* 18:401–444.

Wilmsen, E. 1990. *Land Filled with Flies.* Chicago: University of Chicago Press.

Wilmsen, E., and J. R. Denbow. 1990. "Paradigmatic History of San-Speaking Peoples and Current Attempts at Revision." *Current Anthropology* 31:489–524.

Winter, E. n.d. *Bwamba: A Structural-Functional Analysis of a Patrilineal Society.* Oxford: Oxford University Press.

———. 1963. "The Enemy Within." In *Witchcraft and Sorcery in East Africa,* ed. J. Middleton and E. Winter. London: Routledge & Kegan Paul.

Woodburn, J. 1988. "African Hunter-Gatherer Social Organization: Is It Best Understood as a Product of Encapsulation?" In *Hunters and Gatherers,* vol. 1: *History, Evolution, and Social Change,* ed. T. Ingold, D. Riches, and J. Woodburn. New York: Berg.

Yanagisako, S. J. 1979. "Family and Household: The Analysis of Domestic Groups." *Annual Review of Anthropology* 8:161–205.

Young, C. 1965. *Politics in the Congo: Decolonization and Independence.* Princeton, N.J.: Princeton University Press.

———. 1983. "The Northern Republics." In *The History of Central Africa,* vol. 2, ed. David Birmingham and Phyllis Martin, pp. 291–336. London: Longman.

Young, C., and T. Turner. 1985. *The Rise and Decline of the Zairian State.* Madison: University of Wisconsin Press.

Index

Designer: U. C. Press Staff
Compositor: Maple-Vail
Text: 10/13 Sabon
Display: Sabon
Printer: Maple-Vail Book Manufacturing Group
Binder: Maple-Vail Book Manufacturing Group